REFERENCE

Endangered Wildlife and Plants of the World

Volume 2
BIR–CLA

Marshall Cavendish
New York • London • Toronto • Sydney

Marshall Cavendish Corporation
99 White Plains Road
Tarrytown, NY 10591-9001

Created by Brown Partworks Ltd.
Project Editor: Anne Hildyard
Associate Editors: Paul Thompson, Amy Prior
Managing Editor: Tim Cooke
Design: Whitelight
Picture Research: Helen Simm
Index Editor: Kay Ollerenshaw
Production Editor: Matt Weyland
Illustrations: Barbara Emmons, Jackie Harland, Tracy Williamson

Library of Congress Cataloging-in-Publication Data

Endangered wildlife and plants of the world
p.cm.
Includes bibliographical references (p.).
ISBN 0-7614-7194-4 (set)
ISBN 0-7614-7196-0 (vol. 2)
1. Endangered species--Encyclopedias. I. Marshall Cavendish Corporation.

QH75.E68 2001
333.95'22'03--dc21
99-086194

Printed in Malaysia
Bound in the United States of America
07 06 05 04 03 02 01 00 7 6 5 4 3 2 1

Photo Credits

Cover: Bruce Coleman Ltd: Hans Reinhard
Title page: Natural History Photographic Agency: Manfred
Danegger
Contents page: Nevada Natural Heritage Program, James
Morefield

American Fisheries Society: James E. Johnson/U.S.F.W.S. 259,
260, John N. Rinne/U.S.F.W.S. 257, 260, William N. Roston
268, J.R. Shute 265, Wydoski & Whitney 269; Heather Angel:
207; Ardea London Ltd.: B. "Moose" Peterson 150; Peter
Arnold Inc.: Manfred Danegger 245, Frederick J. Dodd 272,
M. & C. Ederegger 271, Martin Wendler 226; Biological
Photo Services: C.J. James 224; California Native Plant
Society: T. I. Chuang 152; Bruce Coleman Ltd.: Manfred
Danegger 155, Stephen J. Krasemann 209, 258, Hans
Reinhard 274, Kim Taylor 156, Konrad Wothe; Corbis: Susan
Middleton & David Liitschwager 230; D.R.K. Photo: Belinda
Wright; Illinois

Natural History Survey: 279 t & b, 280, 281, 282, 284; Felix
Lopez: 163, 164; Robert Miller: 198; Robert & Linda
Mitchell: 253, 254; Natural History Photographic Agency:
243b; Nevada Natural Heritage Program: James Morefield
182, 217; Russel Norton: 243t; Oxford Scientific Films: Eyal
Bartor 227, Stouffer Productions 169; Ralph Peters: 212, 214,
215, 218, 220; E.S. Ross: 190, 193; Warren D. Thomas: 183;
VIREO: D & M Zimmerman 167, 229; Visuals Unlimited:
276, Patrice Ceisel 273; Wildlife Conseration Society (H.Q. at
the Bronx Zoo): 185; Zoological Society of San Diego: 236,
238, 240, 249, 250, 277, Ron Garrison 154, 166

Cover: Texas cichlid. Bruce Coleman Ltd: Hans Reinhard
Title page: American bison. Natural History Photographic
Agency: Manfred Danegger
Contents page: Schlesser pincushion. Nevada Natural Heritage
Program, James Morefield

TABLE OF CONTENTS/VOLUME 2

Salt marsh bird's-beak 150–151
Soft bird's-beak 151–152
Bison 153
European bison (wisent) 153–154
Wood bison 154–155
Tokyo bitterling 156
Yellow-shouldered blackbird 157
Blindcats 158
Mexican blindcat (Bagre de Muzquiz) 158–159
Toothless blindcat 159–160
Widemouth blindcat 160
Honey blue-eye 161
Boas 162
Mona boa 162–163
Puerto Rican boa 163–164
Virgin Islands tree boa 164–165
Bobcat 166
Masked bobwhite 167–169
Bontebok 170
Abbott's booby 171
Vahl's boxwood 172–173
Buckwheats 173
Clay-loving wild-buckwheat 173–175
Cushenbury buckwheat 175–176
Gypsum wild-buckwheat 177–178
Scrub buckwheat 178–179
Southern mountain wild-buckwheat 180–181
Steamboat buckwheat 181–182
Wild Asiatic water buffalo 183–184
Zanzibar bushbaby 184–186
White-browed bushchat 187
Houbara bustard 188
Butterflies 189–194
Cachorritos 195
Cachorrito boxeador 195–196
Cachorrito cabezon 196–198
Cachorrito cangrejero 198–199
Cachorrito enano de Potosi 199–200
Cachorrito gigante 200–201
Cachorrito lodero 201
Cachorrito de dorsal larga 201–203
Cachorrito del Aguanaval 203
Cachorrito de media luna 203–204
Cachorrito de Mezquital 204

Cacti 205
Blaine pincushion 205–206
Hatchet cactus 207–208
Knowlton cactus 208–210
Lloyd's mariposa cactus 210–211
Mesa Verde cactus 211–213
Peebles Navajo cactus 213–214
San Rafael cactus 214–216
Schlesser pincushion 216–218
Winkler cactus 218–219
Wright fishhook cactus 219–220
Cahow 221–222
Caimans 223
Black caiman 223–225
Broadnosed caiman 225–226
Wild bactrian camel 227–228
Audubon's crested caracara 228–230
Catfishes 231
Cave catfish 231
Giant catfish 232
Incomati rock catlet 233
Cats 234
Flat-headed cat 235
Iriomote cat 235–237
Little spotted cat 237–238
Marbled cat 238–239
Pakistan sand cat 239
Rusty spotted cat 240
Cavefishes 241
Alabama cavefish 241–242
Northern cavefish 242
Ozark cavefish 242–243

Chamois 244
Apennine (Abruzzo) chamois and Chartreuse chamois 244–246
Charals 246
Charal de Alchichica, de Quechulac and de la Preciosa 246–247
Charal del Valle de Mexico 247
Cheetah 248–251
Chimpanzees 252
Common chimpanzee 252–255
Pygmy chimpanzee 255
Chubs 256
Alvord chub 256
Bonytail chub 256–257
Borax lake chub 258
Charalito 258–259
Charalito saltillo 260–261
Least chub 261–262
Oregon chub 262
Pahranagat roundtail chub 262–263
Virgin River roundtail chub 263
Sicklefin chub 264
Slender chub 264–265
Sonora chub 265–266
Spotfin chub 266–267
Sturgeon chub 267–268
Hutton tui chub 268–269
Mohave tui chub 269
Owens tui chub 269–270
Yaqui chub 270
Periodical cicadas 271–272
Lake Victoria cichlids 273–274
Ciscoes 275
Shortjaw cisco 275–276
Shortnose cisco 276
Malagasy civet 277–278
Clams 279
Birdwing pearlymussel 279
Cracking pearlymussel 279
Dromedary pearlymussel 280
Green blossom pearlymussel and tubercled blossom pearlymussel 280
Littlewing pearlymussel 280
White catspaw pearlymussel 281–284
Glossary 285–287
Index 287–288

ESA and IUCN

In this set of endangered animals and plants, each species, where appropriate, is given an ESA status and an IUCN status. The sources consulted to determine the status of each species are the Endangered Species List maintained by the U.S. Fish and Wildlife Service and the Red Lists compiled by IUCN–The World Conservation Union, which is a worldwide organization based in Switzerland.

ENDANGERED SPECIES ACT

The Endangered Species Act (ESA) was initially passed by the U.S. Congress in 1973, and reauthorized in 1988. The aim of the ESA is to rescue species that are in danger of extinction due to human action and to conserve the species and their ecosystems. Endangered plants and animals are listed by the U.S. Fish and Wildlife Service (USFWS), which is part of the Department of Interior. Once a species is listed, the USFWS is required to develop recovery plans, and ensure that the threatened species is not further harmed by any actions of the U.S. government or U.S. citizens. The act specifically forbids the buying, selling, transporting, importing, or exporting of any listed species. It also bans the taking of any listed species in the U.S. and its territories, on both private and public lands. Violators can face heavy fines or imprisonment. However, the ESA requires that the protection of the species is balanced with economic factors.

The ESA recognizes two categories of risk for species:

Endangered: A species that is in danger of extinction throughout all or a significant part of its range.

Threatened: A species that is likely to become endangered in the foreseeable future.

RECOVERY

Recovery takes place when the decline of the endangered or threatened species is halted or reversed, and the circumstances that caused the threat have been removed. The ultimate aim is the recovery of the species to the point where it no longer requires protection under the act.

Recovery can take a long time. Because the decline of the species may have occurred over centuries, the loss cannot be reversed overnight. There are many factors involved: the number of individuals of the species that remain in the wild, how long it takes the species to mature and reproduce, how much habitat is remaining, and whether the reasons for the decline are clear cut and understood. Recovery plans employ a wide range of strategies that involve the following: reintroduction of species into formerly occupied habitat, land aquisition and management, captive breeding, habitat protection, research, population counts, public education projects, and assistance for private landowners.

SUCCESS STORIES

Despite the difficulties, recovery programs do work, and the joint efforts of the USFWS, other federal and state agencies, tribal governments, and private landowners have not been in vain. Only seven species, less than 1 percent of all the species listed between 1968 and 1993, are now known to be extinct. The other 99 percent of listed species have not been lost to extinction, and this confirms the success of the act.

There are some good examples of successful recovery plans. In 1999, the peregrine falcon, the bald eagle, and the Aleutian goose were removed from the endangered species list. The falcon's numbers have risen dramatically. In 1970, there were only 39 pairs of falcons in the United States. By 1999, the number had risen to 1,650 pairs. The credit for the recovery goes to the late Rachel

Carson, who highlighted the dangers of DDT, and also to the Endangered Species Act, which enabled the federal government to breed falcons in captivity, and took steps to protect their habitat.

Young bald eagles were also successfully translocated into habitat that they formerly occupied, and the Aleutian Canada goose has improved due to restoration of its habitat and reintroduction into former habitat.

IUCN–THE WORLD CONSERVATION UNION

The IUCN (International Union for Conservation of Nature) was established in 1947. It is an alliance of governments, governmental agencies, and nongovernmental agencies. The aim of the IUCN is to help and encourage nations to conserve wildlife and natural resources. Organizations such as the Species Survival Commission is one of several IUCN commissions that assesses the conservation status of species and subspecies globally. Taxa that are threatened with extinction are noted and steps are taken for their conservation by programs designed to save, restore, and manage species and their habitats. The Survival Commission is committed to providing objective information on the status of globally threatened species, and produces two publications: the *IUCN Red List of Threatened Animals*, and the *IUCN Red List of Threatened Plants*. They are compiled from scientific data and provide the status of threatened species, depending on their existence in the wild and threats that undermine that existence. The lists for plants and animals differ slightly.

The categories from the *IUCN Red List of Threatened Animals* used in *Endangered Wildlife and Plants of the World* are as follows:

Extinct: A species is extinct when there is no reasonable doubt that the last individual has died.

Extinct in the wild: A species that is known only to survive in captivity, well outside its natural range.

Critically endangered: A species that is facing an extremely high risk of extinction in the wild in the immediate future.

Endangered: A species that is facing a very high risk of extinction in the wild in the near future.

Vulnerable: A species that is facing a high risk of extinction in the wild in the medium-term future.

Lower risk: A species that does not satisfy the criteria for designation as critically endangered, endangered, or vulnerable. Species included in the lower risk category can be separated into three subcategories:

  Conservation dependent: A species that is part of a conservation program. Without the program, the species would qualify for one of the threatened categories within five years.

  Near threatened: A species that does not qualify for conservation dependent, but is close to qualifying as vulnerable.

  Least concern: A species that does not qualify for conservation dependent or near threatened.

Data deficient: A species on which there is inadequate information to make an asssessment of risk of extinction. Because there is a possibility that future research will show that the species is threatened, more information is required.

The categories from the *IUCN Red List of Threatened Plants*, used in *Endangered Wildlife and Plants of the World*, are as follows:

Extinct: A species that has not definitely been located in the wild during the last 50 years.

Endangered: A species whose survival is unlikely if the factors that threaten it continue. Included are species whose numbers have been reduced to a critical level, or whose habitats have been so drastically reduced that they are deemed to be in immediate danger of extinction. Also included in this category are species that may be extinct but have definitely been seen in the wild in the past 50 years.

Vulnerable: A species that is thought likely to move into the endangered category in the near future if the factors that threaten it remain.

Rare: A species with small world populations that are not at present endangered or vulnerable, but are at risk. These species are usually in restricted areas or are thinly spread over a larger range.

Salt Marsh Bird's-beak

(Cordylanthus maritimus ssp. *maritimus)*

ESA: Endangered

IUCN: Endangered

Stems: Upright or spreading, 4–20 in. (10–50 cm) tall, covered with sticky hairs or nearly smooth
Leaves: Alternate, simple, narrow, oblong; up to 1 in. (2.5 cm) long, 2–5 mm wide
Flowers: June to August. Up to 1 in. (2.5 cm) long. Petals have two lips, ¾–1 in. (2–2.5 cm) across, ½–¾ in. (1–2 cm) long: are white or yellow, striped with purple or red, and tipped with yellow, pink, or purple. Sepals are united to form a single structure split nearly to the base, ½–1 in. (1–2.5 cm) long, green, notched at the tip
Pollination: By bees
Seeds: Fruits ellipsoid, up to ½ in. (1 cm) long; seeds up to 2 mm long, curved, brown, 15–20 per capsule
Habitat: High salt marshes and alkaline meadows
Range: California

THE UPPER LIP OF THE flower of *Cordylanthus maritimus* ssp. *maritimus,* like the lip of others in the genus, resembles a bird's-beak, hence its common name: salt marsh bird's-beak. Plants of this genus are hemiparasitic, meaning that while they manufacture their own food through photosynthesis, just like other green plants, they get their water and nutrients from the roots of neighboring plants. This is what allows *Cordylanthus* species to stay green and to flower during the dry summer after other annuals have fruited and died.

Salt marsh bird's-beak is an annual plant found in higher marsh areas above *Spartina foliosa,* typically in the narrow range of elevation between average high tide and extreme high tide, which is dominated by *Salicornia.* It can be found in association with *Salicornia virginica, Jaumea carnosa, Frankenia grandifolia, Monanthochloe littoralis, Limonium californica, Cressa truxillensis,* or *Distichlis spicata.* Occasionally it occurs behind barrier dunes, and it may also occupy low-lying areas, berms, roadsides, and depressions caused by vehicles. This species prefers soil with a pH of 6–9.6. This can include silty clay soil, but the plant prefers sandy loam soils.

Cordylanthus maritimus is considered to have three overlapping subspecies—ssp. *maritimus, palustris,* and *canescens*—based on geographical distribution and

physical characteristics. The subspecies *palustris* is at one extreme and ssp. *canescens* is at the other. The more variable ssp. *maritimus* approaches but does not completely resemble either of the other two in appearance. Differing characteristics include floral and bract color, development, branching patterns, population densities, and seed production.

Pollination and germination

Little is known about the biology of this species. Three possible pollinators have been observed: leaf cutter bees (*Megachile*), sweat bees (*Lasioglossum*), and Sonoran bumblebees (*Bombus sonoras*). Seeds are thought to be dispersed by water and animals. Germination occurs in spring when soil salinity is low and soil moisture is high. Seeds can germinate as soon as they are shed, but the germination rate improves after two years of dry, dark storage. It is also more likely in areas where perennial vegetation has been removed. Germination is inhibited by temperatures greater than 81 degrees Fahrenheit (27

Salt marsh bird's-beak gets water and nutrients from other plants. This keeps it green and allows it to flower in dry weather when other plants have died.

degrees Centigrade) and salinity above 12 parts per thousand. Water levels and salinity appear to be important factors in this species survival.

Salt marsh bird's-beak is found both in dense stands and in small patches mixed with other vegetation. Its occurrence can be patchy in both time and location, with some colonies failing to germinate each season.

Distribution and protection

Cordylanthus maritimus ssp. *maritimus* is found in coastal salt marshes from San Luis Obispo County, California, south. Many of these marshes are small and adjacent to urban areas. In addition to the high marsh habitat in which this plant grows, associated habitats that help maintain the conditions normally found there are also critical to its survival. These associated habitats include the lower marsh and the estuary mouth that maintain tidal influence, upstream areas and the watershed that could affect inflow of fresh water, and adjacent upland areas that have been suggested as possible habitat for pollinators.

The main reason for the endangered status of *Cordylanthus maritimus* ssp. *maritimus* is loss of its southern California coastal salt marsh habitat to marinas, industrial development, beach recreational facilities, and housing.

Salt marsh bird's-beak is protected by the Endangered Species Act of 1973 and the Lacey Act of 1900. The U.S. Fish and Wildlife Service, which has primary responsibility for its protection, drew up the Salt Marsh bird's-beak Recovery Plan in

1984. This plant is also designated as endangered by the state of California under the California Endangered Species Act. The California Department of Fish and Game is the state agency responsible for its protection.

Soft Bird's-beak
(Cordylanthus mollis ssp. mollis)

| ESA: Endangered |
| IUCN: Endangered |

Height: 10–16 in. (25– 41 cm)
Leaves: Oblong to lance-shaped, ½–1 in. (1–0.5 cm) long
Flowers: July to September. White or pale yellow, in spikes 2–6 in. (5–16 cm) long
Pollination: By bees
Habitat: Salt and brackish tidal marshes
Range: San Francisco Bay area of northern California

SOFT BIRD'S-BEAK IS AN annual herb of the snapdragon family (Scrophulariaceae) that grows to a height of 10 to 16 inches (25 to 41 centimeters). It is lightly branched from the middle of its stem upward. This is a hemiparasitic (partially parasitic) species that takes water and nutrients from other plants by attaching its roots to their roots.

The hairy foliage is grayish green and often tinged with a deep red, and the leaves are oblong or lance-shaped. The lower leaf margins are continuous and the upper ones have one to three pairs of lobes.

The flowers of soft bird's-beak are arranged in spikes, and a floral bract with two to three pairs of lobes occurs immediately below each small white or pale yellow flower. The flowers have only two functional stamens. Each egg-shaped seed capsule is 6 to 10 millimeters long and bears 20 to 30 dark brown seeds. The plant blooms between July and September.

Related subspecies
Cordylanthus mollis ssp. *mollis* is distinguished from another *Cordylanthus* found nearby (*C. maritimus* ssp. *palustris*) by its two functional stamens (*C. maritimus* ssp. *palustris* has four) and by its bracts with two to three pairs of lateral lobes (*C. maritimus* ssp. *palustris* has a pair of short teeth on the floral bracts). *C. mollis* ssp. *mollis* is closely related to *C. mollis* ssp. *hispidus*. These two subspecies can be difficult to tell apart, but they can be differentiated most consistently by spike length and seed size.

Habitat
Soft bird's-beak is found primarily in the upper reaches of larger salt grass-pickleweed marshes with fully developed tidal channel networks, at or near the limits of the tide's reach. It lives in association with *Salicornia virginica* (Virginia pickleweed), *Distichlis spicata* (salt grass), *Jaumea carnosa* (fleshy jaumea), *Frankenia salina* (alkali heath), and *Triglochin maritima* (seaside arrow grass). Soft bird's-beak occurs in salt and brackish tidal marshes bordering San Pablo and Suisun Bays in the San Francisco Bay area of northern California, one of the few places along the mountainous California coast where tidal marshes can

form. Since 1850, this habitat has been reduced to about 15 percent of its original area of 30,000 acres (12,000 hectares).

Changing population

Only nine sites hosting this species remain, primarily on private land. The two largest populations are located at Hill Slough and at Concord Naval Weapons Station, each covering approximately 10 acres (4 hectares). The total number of individuals reported varies from one plant at the smallest site to 150,000 plants at the largest. Individual populations fluctuate in size from year to year, which is typical of annual plants.

The greatest threat faced by this species is habitat loss and fragmentation due to hydraulic mining; diking and filling for agricultural use and urbanization; waste disposal; port and industrial development; railroad construction; dredging; salt production; and sedimentation.

The grayish green foliage of soft bird's-beak (*Cordylanthus mollis* ssp. *mollis*) can be seen growing on Grizzly Island, Solano County, California.

Other negative factors include water pollution, increases in salinity of tidal marshes due to upstream removal of fresh water, indirect effects of urbanization, mosquito abatement activities, competition with non-native vegetation, disease, insect predation, erosion, and various other human activities.

Qualified protection

Section 404 of the Clean Water Act is the primary federal law that affords some protection for this species, since it occurs in wetlands, but rare species may receive no special consideration with regard to conservation or protection unless they are listed under the act.

The California Department of Fish and Game has formally designated Soft bird's-beak as rare under the California Endangered Species Act. Although taking state-listed plants is prohibited by the California Native Plant Protection Act, the collection of such plants by means of habitat modification, or by land use changes implemented by the landowner, is exempt. In such

SOFT BIRD'S-BEAK
North America

cases, plans usually involve the transplantation of the species to an existing habitat or to an artificially created habitat, after which the original site is destroyed. However, if transplantation should fail, the source population will have already been lost.

No recovery plan

The U.S. Fish and Wildlife Service, which enforces the federal Endangered Species Act, has not designated a critical habitat for this species because this would not create a significant benefit to the species.

Moreover, any benefit that might be gained by designation of critical habitat is probably outweighed by its drawbacks. Research for drawing up maps depicting precise locations of critical habitat, which would be required for such designation, would most likely contribute to the further decline of soft bird's-beak. Such information would encourage trespassing and collecting and would hinder recovery efforts.

For these reasons there is no approved recovery plan for this species.

Rick Imes

BISON

Class: Mammalia
Order: Artiodactyla
Family: Bovidae
Subfamily: Bovinae
Tribe: Bovini

Bison were originally found in North America and Europe in large populations. The European varieties actually covered a very wide range of Eurasia, while those in the Western Hemisphere once roamed across nearly all of North America.

Bison are found generally in small family groups. They have no major predators other than humans. Wolves and brown bears were once menaces, but neither is a factor today.

European bison have longer legs than their North American counterparts; therefore, they are slightly taller. A long mane and heavily-muscled withers give the bison the appearance of being much taller than it really is. Like all bison, the European variety is not particularly dangerous in the wild unless it feels trapped, when it can defend itself well.

Both the European and North American bison share a common relationship with humans: although humans were responsible for their decline, humans can also take credit for their recovery. Bison have been protected now for nearly three generations, allowing their numbers to increase substantially. One wild herd protected in Yellowstone National Park (in Wyoming) has at least 2,000 individuals.

European Bison (Wisent)

(Bison bonasus)

IUCN: Endangered

Weight: 1,760–2,425 lb. (800–1100 kg)
Shoulder height: 71–79 in. (180–200 cm)
Diet: Leaves, shoots, twigs, and grasses
Gestation period: 254–272 days
Longevity: 20–25 years
Habitat: Open forest
Range: Poland, Russia

IN HISTORIC TIMES there were two type of European bison: the common European species (*B. bonasus*) found on that continent, and the Caucasian bison (*B. bonasus caucasicus*) found in the Caucasus Mountains region, which is between the Caspian and Black Seas.

The European bison were primarily animals of the open forest. They were not plains animals at all, as we often see them pictured in North America. European bison lived by eating leaves and grass in forest glades. When threatened, they retreated to denser portions of the forest. However, as forests were cut down for farming, the range of the European bison shrunk. In fact, the only original forest left today that is the European bison's natural range is in a place called Bialowieza, in Poland. This forest along the Polish-Russian border is the last holdout of the wisent, or European bison.

This impressive animal once lived in small family groups, never in large numbers as did the North American plains bison. It was not uncommon to find old bulls by themselves. European bison were well adapted to their environment, so their demise in the wild was a direct result of habitat destruction. The last truly wild specimen was killed in 1921 in the Bialowieza forest. From then on, European bison did not exist in their original wild state. However, through the efforts of Jan Sztolcman, a Polish zoologist, and Erna Mohr of the Prague

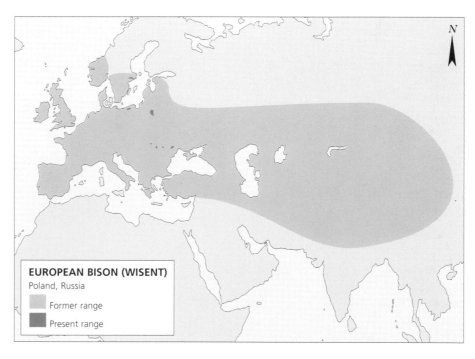

EUROPEAN BISON (WISENT)
Poland, Russia
Former range
Present range

Zoo in Hungary (who kept a log of survivors in captivity), this animal was saved from extinction. After World War II, the bison were reintroduced into the Bialowieza forest, where they now exist in a stable situation.

The Caucasian bison, however, did not have the same good fortune. A few were brought into captivity, but were hybridized (interbred) with the common European variety. When they were later reintroduced into the Caucasus, they were no longer the same Caucasian species.

Bison take to captivity well. They are quite long-lived and are reproductive for a long period of time. All they require is protection. Today, with both a healthy captive population and protected forms in the wild, it seems probable that the future of the European bison is assured.

Wood Bison

(Bison bison athabascae)

ESA: Endangered

Weight: 1,760–2,425 lb. (800–1,100 kg)
Shoulder height: 75–79 in. (190–200 cm)
Diet: Grasses and leaves
Gestation period: 270–300 days
Longevity: 25 years
Habitat: Open forest, grasslands
Range: Canada, Alaska

NORTH AMERICA once had a very large population of three different kinds of bison. The most familiar to Americans is the great plains bison (*B. bison bison*) that once numbered literally in the

The European bison is also known as the wisent. Today, both the captive and the wild populations of these animals are stable, and there is optimism about their survival.

millions. It roamed the open prairie of North America.

Another eastern variety was a forest dweller that inhabited Pennsylvania, Ohio, and the Great Lakes region. By all accounts, it was a relatively large variety. Its range, however, was directly in the path of colonial settlement, and the last animals were killed around the time of the American Revolution. This bison could not survive the settler's agriculture practices.

Forest dweller

The third variety is the wood bison, which lived in the northernmost part of the continent. A few still exist today in small num-

WOOD BISON
North America

Former Range

Present Range

The mistakes of humans

Aside from causing their habitat to shrink, humans did the wood bison a great disservice when they transplanted some plains bison to the wood bison's range. The result was that hybridization (or inbreeding) reduced the bloodlines of the wood bison. Wood bison have been set aside in protected areas of Canada and Alaska. The number of full-blooded individuals is small and the wood bison is thought to be endangered. There is a small captive population, but it is not as large as it should be to offer the wood bison sufficient protection from extinction in the wild.

Warren D. Thomas

The American bison (*Bison bison*) once roamed the plains of North America in vast herds numbering millions. By the 19th century they were almost wiped out. The population today is estimated at about 100,000, mainly in eastern and central North America.

bers. The wood bison differs from the plains bison in that it is taller and tends to be a little longer-legged.

Its coat is much darker, and it lacks the light buff color on its forequarters that can be seen on the plains bison. The wood bison's habits, however, are less like the plains bison and more like the European bison or wisent; in other words, the wood bison is a forest dweller.

Its diet consists of grass and leaves—and almost any available vegetation.

Tokyo Bitterling
(Tanakia tanago)

ESA: Endangered

IUCN: Vulnerable

Class: Actinopterygii
Order: Cypriniformes
Family: Cyprinidae
Length: 4 in. (10 cm)
Reproduction: Egg layer
Habitat: Small streams
Range: Kanto Plain, Japan

THE TOKYO bitterling belongs to the diverse family of fishes called Cyprinidae which includes carps, minnows, shiners, daces, and similar groups. Worldwide, there are over 1,500 species of Cyprinidae and many occupy the Asian continent. This fish is a victim of urbanization and pollution. The Kanto Plain, an area very near the capital city of Tokyo and sole inhabited range of the Tokyo bitterling, has been overrun by people and the pollution that invariably follows.

TOKYO BITTERLING
Japan

Many of the small streams once occupied by this fish have been destroyed, and the remaining waterways have been fouled by pesticides. As a result, the Tokyo bitterling is considered to be vulnerable.

Another key factor in the decline of this handsome freshwater species is competition from one of its relatives, the rose bitterling. Bitterlings lay their eggs within the shells of freshwater mussels. The Tokyo bitterling relies on one particular species of mussel for this purpose. The rose bitterling is not as choosy and lays eggs in any mussel variety. In addition, the rose bitterling is much more aggressive than the Tokyo bitterling and out-com-

This species, *Rhodeus ocellatus* (pictured here), belongs to the same family as the bitterling. It is not so protected as the bitterling, and is classified as critically endangered.

petes its cousin for breeding space within the Tokyo bitterling's preferred mussel.

Rescue measures

What may save the Tokyo bitterling is that as a result of its drastically diminished numbers and declining habitat, it has been formally designated by the Japanese government as a national monument. Hopefully, with this kind of strong protection, the Tokyo bitterling will be able to survive and flourish.

William E. Manci

Yellow-shouldered Blackbird

(Agelaius xanthomus)

ESA: Endangered

IUCN: Endangered

Class: Aves
Order: Passeriformes
Family: Icteridae
Subfamily: Icterinae
Length: 8–9 in. (20–23 cm)
Weight: 1.5–2¼ oz. (43–65 g), males slightly larger than females
Clutch Size: 2–4 eggs, usually 3
Incubation: 12–13 days
Diet: Insects, fruits, and seeds
Habitat: Originally coastal lowlands of savannah-like growth (scattered trees among open grassy areas); now nests almost exclusively in off-shore mangroves; feeds in various habitats, including some agricultural and urban settings
Range: Puerto Rico, and Mona Island in the Greater Antilles

VERY FEW ENDANGERED songbirds have been so well studied as the yellow-shouldered blackbird. Specific measures to protect or recover an endangered species require a thorough understanding of that species' natural history, the survival rates of young birds, their age at first breeding, individual longevity, their predators and diseases, and how they compete with other species. This knowledge is needed before recovery measures and direct action can be taken on behalf of any species.

This bird's limited distribution has contributed to successful research and made it easier to study. The bird is not migratory, but remains in its limited habitat on Puerto Rico all year.

Where they occur on Puerto Rico, yellow-shouldered blackbirds use various habitats including suburban areas, pastures, and coastal islets densely grown with mangroves. Nesting success, however, varies considerably. Black rats (*Rattus rattus*) climb trees to prey on eggs and nestlings. Shiny cowbirds (*Molothrus bonariensis*) are now a problem as they have extended their range. As nest parasites, the shiny cowbirds do not care for their own young but lay their eggs in other birds' nests. The cowbird nestlings hatch and develop faster than the eggs and chicks of their foster parents. Often, the species invaded by cowbirds fail to raise any chicks of their own; instead, the parents spend time tending to the more aggressive cowbird young.

On the main island, the blackbirds usually succeed more often when they nest in trees such as palms, which form natural "rat guards." The most successful nesting, however, occurs on the mangrove islets where the rats cannot reach the blackbirds' nests and the shiny cowbirds have not yet begun parasitizing the blackbird nests.

By the late 1970s, the population was less than 3,000 birds, most along Puerto Rico's southwestern coast. The remaining bird population was equally split between the eastern coast of Puerto Rico and Mona Island. By the late 1980s, the estimate was about 1,500 birds. Some accounts of the yellow-shouldered blackbird have attributed its demise to marsh drainage on Puerto Rico, but the bird does not occupy marshes. Nest predation and parasitism are more likely factors in its decline. In addition, the birds have been driven to nest on the small islets—a considerable distance from their feeding grounds.

The Mona Island subspecies has been threatened by government proposals to make the island a port for supertankers, and to use Mona Island as a target range for American naval warplanes. If either proposal were implemented, the yellow-shouldered blackbird would almost certainly perish on Mona.

Kevin Cook

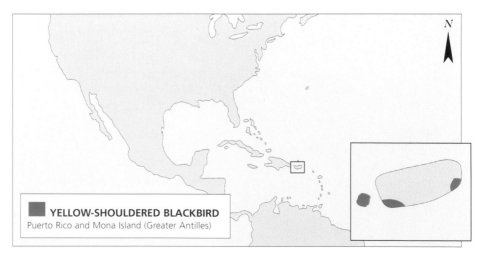

YELLOW-SHOULDERED BLACKBIRD
Puerto Rico and Mona Island (Greater Antilles)

BLINDCATS

Class: Actinopterygii

Order: Siluriformes

Family: Ictaluridae

When we think of caves, we think of creatures like bats, large insects, or other creatures that shun bright light. We seldom consider that many caves hold water or are completely filled with water, and that fish live in these underground recesses, pools, and streams. Many fishes have evolved underground without light and other physical qualities of our environment that we take for granted.

Caves offer conditions that are very different from those at the surface. Cave-dwelling animals live in total darkness in an "energy-poor" environment. Caves cannot sustain green plants that capture sunlight and turn it into food for other plants and animals. Because of their isolation from the surface and a lack of life-giving sunlight, subterranean fishes depend completely on the movement of food items from the surface to their underground domain. Caves have a stable temperature that varies little if at all.

In response to their unusual environment, cave-dwelling fishes have developed unique features. They lack eyes, which would be useless, could be damaged in the darkness, and would require energy to develop and maintain. However the exterior of these fishes is packed with other sensory organs that provide touch, taste, and smell capabilities. They lack skin pigmentation, and all of these fishes are white and pink (albino). Camouflage to avoid predators and protect the skin from the sun is not required in this cavernous environment. To cope with the reduced availability of food, these fishes have a slower metabolism than many others, and have larger fins for more efficient swimming. Also, cave-dwelling fishes are able to store fat more efficiently. Blindcats lack a swim bladder, an organ used by most fish to regulate buoyancy, but rely on fat stores to provide buoyancy and energy when food is scarce.

Bats can play an important role in the lives of some cave-dwelling fishes. In caves that are not completely filled with water, bats are a transport mechanism that supports fish populations. Solids wastes such as bat guano, and dead bats are key sources of food for cave fishes and other inhabitants of the cave ecosystem. Aquatic plankton, fungus, decaying organic material, small amphibians, and other fish are also food sources.

Given the thin margin between death and survival for blindcats, it is not surprising that little energy remains available for reproduction. They do not breed regularly and, depending on the food supply, may not breed even once in a year. When breeding occurs, relatively few eggs are produced. An important adaptation of the blindcats is their ability to protect newly hatched fish by holding them in their mouths, thereby decreasing predation on the offspring.

Only three species of blindcat fishes within the family Ictaluridae are known, and each is different enough to earn its own genus. There are other blindcat fishes in the family Clariidae such as Africa's endangered cave catfish (*Clarias cavernicola*). Less is known about blindcats than about cavefishes, because of limited access to the fish. Blindcats inhabit deep underground water reservoirs that are difficult or impossible for people to penetrate, while cavefishes occupy more accessible areas. The toothless and widemouth blindcats and the Mexican blindcats are included in the group.

Mexican Blindcat (Bagre de Muzquiz)

(Prietella phreatophila)

ESA: Endangered

IUCN: Endangered

Length: 2½ in. (6 cm)
Reproduction: Egg layer
Habitat: Underground waterways
Range: Coahuila, Mexico

THE MEXICAN BLINDCAT, or bagre de Muzquiz, is very rare. While a good estimate of the total number of fish and their locations is difficult to determine, we do know that pollution and human use of underground water supplies are the principal threats to this unusual fish.

Leaching of agricultural pesticides and improper disposal of industrial chemical wastes jeopardize the survival of the few remaining specimens. As human demands on the water supply grow, water tables will inevitably fall, most probably to the detriment of the bagre de Muzquiz. Although they occupy similar kinds of habitat, the bagre de Muzquiz is quite different from other blindcats and is classified in a different genus, *Prietella*. All blindcats arose from different evolutionary lines, but have adapted in similar ways to deal with the underground environment. The bagre de Muzquiz lacks eyes and skin coloration, and has extremely sensitive senses of taste and touch. It feeds on a wide variety of food items, taking whatever the environment offers in terms of nourishment including fish, plankton, and other organic material. Little else is known about the biology of this creature.

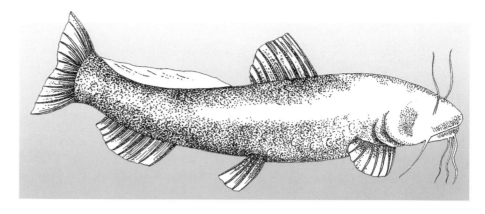

Toothless Blindcat

(Trogloglanis pattersoni)

IUCN: Vulnerable

Length: 3½ in. (9 cm)
Reproduction: Egg layer
Habitat: Deep, thermal artesian wells
Range: San Antonio, Texas

THE ONLY KNOWN populations of toothless blindcat are located in an underground water formation called the Edwards Aquifer near San Antonio, Texas. This aquifer, situated 500 feet (150 meters) below the surface, is large—about 200 miles (320 kilometers) long. Since it is the only source of drinking water around for the city of San Antonio, the demand for water by the city is potentially a major threat to the survival of

the toothless blindcat. Several 1,000-foot (305-meter) deep wells enter the prime habitat of this fish in an area of the aquifer called the San Antonio Pool, and hundreds of other agricultural irrigation wells tap the Edwards Aquifer at other locations. This water source is resupplied by rainfall that percolates through the soil, but experts estimate that additional water demand resulting from an increase in San Antonio's population could outstrip the natural resupply.

Pollution problems

Compounding the problem of water consumption is pollution from industrial and agricultural sources. While their effects on the toothless blindcat are unclear, concern about the effects on people may save the blindcat. Because the Edwards Aquifer

The bagre de Muzquiz is so different from other blindcats that it is in a different genus, called *Prietella*.

and San Antonio Pool are used as drinking water sources, steps taken to protect the public safety will also be beneficial to the toothless blindcat.

This species occupies some areas of the San Antonio Pool as the sole resident, and shares other areas with its close relative, the widemouth blindcat. Because of its lack of teeth and very delicate jaw, this white- and pink-skinned fish is believed to survive on a diet of fungus and organic material. The toothless blindcat has a long digestive tract for efficient absorption of food and an intricate system of taste buds over its body that allows it to find and identify its food.

Despite its harmless nature and willingness to cohabit with its relative, the widemouth blindcat, fishery scientists believe that the toothless blindcat may be preyed on by its less-hospitable cousin. Predation by other animals, including the widemouth blindcat, hinders the toothless blindcat's struggle for survival.

The toothless blindcat grows to about four inches (10 centimeters) in length and is oddly shaped. It has a catfish-like body but the head is highly specialized.

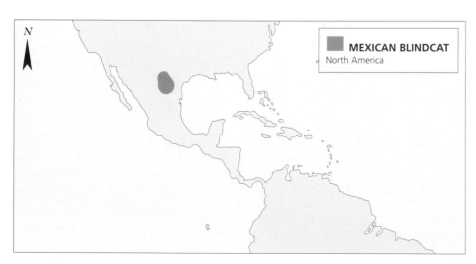

N

MEXICAN BLINDCAT
North America

To make up for its lack of eyes, the white and pink head and body have many sensors to detect taste, and to smell cues from food. The dorsal fin on the back and the pectoral fins on the sides (just behind the gills) each have a single stout spine to deter predators. The large anal fin (behind the anus) helps the mouth to point slightly downward.

Widemouth Blindcat

(Satan eurystomus)

IUCN: Vulnerable

Length: 4 in. (11 cm)
Reproduction: Egg layer
Habitat: Deep, thermal artesian wells
Range: San Antonio, Texas

LIKE THE TOOTHLESS blindcat, the only known populations of widemouth blindcats are located in an underground water formation called Edwards Aquifer near San Antonio, Texas, which is the only source of drinking water for the city of San Antonio and the surrounding area. The demand for water by the city is a threat to the survival of the blindcat. Several 1,000-foot (305-meter) wells enter the prime habitat of this fish in an area of the aquifer called the San Antonio Pool, and hundreds of other irrigation wells tap the Edwards Aquifer at other locations. This water source is resupplied by rainfall that perco-

The toothless blindcat is thought to survive on a diet of fungus and other organic material, an adaptation that helps it survive in its cave environment.

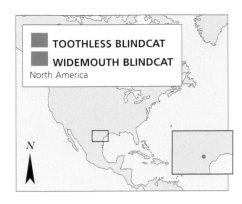

TOOTHLESS BLINDCAT
WIDEMOUTH BLINDCAT
North America

N

lates through the soil, but experts estimate that additional water demand resulting from an increase in San Antonio's population could outstrip the supply. As well as the problem of water consumption there is pollution from industrial and agricultural sources. While their effects on the blindcat are unclear, worries about the effects on people may be the blindcat's "saving grace." Because the Edwards Aquifer and San Antonio Pool are sources of drinking water, steps taken to protect public safety will also be beneficial to the blindcat.

This species occupies some areas of the San Antonio Pool as the sole resident and shares other areas with its close relative, the toothless blindcat. However, the widemouth blindcat is built somewhat differently. This white- and pink-bodied albino has a broad, toothed jaw and is larger. Unlike the toothless blindcat, the head and body are loaded with sensors to detect motion; taste and smell are far less developed. The two blindcats live side by side in some locations, and scientists believe—because of its well-developed mouth and sense of touch geared toward detecting movement—that the widemouth blindcat preys on the slightly smaller toothless blindcat.

The widemouth blindcat grows to around 5 inches (12.5 centimeters) and is oddly shaped. It has a catfish-like body but the head and body are highly specialized. A series of canals on the head and sides detect pressure waves from moving prey. These waves move hairs in the canals, stimulating nerves at their base. This fish can determine the size and direction of very small prey, as small as 0.03 inches (1 millimeter) by using this system—even in total darkness. The dorsal fin on the back and the pectoral fins on the sides each have a single stout spine to deter predators. The anal fin helps the mouth to point downward during swimming. This serves as an aid in finding and recognizing food.

William E. Manci

Honey Blue-eye
(Pseudomugil mellis)

IUCN: Endangered

Class: Actinopterygii
Order: Mugiliformes
Family: Pseudomugilidae
Length: 1 in. (3 cm)
Reproduction: Egg layer
Habitat: Small streams and pools
Range: Queensland, Australia

As a result of its geographic isolation and scarcity of fresh water, Australia has relatively few native freshwater fishes. Only about 190 fish species occupy fresh water across the entire continent, and many of these are derived from marine ancestors. Despite low human population density across the continent, people tend to live in many of the same places as these freshwater species. An alarmingly high percentage of these fishes (34 percent) is threatened by extinction to one degree or another.

In common with many other continents, hydroelectric, flood-control, and irrigation dams play a significant role in the destruction of habitat, and act as barriers to the free movement of fishes up and down river systems. Associated modifications may include the construction of flood-control dikes, the removal of streambed vegetation, and the destruction of breeding and nursery areas. These changes restrict movement, and can cause problems of siltation, unacceptable temperature patterns, and reduced or inappropriate water flow patterns.

Agricultural practices that lead to deforestation and also to overgrazing are particularly destructive and cause erosion, thereby producing too much silt in the water. Other water quality changes resulting from pollution are equally traumatic.

Overfishing and the introduction of exotic species can reduce or eliminate populations of fishes. Fishing pressure and competition for habitat and food by more aggressive, non-native species play important roles in the decline of many of Australia's threatened fishes. The honey blue-eye and other blue-eyes are also in demand as ornamental aquarium fishes.

Finally, "natural" occurrences such as disease add to the threat, causing many to die off; however, pollution and other man-made habitat alterations can trigger these disease episodes as well.

Positive steps
In light of the challenges to many of Australia's native fishes, the government is beginning to take steps to remedy the situation. New laws to protect existing populations from current and future threats are being put in place. For example, scheduled releases of water from dams during critical spawning and nursery periods should help to increase reproductive success. Also, efforts are increasing to collect more basic biological information about these fishes.

A small and brightly colored warmwater fish, the honey blue-eye is found in the tropical regions of northeastern Australia in Queensland. It lives in small quiet streams and pools, along stream banks in dense aquatic vegetation, and in areas where roots from terrestrial plants hang down into the water. The honey blue-eye consumes small insects and plankton and is prone to eat small eggs of other fishes and those of its own species. The male is the flashiest of the two sexes and has large fins used for swimming and to display to a potential mate. Honey blue-eyes in breeding condition swim closely together as the female chooses a plant on which to deposit her eggs. She then lays a few eggs and moves on to other vegetation to repeat the process. As eggs are laid, the male immediately releases sperm to fertilize them.

William E. Manci

N

HONEY BLUE-EYE
Australia

BOAS

Class: Reptilia

Order: Serpentes

Family: Boidae

Members of the Boidae family are the largest snakes alive. The family includes small-to-medium-sized species. Boas share the family with three other subfamilies: Loxoceminae, a single species; Pythoninae; and Round Island Bolyeriinae.

Conservation efforts for all reptiles have begun only recently, but snakes have been particularly neglected. This may be because humans traditionally have been taught to fear snakes. Public opinion has made saving snakes more difficult than protecting "preferred" animals such as members of the cat family or whales. Few people have expressed interest in saving these intriguing animals in the past, but today more people are devoting their time to the conservation of snakes. As the public learns that boids are virtually harmless to humans, perhaps snakes such as boas will finally be protected.

Mona Boa

(Epicrates monensis monensis)

ESA: Threatened

IUCN: Endangered

Length: Approximately 3 ft. (1 m)

Diet: Uncertain; probably anoles, rats, mice, and bats

Habitat: Forests, or subtropical, semideciduous scrub lands

Range: Found only on Mona Island in the Greater Antilles

THE MONA BOA is endemic to Mona Island, a rocky limestone island located between Puerto Rico and Hispaniola. Only 12 specimens have been collected by scientists; all but one were juveniles. The ground color of the adult boa was found to be light brown with 44 dark brown markings, while the underside was beige with a few scattered spots. The juveniles are a very light yellowish brown with dark brown markings as the ground color.

Found only on Mona Island, one Mona boa has been captured on a small branch in a subtropical, dry, deciduous forest. Others were observed on the island's southwestern coastal plain on branches of a pine.

Still others have been captured on spiny shrubs on a coastal road. Such varied sightings suggest that the mona boa is widely distributed across the island.

Varied habitat

The island of Mona is a flat plateau that slopes gently upland, terminating in high, sheer cliffs along the northern and southern coasts, with less steep cliffs on the western margin. A great deal of the island is covered by solid limestone, which encourages the growth of dry scrub vegetation such as low trees, shrubs, and cacti. Over the rest of the plateau, a thin soil layer permits tree growth only in soil pockets; thus, the tree canopy is particularly low and the forest discontinuous. Large areas of the coastal terrace were cleared and planted with West Indian mahogany and Australian pine in the 1930s and 1940s. The terrain and growth on Mona Island is fairly diverse, and it appears that the boa is adapted to a large number of habitats.

Food and reproduction

Little is known of the Mona boa's feeding habits, but observations of three snakes in captivity suggest that lizards of the genus *Anolis* probably constitute an important part of its diet.

Some of the other species of *Epicrates* eat various rodents and bats, and it is possible that these animals also make up part of the Mona boa's diet. In common with all species of the genus, this boa kills its prey by constriction and swallows it head first.

The reproductive habits of this reptile are unknown. Other species of the genus usually have eight to thirty young. The only data that is available about the Mona boa show that one specimen collected in 1979 aborted four young while in captivity.

Secretive snake

Because of the lack of field data on the Mona boa, the cause of its endangered status is speculative. Many think it is the result of habitat modification. For example, the introduction of mammals such as goats and pigs has altered the island's plant life, which may be vital to the boa's survival.

It is likely that the large population of feral cats on the island may prey on the boa. These cats also consume reptiles and birds, possibly competing with the snake for food.

Many scientists think that the Mona boa's nocturnal habits may make it hard to locate during the daytime. Also, because most of the specimens collected have been juveniles, the adult snakes' habits may become such that they are more difficult to collect. The nocturnal and secretive habits of the snake, together with the spiny vegetation on Mona Island, make research difficult—possibly exaggerating the image of the boa's endangered status. There is no past or present information on population, so it is uncertain if the boa has declined.

To date there have been no direct conservation efforts to protect the Mona boa. Mona Island has been managed by the U.S. Department of Natural Resources since 1973 to protect its wildlife and vegetation. Rangers work on the island with a resident biologist to enforce protective legislation and educate visitors on the importance of native wildlife and flora.

Because so little is known about the Mona boa, it is difficult to protect it or initiate a recovery plan. Until adequate information is obtained about the snake's habits, its role as prey to feral animals, and its population density, it will be difficult to know whether the boa is surviving.

Puerto Rican Boa

(Epicrates inornatus)

ESA: Endangered

IUCN: Lower risk

Length: Approximately 5.9–7.2 ft. (1.8–2.2 m)
Diet: Uncertain; probably bats, birds, mice, rats, and lizards
Habitat: Various, ranging from wet montane to subtropical dry forest
Range: Endemic to Puerto Rico

THE PUERTO RICAN boa is the largest snake of the Puerto Rican Island Shelf. Based on examinations of existing museum specimens and the descriptions of biologists, its color and pattern are highly variable. The ground color ranges from tan to dark brown with 70 to 80 markings on the back. Some individuals appear to lack markings altogether. Young of the species are reddish brown in ground color with numerous markings. Females appear to be larger than males. The Puerto Rican boa differs from the Mona boa and the Virgin Island boa—two other species of the Puerto Rico Island Shelf—because of its larger size, darker coloration, and less pronounced patterns.

The boa occurs in a wide variety of habitats ranging from wet montane to subtropical dry forest. One specimen was found on a mangrove island off southwestern Puerto Rico. In Loquillo National Forest, these boas are found in both virgin forests and areas that have seen varying degrees of human disturbance such as managed tree plantations or the construction of roads. However, the snake is most often encountered in the northern limestone karst, an irregular region with sinks, underground streams, and caverns. This area supports a subtropical, moist forest and has a mean temperature of 65 to 75 degrees Fahrenheit (18 to 24 degrees Celsius). In this habitat, Puerto Rican boas have been seen on tree branches, on rotting stumps, and basking in cave entrances.

All species of *Epicrates* are nocturnal, tending to be active at night but remaining concealed or basking in the sun during the day. Basking may help raise the body temperature, which aids in digestion and embryo development. The feeding habits of the Puerto Rican boa are uncertain, but in captivity it eats birds, mice, rats, and lizards. First it constricts the prey, then consumes it head first. In the wild, an individual was observed preying on a bat. Examination of

Little is known about the habits and natural history of the Mona boa, so it is difficult to say with certainty what has caused the population to decline.

stomach matter of this boa has also displayed an adult rat and a small firefly.

Little information is available about the snake's reproductive habits in nature. As with all boids, it lays eggs that develop and hatch outside of the body. Apparently these snakes mate between February and April and birth occurs in September or October. From 17 to 32 young in a clutch have been reported. Two organizations have bred the Puerto Rican boa in captivity. In these cases, the age at first reproduction was between six and seven years and mating occurred on branches. At one institution, the snake was seen to breed annually; at the other breeding was biennial. The reason for this difference is unknown.

Opinions are divided among biologists about the status of the Puerto Rican boa. The U.S. Fish and Wildlife Service concluded that it was endangered in 1970. However, because the boa has been seen relatively frequently in adequate habitat, the Puerto Rico Natural Heritage Program does not consider it to be endangered. It is, however, protected from collecting and hunting by the Commonwealth of Puerto Rico's Wildlife and Hunting Regulations.

No truly reliable population estimate exists for the boa at this time. One report recorded 75 different individuals from 18 localities, but the biologists who collected this data visited only a small percentage of the areas that are reported to have a suitable habitat for the species. There is information that suggests a historical decline in numbers. Data compiled by a writer in 1788 described snakes with size, color, and habits resembling the Puerto Rican boa, stating that the snakes were very abundant, even entering homes at night in search of rats or other prey. By 1904, however, biologists on expedition to Puerto Rico failed to secure specimens of the snake.

Widespread deforestation during the 1800s probably reduced the boa populations. The human fear of snakes, together with using the animal for medicinal extracts, and mongoose predation, may have played a role in the boa's decline. Increased sightings in the past decade, however, suggest that the species may be reestablishing itself.

Virgin Islands Tree Boa
(Epicrates monensis granti)

ESA: Endangered

IUCN: Endangered

Length: Approximately 31–40 in. (79–101 cm)
Diet: Primarily anoles
Habitat: Dry forest habitat
Range: Endemic to the Puerto Rico Bank

THE VIRGIN ISLANDS tree boa was first described in 1933, but has been rarely seen since that time. Only 13 specimens have been recorded. Initially, this snake was thought to be a subspecies of the Puerto Rican boa until its similarities with the Mona Boa were described in 1974. While the Mona boa is endemic to Mona Island, the Virgin Islands tree boa is found on several islands of the Puerto Rico Bank east of Puerto Rico. The Virgin Islands tree boa is absent from the island of Puerto Rico itself, probably because of the extinction of xeric fauna there.

Biology and natural history
The adult Virgin Islands tree boa's body color is light brown with darker markings partially edged in black. The slender boa grows to about three feet (0.9 meters) in length, but it is probable that a larger specimen will be

Widespread deforestation is probably responsible for reducing the Puerto Rican boa populations. Humans, who have killed the boa out of fear and for use in medicinal extracts, have also done their share to deplete the numbers of this species.

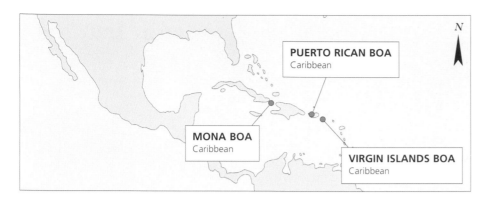

discovered. The Virgin Islands tree boa is nocturnal, and captive snakes rapidly seek cover when exposed to light. However, during later stages of gestation, females may bask in the sun to raise body temperature and aid in the development of the embryos. Snakes of the *Epicrates* genus generally copulate between February and May; birth usually occurs from August through October. It seems most species of the genus reproduce biennially, but there are indications that the Virgin Islands tree boa may reproduce annually. The species may not reach reproductive maturity until about three years of age. Snakes of the genus *Epicrates* tend to live in excess of 10 years, and this may also be true of the Virgin Islands tree boa. Very large animals with faded patterns suggest longevity.

The boa seems to feed primarily on a specific species of anole. It feeds by gliding slowly along small branches and attacking sleeping lizards. The snake has been observed or captured most frequently where the population of this anole is most dense, suggesting it is dependent upon the anole as the staple of its diet.

This tree boa occurs in an arid forest habitat with steep slopes and rocky soils. It is found in almost every type of vegetation in

the range except very low, succulent cover close to the high-tide line. This snake has been found on branches of a small Mimosa tree of only about three feet (0.9 meters) in height; prowling in tangled vines three feet (0.9 meters) above ground; and in low shrubs around the perimeter of the island just above the high-tide mark. Observers in Las Croabas note that the snake seems to be limited to dry, savannah-like habitats on islets off the eastern coast of Puerto Rico.

The current distribution of the Virgin Islands tree boa suggests that it was once more widespread. A population estimate is not possible due to lack of data. Because the boa's distribution is patchy, several populations probably became extinct in prehistoric times, perhaps due to climate changes, decline in xeric fauna, or natural disasters such as hurricanes. More recent causes of decline include habitat disturbance; increased human and domestic animal populations; and the introduction of the mongoose in the late 19th century, which had a devastating effect on endemic reptiles. On the island of Cayo Diablo, a recent count of 58 boas indicates that the population may be thriving. There is also potential for high populations on other

islands where Indian mongooses and other predators are absent. The nocturnal and arboreal activity of the boa probably protects it by day.

While there are no direct local efforts to protect this boa, its status is regarded as endangered. Live specimens captured by the public are released by the U.S. Fish and Wildlife Service into areas within its known range. In addition, captive breeding of the species began in 1985 under the management of the Departmento de Recursos Naturales de Puerto Rico, the U.S. Fish and Wildlife Service, and the Toledo Zoological Society. Studies of wild populations were coupled with reproductive research programs that established environmental and social factors critical to reproduction of the species.

Captive breeding of the Virgin Islands tree boa has been successful, with 48 offspring produced by ten adults; 40 of the young have survived. Fortunately, environmental factors necessary for reproduction can be easily duplicated in captivity, and the survival rate of the offspring is very high. Also, because the species is long-lived, lifetime reproductive output can be very high. Reintroduction of captive-reared individuals appears to be a viable strategy for the survival of this boa. A significant barrier to overcome is the eradication of potential predators of the snake. Snakes cannot be released in an area until control programs of these animals are successful. Initial releases may involve tracking of captive-bred individuals with transmitters to ensure that they can exist with wild snakes.

Elizabeth Sirimarco

Bobcat
(Felis rufus)

Class: Mammalia
Order: Carnivora
Family: Felidae
Length: 24–36 in. (62–95 cm)
Shoulder height: 20–24 in. (12-19 cm)
Weight: 9–41 lb. (4–18.5 kg)
Diet: Birds, hares, wild rabbits, other mammals up to the size of a deer
Gestation period: 60–70 days
Litter size: 1–4, seldom to 6
Habitat: Brush and grasslands in damp and dry regions
Range: From Canada through the United States, south to Mexico and the Yucatan Peninsula forests

BOBCAT
Canada, United States, Mexico

THE BOBCAT IS yellowish gray in the northeastern parts of its range, and brown and reddish as it moves to the southwest and into Central America. It is covered with small spots, or rosettes, and bands. It has ear brushes, or tufts, that rise up from the ears. It gets its name from its short, stumpy tail. It is a relative of the lynx, but is smaller, with shorter legs and a slightly longer tail that is marked with black bands on its upper surface.

Natural history

The bobcat was once the most prevalent wild felid in the United States. It can occur in nearly every habitat, from high altitude forests to subtropical swamps or arid plains. This cat will cover a territory from one square mile (2.5 square kilometers) to 18 square miles (47 square kilometers). Females are less tolerant than the males in protecting their territory from other bobcats. Males will often share border areas. The male and female may stay together after mating for some time. The female builds a den of dry moss or leaves in a hollow log, or rock crevice. After the litter is born, the male is not allowed near the young until they eat solid food, when he helps by bringing food for them. The female then leaves her cubs to join the male. The breeding season is in winter, and after a gestation period of 60 to 70 days, the female bears up to four offspring, which stay and hunt with the mother until the next season.

Killed for fashion

The bobcat's fur was not in fashion until the early 1970s, because the fur was not durable. Chemical treatments solved this problem. As more desirable species such as the ocelot became endangered, they were protected by CITES, and the fur industry saw the bobcat as a moneymaker. Bobcats possess unique markings and long winter coats, and the price of their coats rose to $500 dollars, and rose until the animal became threatened.

By 1976 most states in the U.S. restricted or prohibited hunting of the bobcat, but it had already been eliminated from many areas. The last count estimated that there were between 725,000 and one million bobcats in the wild, and the bobcat is no longer considered to be endangered, although a subspecies, the Mexican bobcat (*Felis rufus escuinapae*), is now endangered.

Elizabeth Sirimarco

The bobcat is one of the smaller North American wild felids. It is a relative of the lynx, but is much smaller.

Masked Bobwhite

(Colinus virginianus ridgwayi)

ESA: Endangered

Class: Aves
Order: Galliformes
Family: Phasianidae
Subfamily: Odontophorinae
Length: 9–11 in. (23–28 cm)
Weight: 5 oz. (142 g)
Clutch size: Extremes of 7–28 eggs reported for the species, averages 12–16 eggs
Incubation: 23–24 days
Diet: Seeds, buds, insects
Habitat: Open desert grassland and semi-desert shrub lands well interspersed with grass
Range: From Altar and Santa Cruz Valleys of southern Arizona south into plains of Sonora, Mexico

The bobwhite is an attractive bird that has long been the prey of American sport hunters.

MILLIONS OF AMERICANS recognize the sharp, cheery, two-note whistle that gave a bird its name. "Bob-white!" rings through grassy shrub lands and woodlands across the Great Plains into the Midwest, East, and Southeast. A tiny population of these birds struggles to survive in the Desert Southwest.

The only quail native to the eastern United States, the northern bobwhite naturally occupies all or portions of 39 states, extreme southern Canada, Cuba, and large sections of Mexico. It has also been introduced into at least three additional states plus many islands and foreign countries. The success of the introductions has been highly variable. Throughout its vast native range, the northern bob- white has specialized into 21 or 22 recognizable subspecies. As with all birds, it is more abundant in some places, less abundant within others. The key factor is habitat quality.

As a species, the northern bobwhite inhabits shrubby woodlands where the ground is well covered by grass and other herbaceous plants. A terrestrial species, it nests on the ground and needs good cover to hide its nests and to shelter its chicks. Good cover is not always enough protection, however. As a secondary defense, the northern bobwhite lays large clutches of eggs so that at least a few chicks may survive to adulthood. Even so, predators as diverse as snakes and rodents, weasels and foxes, even some hawks and owls prey heavily on the bird. A hen may have to lay two or three, even four, clutches to hatch a brood successfully and have a chance to raise chicks.

Typically, river floodplains support ideal bobwhite habitat. For many years, fallow fields, pastures, and creek bottoms on farms provided good habitat also. Changing farm methods, commercial land development, conversion of rural land to suburban land, and other factors, have caused some of the northern bobwhite populations to decline. The bird's popularity has been its most important asset.

Popular with hunters

Quick, explosive flight and agreeable flavor have made the northern bobwhite a favored game bird since colonial times. Various hunters' groups and state wildlife agencies have worked hard to manage the species to sustain populations. Private citizens and organizations even raise northern bobwhites just to release them into the wild. Some raise the birds on game farms for private hunting access. For the most part, then, the northern bob-

white has fared well, except for that isolated population in the Desert Southwest—a subspecies known as the masked bobwhite. It steadily declined for decades before disappearing from the United States altogether. Some accounts indicate the masked bobwhite may have vanished from Arizona as early as 1900.

The masked bobwhite originally inhabited desert grasslands in low mountain valleys and river plains in extreme southern Arizona southward into Sonora, Mexico. These grasslands became highly prized for grazing cattle; but desert plant communities are fragile, especially desert grasslands. The grasses grow very quickly with seasonal rains. The masked bobwhite depends on this flush of growth to produce the thick ground cover needed for hiding its nests and chicks. If the rains are late, the masked bobwhite will delay its nesting. If the rains fail, it may skip a season without breeding. Moreover, these grasslands cannot sustain grazing for very long. Woody shrubs gradually replace the grasses and slowly change grasslands to shrub lands. Other quail species, such as the scaled (*Callipepla*

squamata) and the Gambel's (*Callipepla gambelii*), then move into the shrub lands. The masked bobwhite cannot compete with the other quails in their preferred habitat. As cattle grazing has steadily expanded through the masked bobwhite's range, the bird has slowly disappeared from its habitats.

Appearance

The male bobwhite is a reddish brown or cinnamon on the breast and belly; the head and throat are black with a variable white line above and behind the eye. The back, wings, and tail are mottled in browns (for camouflage), and the head is tufted. The females lack the black head and throat and cinnamon underparts of the male; the head is brown, and the throat a dirty white leading to a buff breast and belly.

The bobwhite's decline has been recognized since the 1930s. Both captive and wild birds were released through the 1940s into 1950. The releases were outside the subspecies' natural range and did not include good quality habitat. The program utterly failed. In 1966, a successful captive breeding began at Patuxent Wildlife Research Center in Maryland. The facility was able to produce 3,000 masked bobwhite chicks a year, but despite great care to release chicks into the best available habitat, losses remained very high, probably owing to coyotes preying on the released birds. For many years, experts believed that captive-bred birds lacked the experience to survive natural conditions after release. Wild-caught birds would have a better chance to survive, but the only wild masked

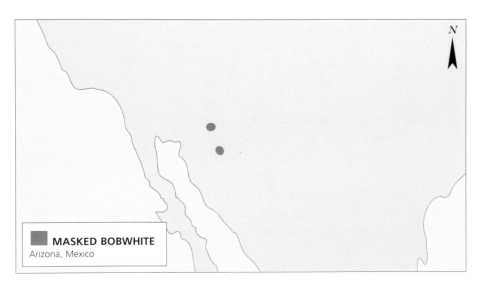

MASKED BOBWHITE
Arizona, Mexico

predator avoidance was vital to the quails' survival.

Another approach used a different subspecies of northern bobwhite, the Texas bobwhite (*Colinus virginianus texanus*), as a foster parent. Male birds accept chicks, and as they can be easily neutered, they cannot interbreed and thus dilute the genetic purity of the endangered subspecies.

Both techniques yielded satisfactory results. The difficulty was finding suitable habitat that would sustain bobwhites. The best remaining habitat was in Arizona on a privately owned ranch 60 miles southwest of Tucson on the Mexican border. The federal government purchased the ranch in 1985, and the U.S. Fish and Wildlife Service administers it as the Buenos Aires National Wildlife Refuge. A program of controlled burning maintains the grassland qualities and prevents mesquite from invading. Heavy grazing in the last century damaged the land, then exotic grasses were brought in to help to stabilize the soil. Although the refuge cannot offer the most ideal natural habitat, it seems capable of sustaining a population. About 12,000 chicks produced at Patuxent have been released with the neutered Texas bobwhites. By 1991, 300 to 500 birds survived, and some natural, wild reproduction had taken place. The Mexican population has declined to about 300 pairs on a privately owned ranch in Sonora. A recent cooperative agreement between the United States and Mexican governments promises new opportunities for research and management to preserve the masked bobwhite.

Kevin Cook

bobwhites lived in Sonora. Expanding cattle grazing in Sonora likewise pressured the masked bobwhite in Mexico. The possibility of an international agreement to live-trap masked bobwhites in Mexico so they could be released into another poor habitat in the United States was unlikely to be successful. Other options had to be found.

Other plans

Several other recovery strategies were tested during the 1970s. Eggs of the masked bobwhite were placed in the nest of a scaled quail who hatched the eggs and tended the young bobwhite chicks as her own. This technique, known as "cross-fostering," offered some promise. It was abandoned, however, because locating the nests of wild quails proved extremely tedious. Another approach to cross-fostering called for domestic chickens to raise masked bobwhite chicks, but the chickens proved hostile to the quail chicks. The best option seemed to rest

Because the bobwhite nests on the ground, it chooses territory with good cover that will effectively camouflage it from would-be predators.

on releasing captive-bred birds but with better care.

Special rearing and holding pens were designed so the birds would not damage their feathers or beaks while in captivity. This meant the birds would be in better condition when released. The birds were then transferred to areas where they would be released and held in special pens where they could become familiar with the vegetation and general habitat where they would live after release. Special boxes with captive birds were used to lure the semi-free birds back each night. The captives would call and the birds would return where they could be protected. Before the final release, the masked bobwhites were harassed by people on foot, trained dogs, and trained hawks. The intention was to build their instincts for when to fly and when to crouch, and to develop their flight strength. Learning

Bontebok

(Damaliscus dorcas dorcas)

ESA: Endangered

IUCN: Vulnerable

Class: Mammalia
Order: Artiodactyla
Family: Bovidae
Tribe: Alcephalini
Weight: 132–220 lb. (60–100 kg)
Shoulder height: 31.5–39.5 in. (80–100 cm)
Diet: Grasses
Gestation period: 7.5 months
Longevity: 12–14 years (20 years in captivity)
Habitat: Grasslands
Range: South Africa

THE BONTEBOK is one of the smallest members of the harte-beeste tribe. Its name means "many colored," and it is one of the most colorful of all the ante-lope. There are many shades of brown, white, fawn and purple in its hide. The darker areas glisten, and almost glow under bright light. In their habits they are almost exclusively grazers. They do eat some leafy material, but feed mainly on grasses. They especially eat many of the short grasses that occur in the veldt or grasslands of South Africa.

Like other hartebeestes, bon-tebok are very territorial. They exhibit a strict code of domi-nance. The males probably begin to stake out territory and defend it at about three or four years of age. They make every attempt to attract females. Females have a dominance hierarchy within their gender groups, so it is difficult to keep bontebok in captivity in a confined area. Unlike other ante-lope, they do not show tolerance for each other.

A problem for farmers

Bontebok were once numerous in southwestern South Africa, but in an area that was coveted by the settler, and bonteboks and farming did not coexist well. The Boer farmers of the South African grasslands have system-atically destroyed this animal.

There were actually three species of antelope that have been reduced or completely elim-inated in southern Africa. One was the blaubok or bluebuck (*Hippotragus leucophaeus*), which was driven to extinction in the 19th century. Another was the white-tailed wildebeest (*Con-nochates gnou*), saved by major efforts in the 20th century. The third was the bontebok.

The bontebok owes its sur-vival to a handful of people and three families, in particular. They were the Vanderbyl family, the Van Bredas, and the Albertuins. They recognized that the bonte-

BONTEBOK
South Africa

N

bok was declining, so they set aside land for the animals, and tried to save the few that were left. The Vanderbyls set up a pri-vate reserve on their own farm in 1837, starting with 27 animals.

All the bontebok that exist today are descendants from those few survivors. Apparently these were strong individuals, because the generations since then have not suffered genetically (inbreed-ing can cause the species to die out). In 1931, an area adjacent to the Vanderbyl farm was set aside as Bontebok National Park, and 84 individuals were moved there by truck. This is the stronghold of the bontebok population today.

Since then, many bonteboks have been moved to other areas of South Africa, and numbers have increased. More than 1,000 are doing well in the wild. They are vulnerable only because of their restricted range and their small numbers, but protection efforts are succeeding.

In captivity, given enough space and good management, bonteboks reproduce and adapt fairly well. It takes a fair amount of space to lessen their dominat-ing behavior and their intolerance for others, and not all zoos have sufficient space for this purpose.

Warren D. Thomas

Compared to other antelope the bontebok do not display much tolerance of one another, and exhibit a strict code of dominance among themselves. Nonetheless, they can be seen grazing together in groups.

Abbott's Booby
(Papasula abbotti)

ESA: Endangered

IUCN: Vulnerable

Class: Aves
Order: Pelecaniformes
Family: Sulidae
Length: 30–31 in. (76–79 cm)
Weight: Females 3–3½ lb.
(1.4–1.6 kg); males 2¾–3¼ lb.
(1.3–1.5 kg)
Clutch size: 1 egg
Incubation: 56–57 days
Diet: Mostly fish but also squid
Habitat: Pelagic, comes ashore
to nest on Christmas Island
Range: Indian Ocean

AMERICAN NATURALIST W. L. Abbott collected a booby from one of the islands in the western Indian Ocean, which he sent to Robert Ridgway at the U.S. National Museum. Ridgway pronounced it a new species and named the bird after its collector. Abbott attributed the booby to Assumption Island, but his notes identify a unique booby breeding on Glorioso Island. This caused confusion regarding the bird's historic breeding distribution.

Bones identified as those of Abbott's booby have been recovered on Rodrigues Island, several hundred miles east of Madagascar. A written account puts a nesting booby fitting Abbott's description on Rodrigues in 1761. At that time, the little island was heavily forested, then forest cutting stripped the island nearly bare. A nesting colony on Rodrigues would account for Abbott's boobies being reported from the western Indian Ocean, as would a breeding population on Glorioso. Assumption Island was too low and void of forest trees to support breeding Abbott's boobies.

The head, chin, throat, breast, and belly of the Abbott's booby are pure white, with some black on the underwings. The back and rump are mostly white, but have some black markings. The tail is black with very slight white tips to the individual feathers, while the flank is black from the rear edge of the leg to under the tail. The beak is stout and hooked. The male bird has a pale blue-gray beak with light pink wash and a black tip. On both sexes, the skin around the eye and the base of the beak is a blue-black.

Forests and the character of individual trees seem equally vital to the booby. On Christmas Island it disperses itself irregularly, seeming to ignore perfectly usable trees. The bird usually selects a site about 500 feet (153 meters) above the sea. Typically, it builds a nest 60 feet (18 meters) above ground in a large tree that emerges from the forest canopy. When leaving their nests, Abbott's boobies regularly drop 25 to 30 feet (8 to 9 meters) before taking flight. Trees with dense foliage are not used by boobies. Nesting trees often grow on steep terrain. Most of these trees, and the nesting boobies, appear on the western side of the island. Abbott's booby does not form expansive colonies. Pairs may share nesting trees, and adjoining trees may harbor additional pairs, but unlike other colonial species, there is little interaction. Boobies are suited for life at sea. They forage by flying 10 to 100 feet (3 to 31 meters) above the water, with their heads down. When they locate fish, they fold their wings and plunge dive, with their nostrils closed. The serrated edge on their beaks helps them hold the prey before swallowing. Incubating adults relieve each other at four-day intervals, to give them time to fly long distances. The proximity of feeding waters to nesting habitat could be the clue to preserving Abbott's booby.

Protective measures have concentrated on preserving the boobies' nesting habitat on Christmas Island.

Through the 1970s, phosphate mining on Christmas Island destroyed nesting habitat for boobies. Efforts made to reduce the impact of the mining partially succeeded, although it continued into the 1980s.

Abbott's is vulnerable because it has such a low rate of reproduction, and lays only one egg per nesting, and it takes more than 600 days to produce an independent offspring. Producing only one chick every two years makes recovering a diminishing population in a declining habitat very difficult. It was estimated that the Abbott's booby population was at about 3,000 pairs in 1991.

Kevin Cook

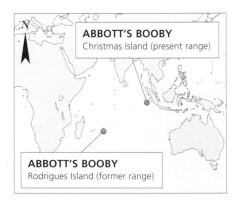

ABBOTT'S BOOBY
Christmas Island (present range)

ABBOTT'S BOOBY
Rodrigues Island (former range)

Vahl's Boxwood
(Buxus vahlii)

ESA: Endangered

IUCN: Endangered

Class: Magnoliopsida
Order: Euphorbiales
Family: Buxaceae
Size: Shrub or small tree, to 15 ft. (4.5 cm) in height and 6 in. (15 cm) in trunk diameter
Leaves: Opposite, oblong to ovate, ¾–1½ in. (2–4 cm) long, ¾ in. (2 cm) wide
Flowers: White or yellowish, less than ⅛ in. (3 mm) in diameter
Fruit: A three-horned capsule to ¼ in. (6 mm) long, split into three, with shiny black seeds
Habitat: Thickets or forests on rocky limestone or sandy soils
Range: Puerto Rico and St. Croix, U.S. Virgin Islands

FRENCH TAXONOMIST M.H. Baillon recognized Vahl's boxwood as a new species in 1859. He designated the specific name in honor of Martin Hendrickson Vahl (1749-1804), an early Danish botanist who had described several new plants in the Caribbean. Today this species is found only at two locations on Puerto Rico and two on the island of St. Croix. On Puerto Rico, one stand exists on the Nuclear Power Plant site at Rincon. This population occupies a ravine, growing in partial shade on shallow, friable clay, with small limestone rocks over limestone bedrock. The second Puerto Rican stand, about 70 miles (110 kilometers) from Rincon, is found in the hills of Hato Tejas, Bayamon,

at the edge of an old limestone quarry near a shopping center. The site contains specimens of various ages, from 3 feet to 16 feet (1–5 meters) in height. The soil is shallow and stony, once again with bedrock of limestone. Rainfall in both locations averages 50–70 inches (125–180 centimeters) each year and is divided into distinct wet and dry seasons.

Outside Puerto Rico, Vahl's boxwood occurs only on St. Croix, about 60 miles (95 kilometers) to the southeast. Two small populations exist there, one at the west end of the island at Sandy Point, the other in the central portion of the island on Recovery Hill. The Sandy Point population is found in a mixed xerophytic community of drought-resistant plants and

thorn-scrub on thin, sandy soil. Measuring 12–14 feet (3.5–4 meters) in height, Vahl's boxwood forms the mature canopy in one area. The annual rainfall is about 22 inches (55 centimeters) and the stand holds specimens at stages of development from seedlings to mature flowering and fruiting plants. Although the population is small, only covering an area of 150 by 300 feet (45 by 90 meters), the varying degrees of maturity points to a viable community. The second population is on the summit of Recovery Hill and the west-facing slope. It is a larger stand than on Sandy Point and is found on thin, rocky limestone soil with an average rainfall of 30 inches (76

The leaves of the endangered shrub, Vahl's boxwood, are dark, shiny green above, and a lighter and duller green underneath.

VAHL'S BOXWOOD
Caribbean

centimeters). Because of the slope, it is unlikely that there will be land development. However, the location is vulnerable to natural disasters such as hurricanes.

Reasons for concern

In Puerto Rico, the government-owned Rincon location was once proposed as a possible site for a coal-fueled power plant. Development of this type could result in the destruction or extreme modification of the species' habitat, or affect the population through air pollution or polluted water run-off. In addition, local residents adjacent to the government property raise goats that could damage the habitat if they were allowed to roam freely. The Hato Tejas stand, located at the edge of an old limestone quarry, is surrounded by residential and commercial enterprises and is vulnerable to future development. If the quarry is reactivated, the plant's habitat could be destroyed. Also half of the known plants are on private lands with little legislation to protect endangered species. Site destruction by development is likely, although populations are isolated and inaccessible. The threat of hurricanes and fires is a constant hazard.

Current status

Because of its limited numbers and its restricted range, the species was included on the U.S. Fish and Wildlife Federal Register of Endangered Species on August 13, 1985, because of alteration or destruction of habitat and inadequate regulatory legislation. Vahl's boxwood is now protected by law enforcement to ensure its continued existence in Puerto Rico and St. Croix. The Center for Plant Conservation (CPC) has included it in the National Collection of Endangered Species.

The St. George Village Botanical Garden of St. Croix, an Affiliate Institution of the CPC, is also growing and monitoring specimens to reintroduce progeny back into the wild.

Vahl's boxwood is a little known but highly ornamental species with landscape potential. With current protection and proper management, it may one day find its way into the mainstream of horticultural endeavors and shed its endangered status.

Kenneth D. Jones

BUCKWHEATS

Phylum: Anthophyta
(flowering plants)
Order: Polygonales
Family: Polygonaceae
Subfamily: Eriogonoideae
Tribe: Eriogoneae
Genus: *Eriogonum*

Wild buckwheats are shrubs, herbs, and dwarf cushion plants belonging to the knotweed family (Polygonaceae), which includes food crops such as buckwheat (*Fagopyrum esculentum*) and rhubarb (*Rheum rhaponticum*). All together there are about 240 species of wild-buckwheats (*Eriogonum*) distributed in western and southern North America. The plants bear flowers in heads of various shapes. Several of the species are cultivated for ornament, particularly as rock garden plants, or for their edible leaves and roots. In Montana, one species is even used as an indicator of silver in the ground. Several species of wild-buckwheat have extremely small natural distributions, and small population sizes. They are threatened by habitat damage and destruction caused by mining and construction activities.

Clay-loving Wild-buckwheat

(Eriogonum pelinophilum)

ESA: Endangered

IUCN: Vulnerable

Size: Low, rounded shrublet
Leaves: Spear-shaped leaf blades, 1–1.5 mm long
Flowers: White, with segments 3–3.5 mm long
Seeds: 3–3.5 mm long
Habitat: Barren, gray clay hills, toe slopes, and runoff plains of the Mancos Shale
Range: Near Montrose in southwestern Colorado

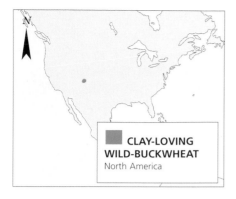

CLAY-LOVING
WILD-BUCKWHEAT
North America

IT MAY SEEM STRANGE that clay-loving wild-buckwheat is a plant in danger, since it inhabits a part of Colorado that has a very sparse human population. However, the species is seriously threatened by destruction or alteration of its habitat through agriculture, livestock grazing, off-road vehicle use, irrigation projects, residential development, oil and gas exploration, and potential gypsum mining.

Areas used for livestock grazing are not suitable for habitat for this plant, because the productivity of the vegetation is very low. Grazing damages the habitat because the animals trample the clay soils, especially during wet weather, and this sometimes leads to severe soil erosion.

Dry environment

The Mancos Shale is a saline, calcium-rich deposit that was formed during the Cretaceous period (about 144 to 65 million years ago). Its outcrops form almost barren clay hills at altitudes from about 5,200 to 6,200 feet (1,600 to 1,900 meters). The nature of these soils and the low rainfall—about 9 inches (23 centimeters) annually—create an extreme environment in which the plants compete intensively for water. The vegetation therefore tends to be low and sparse, with very little growth each year and a fairly low diversity of species.

Those plants able to survive are adapted to dry conditions, and the dominant species are mainly shrublets. Companion plants for clay-loving wild-buckwheat include black sagebrush (*Artemisia nova*), bottlebrush squirreltail (*Elymus elymoide*), Castle Valley clover (*Atriplex cuneata*), Douglas rabbitbrush (*Chrysothamnus viscidiflorus*), mat saltbush (*Atriplex corrugata*), shadscale or spiny saltbush (*Atriplex confertifolia*), and winterfat (*Eurotia lanata*).

Clay loving wild-buckwheat is a low, rounded, cushion-shaped shrublet. It is many branched, with persistent lower branches and herbaceous upper ones. The spear-shaped leaves are white and hairy underneath and hairless, or nearly hairless, above. The 1–1.5 millimeter leaf blades grow among the herbaceous branches.

The flowers are white and occur from June to August. The flower stems are slender, 5–10 millimeters long, ending in a compact cluster of top-shaped bract whorls.

The total world population of clay-loving wild-buckwheat is approximately 65,000 plants. The individual populations range in size from 1 to 74 acres (0.5 to 30 hectares) and from 100 to 10,000 plants. The averages are about 22 acres (9 hectares) and about 2,800 plants.

Clay-loving wild-buckwheat likes to grow in swales and valley bottoms where the competition for water is less intense. In suitable habitat, the plant can be a dominant species living with other shrubs or shrublets. The wild-buckwheat has the potential to grow anywhere where there are outcrops of Mancos Shale forming characteristically barren clay hills. The flat lands at the feet of these clay hills may also have wild-buckwheat plants. Unfortunately, though, most of this type of land has now been converted either to fields of alfalfa, residential sites, roads, or railroads, or the soil has become severely compacted by livestock grazing (in wet weather, large, deep footprints are made in the soil by the animals). The clay hills themselves attract the recreational use of off-road vehicles from over a wide area. Such activity may seem like harmless fun in such a barren-looking environment, but this habitat is actually unique, with its own special assemblage of plant species, and should not be used in this way. The hills are prone to serious erosion because of their clay soils and sparse vegetation. Deep erosion channels have formed on those hills that suffer the heaviest use of off-road vehicles.

The whole area also has a high potential for oil and gas development because of the nature of the Mancos Shale and its underlying strata. There are also gypsum deposits, which could be mined. If the need for these resources were to increase, the clay-loving wild-buckwheat's habitat would suffer even more with the impact of heavy equipment used for oil and gas exploration or surface mining for gypsum deposits.

Urban threat

Urban sprawl is already about to destroy populations of clay-loving wild-buckwheat near the towns of Montrose and Delta. Expansion of the human population in these towns has resulted in residential sites creeping onto the habitat that used to support the wild-buckwheat.

There is one good example that illustrates how residential development and agriculture have displaced the species: there is a fenced area, which has so far escaped conversion into home sites or pasture, with a high density of clay-loving wild-buckwheat plants. Nearby, identical habitat presumably also once supported the plant, but does so no longer.

Clay-loving wild-buckwheat was listed by the U.S. Fish and Wildlife Service as endangered in 1984, and there is now an officially approved recovery plan for the species. It is hoped that the plan will prove effective in controlling some of the threats faced by this rare plant.

Nick Turland

Cushenbury Buckwheat

(Eriogonum ovalifolium var. *vineum)*

ESA: Endangered

IUCN: Endangered

Height: 4 in. (10 cm)
Leaves: Round to oval, up to 15 mm long
Flowers: May to June. Small; creamy white, reddish, or purple, ⅛ in. (3 mm) long
Habitat: Occurs within openings of Juniper, pinyon, Joshua tree, and blackbrush scrub
Range: San Bernardino Mountains, California

CUSHENBURY BUCKWHEAT is a low, densely matted perennial of the buckwheat family (Polygonaceae). The tiny flowers are creamy white at the outset but darken to a reddish or purple color with age. They are borne in heads 1 inch (2.5 centimeters) in diameter on flowering stalks reaching 4 inches (10 centimeters) in height. Individual flowers are about ⅛ inch (3 millimeters) long, with six petal-like segments. The round to oval leaves are white and woolly on both surfaces and are 7 to 15 millimeters long. The mats of basal leaves are typically 6 to 10 inches (15 to 25 centimeters) in diameter, but may reach up to 20 inches (51 centimeters) in larger individuals.

Habitat

Cushenbury buckwheat grows primarily on carbonate deposits or soils originating from them. This species and other plants that occur on carbonate deposits have commonly been referred to as limestone endemics by botanists, whether they occur on limestone or dolomite. Cushenbury buckwheat occurs within openings of pinyon woodland, pinyon-juniper woodland, Joshua tree woodland, and blackbrush scrub communities between 4,600 and 7,900 feet (1,400 and 2,400 meters) in elevation. Other habitat characteristics include open areas with little accumulation of organic material, a canopy cover usually less than 15 percent, and powdery fine soils with rock cover exceeding 50 percent.

The plant is typically found on moderate slopes, although a few occurrences are on slopes over 60 percent. On milder, north-facing slopes, it occurs

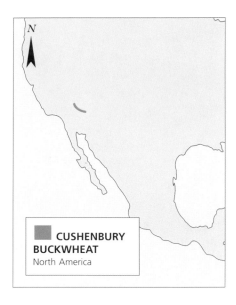

CUSHENBURY
BUCKWHEAT
North America

with Cushenbury milk vetch (*Astragalus albens*).

The distribution of *Eriogonum ovalifolium* var. *vineum* is limited to the belt of carbonate substrates (limestone and dolomite) of the north slopes of the San Bernardino Mountains in San Bernardino County, California. Outcrops of these carbonate substrates occur in several bands running on an east-west axis along the desert-facing slopes of the San Bernardino Mountains, with separate patches occurring just to the south of Sugarlump Ridge and to the east as far as the Sawtooth Hills. The plant is currently known to occur on approximately 20 sites over a distance of about 40 kilometers (25 miles) from the White Knob area east to Rattlesnake Canyon. Only one quarter of those occurrences comprise more than 1,000 individuals each, with the total population estimated at 13,000 individuals.

Habitat destruction

Much of the Cushenbury buckwheat's habitat occurs within areas that are currently mined for rocks and minerals using strip

and terraced mining techniques. These techniques, combined with road construction for access to mines and the dumping of mining waste, cause direct destruction of the plant's habitat. The plant is further threatened by energy development projects, off-road vehicle use, and urban expansion near the community of Big Bear. It may also be vulnerable to random extinction in some areas because of the small number of populations and total number of individuals.

Protection

Cushenbury buckwheat is protected by the federal Endangered Species Act, which requires that, to the maximum extent prudent and possible, critical habitat be identified at the time a species is determined to be endangered or threatened. The U.S. Fish and Wildlife Service decided that designation of critical habitat for Cushenbury buckwheat was not prudent, because the publication of habitat descriptions and maps required for critical habitat designation would increase the threat to these plants from possible collection or vandalism and could contribute to their decline. The listing of species as either endangered or threatened publicizes the rarity of the plants and can make these plants attractive to researchers, curiosity seekers, or collectors of rare plants. According to the U.S.F.W.S., all appropriate federal agencies and local planning agencies have been

Cushenbury buckwheat grows on the slopes of the San Bernardino Mountains, California.

notified of the location of this species and importance of protecting its habitat. The federal Endangered Species Act also requires federal agencies to ensure that activities they authorize, fund, or carry out are not likely to jeopardize the existence of a listed species or to destroy or adversely modify its habitat.

The U.S. Fish and Wildlife Service has developed a recovery plan for five plant species endemic to carbonate substrates in southern California mountains, including Cushenbury buckwheat.

Rick Imes

Gypsum Wild-buckwheat

(Eriogonum gypsophilum)

ESA: Threatened

IUCN: Endangered

Height: 4–8 in. (10–20 cm) tall, arising from a thick, woody, tufted base

Leaves: 1–2 basal leaves, oval to circular (rarely kidney-shaped), ¾–1 in. (2–3 cm) long, somewhat thickened and succulent

Flowers: Mid-May to early July. The branched flowering stem bears numerous bell-shaped whorls of bracts, each containing 6 flowers; each flower is broadly bell-shaped, 1–2 mm long, with bright yellow oval segments and a greenish midvein

Seeds: Fruits late July to August. The seeds are 1–1.8 mm long

Habitat: Desert scrub on gypsum substrates

Range: Known only from the Seven Rivers Gypsum Hills in the Chihuahuan Desert of New Mexico

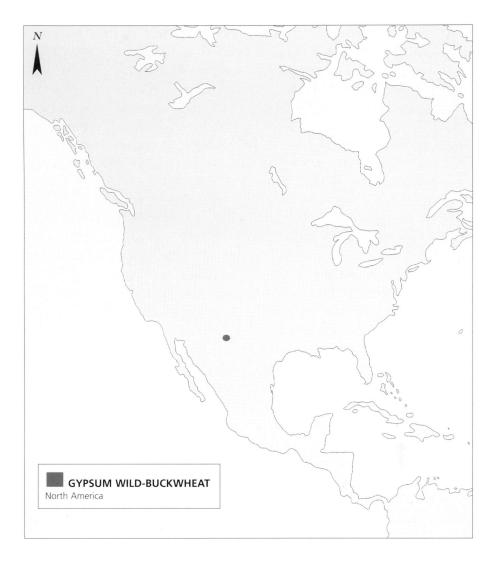

GYPSUM WILD-BUCKWHEAT
North America

GYPSUM WILD-BUCKWHEAT is an extremely rare plant of the Chihuahuan Desert of New Mexico. It is known from only one locality covering some 590 acres (240 hectares), with an estimated total population of about 10,000 individual plants. With such a tiny distribution, this species is highly vulnerable to extinction caused by disturbance of the plants or damage and destruction of its habitat. In the early 21st century, threats to gypsum wild-buckwheat included the use of off-road vehicles, exploration for oil and gas deposits, and excessive grazing by cattle.

Future development

Already plants and habitat have been damaged by off-road vehicles, and the Bureau of Land Management has responded by closing the area to off-road vehicle use. Currently, oil or gas exploration is not active in the area inhabited by gypsum wild-buckwheat. However, there are five leases there, and the possibility of future oil and gas drilling cannot be ruled out. Cattle may also pose a threat if present in large numbers, because they increase trampling and browsing of the wild-buckwheat plants.

On top of these threats, there is the proposed building of the Brantley Dam Reservoir in the area, which has the potential to flood a small portion of the population, but more serious would be the secondary effects of a large body of water next to the wild-buckwheat's habitat. Such effects would include road construction to relocate the existing road away from the flooded area; the dissolving of underground gypsum, causing subsidence and physical disruption of the plant's habitat; wave action from the water that could erode the gypsum surface; changes in microclimate that could increase humidity and wind speed and frequency; and changes in habitat that would allow weedy species to intrude and compete with gypsum wild-buckwheat.

Specific substrate

Gypsum wild-buckwheat grows in a special habitat in the Seven Rivers Gypsum Hills, where the substrate is made up of beds of gypsum 1–5 feet (0.3–1.5 meters) thick, inter-layered with siltstones and red shales. Altogether the gypsum bed formation is about 20 feet (6 meters) thick beneath the wild-buckwheat. The plants grow on the eroded sides and tops of the gypsum hills, as well as on the gypsum wash fans at the bases of the hills. The vegetation is made up of several dominant species, including Apache plume (*Fallugia paradoxa*), gypsum grama (*Bouteloua breviseta*), gypsum ringstem (*Anulocaulis gypsogenus*), littleleaf (*Rhus microphylla*), prickly coldenia (*Coldenia hispidissima*), and White Sands fanmustard (*Nerisyrenia linearifolia*).

There is an interesting connection between disturbance of the ground surface and the density of gypsum wild-buckwheat plants: the density increases when the hard surface crust of the gypsum is broken. It seems that young plants can more easily establish themselves when this happens. Certainly, gypsum wild-buckwheat tends to establish itself rapidly. As might be expected, the plant tends to be commoner by erosion channels on the hillsides, and by roads at the base. Chemically, gypsum is hydrated calcium sulfate, $CaSO_4-2(H_2O)$; it is usually formed by precipitation out of

highly saline waters. It is an unusual material to find on the surface of the ground because it is completely soluble in water and will eventually erode away to nothing. In contrast, sandstone erodes into grains of sand, while limestone partially dissolves, leaving behind clay. Gypsum comprises various forms and textures, including translucent crystals, porous rock, and exceedingly fine powder. It is usually white. The gypsum where the wild-buckwheat grows was deposited during the Permian period, from about 286 to 245 million years ago. Gypsum wild-buckwheat was designated as a threatened species by the U.S. Fish and Wildlife Service (U.S.F.W.S.) in 1981, under the Endangered Species Act of 1973. The plants have also been given protected status in New Mexico by the New Mexico Department of Natural Resources.

The U.S.F.W.S. has approved a recovery plan for gypsum wild-buckwheat. The plan's objectives include monitoring the long-term effects of cattle grazing, regulating recreational use of off-road vehicles in the habitat, regulating access by livestock to the proposed Brantley Dam Reservoir, so that trampling and habitat destruction do not occur, as well as monitoring the likely effects of the reservoir (flooding of plants, wave action on gypsum hills, raised water table dissolving gypsum, altered wind patterns, and weedy species invading altered habitat).

The recovery plan also aims to encourage the general public to appreciate gypsum wild-buckwheat and to support its conservation and protection.

Scrub Buckwheat
(Eriogonum longifolium var. gnaphalifolium)

ESA: Threatened

IUCN: Rare

Height: 3 ft. (1 m) tall
Leaves: Mostly at the base of the stem, narrowly spear-shaped, 6–8 in. (15–20 cm) long, green or bronzed above, densely white and woolly beneath
Flowers: Silvery, silky-haired, in an open, branching cluster, each branch ending in a cup-shaped whorl of bracts enclosing 15–20 flowers, each 6–8 mm long, with 6 narrow segments. Flowers are at first erect but later hang down
Habitat: Dry, upland vegetation, including scrub, high pine (sandhills), or turkey oak (*Quercus laevis*) barrens intermediate between scrub and high pine
Range: Marion County southward to Highlands County, central peninsular Florida

SCRUB BUCKWHEAT is a large, conspicuous plant of scrub and open, woodland habitats in central Florida. It is a variety of the variable species *Eriogonum longifolium*, which has a wide range and is represented east of the Mississippi River not only by scrub buckwheat but also by the rare Harper's umbrella-plant (*E. longifolium* var. *harperi*), from northern Alabama, Kentucky, and Tennessee. Florida has only one other species of wild-buck-wheat: *Eriogonum tomentosum*, which is also native to high pine vegetation but is common throughout the northern part of the state.

Threatened species

Scrub buckwheat grows as far north as the town of Ocala in Marion County. It also grows near Clermont in Lake County, in southwestern Orange County, northwestern Osceola County and reaches the southern limit of its small range on the Lake Wales ridge spanning Polk and Highlands Counties. The main threats to the species are loss of habitat through agricultural and residential developments, as well as habitat damage from non-natural fires. Scrub buckwheat was listed by the U.S. Fish and Wildlife Service as a threatened species in 1993, and there is now an officially approved recovery plan for the plant. Action is being taken to conserve the upland flora of central Florida, and especially to protect endangered species that live in scrub vegetation.

Conservation measures

The Conservation and Recreation Lands (CARL) Program of the State of Florida is buying land in Highlands and Polk Counties. The Nature Conservancy has also purchased land at various sites, and the U.S.F.W.S. has proposed a 10,000-acre (4,000-hectare) Lake Wales Ridge National Wildlife Refuge.

Effective conservation of these lands will require careful planning and management, and the areas may well require extensive habitat restoration. The scrub vegetation where scrub buck-wheat still grows is a shrub community adapted to dry conditions, occupying sandy, well-drained, infertile soils, and dominated by a layer of evergreen or nearly evergreen oaks (*Quercus* species) and/or Florida rosemary (*Ceratiola ericoides*). There may also be a higher layer of pines, usually sand pine (*Pinus clausa*). This special scrub also provides habitat for the Florida, or scrub, jay (*Aphelocoma coerulescens coerulescens*), which is listed by the U.S.F.W.S. as a threatened bird species. The scrub exists on dune ridges along the Gulf and Atlantic coasts of Florida and on older ridges of sand inland. Endemic plant species (those that grow nowhere else) are found in this scrub in various parts of Florida, with the biggest hot spot for endemism on the Lake Wales Ridge (the southernmost, high, interior ridge), northwest of Lake Okeechobee.

The scrub ecosystem is maintained by natural fires, which are infrequent but fierce, occurring every 10 to 100 years depending on the density of the scrub (the denser the scrub, the more frequent the fires). High pine vegetation (also known as sandhills vegetation) is the other main type of natural vegetation in the dry uplands of central Florida. It used to be a very widespread type of forest in the southeastern United States, all the way from Texas to Virginia. High pine is a forest of longleaf pine (*Pinus palustris*) with an underlying ground layer of grasses, including pineland threeawn (*Aristida stricta*), various herbs, and deciduous hardwoods such as turkey oak (*Quercus laevis*) and bluejack oak (*Q. incana*).

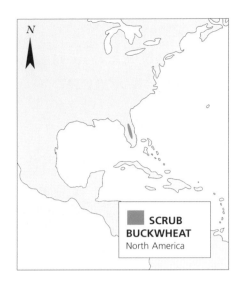

SCRUB BUCKWHEAT
North America

Fire tolerance

High pine species can tolerate being burned to the ground from time to time. Frequent fires of low intensity prevent the hardwoods from becoming canopy trees and maintain the grassy ground layer.

In central Florida, high pine is mixed with scrub, and the intermediate vegetation is known as turkey oak barrens. Most of today's barrens may just be the results of logging of longleaf pine followed by suppression of natural fires, which have allowed the turkey oaks to grow into full-sized trees and also evergreen oaks to invade. However, some of the barrens may be much older.

Creation of citrus glades

On Lake Wales Ridge, most of the high pine was converted to citrus groves long ago. Today, scrub vegetation is also being converted to citrus glades.

Habitat encroachment in the form of urban development is also destroying tracts of upland vegetation. Only about 15 percent of the original 550,000 acres (220,000 hectares) of dry, upland vegetation in Highlands and Polk Counties remain intact today.

Southern Mountain Wild-buckwheat

(Eriogonum kennedyi var. *austromontanum)*

ESA: Threatened

IUCN: Vulnerable

Size: Woody-based perennial forming loose, cushion-shaped, leafy mats 2–14 in. (5–35 cm) wide

Leaves: Spear-shaped, broader toward the tips, 6–10 mm long, white and densely hairy

Flowers: July to September. Woolly stems bear heads of white to rose flowers with similar inner and outer segments

Seeds: 3.5–4 mm long

Habitat: Pebble plains

Range: San Bernardino Mountains, southern California

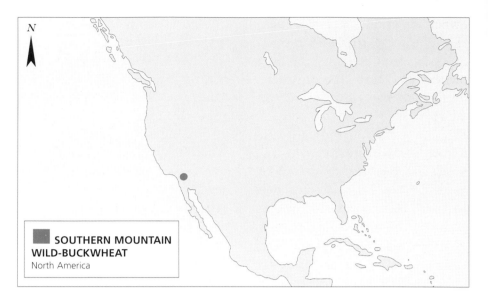

SOUTHERN MOUNTAIN WILD-BUCKWHEAT
North America

SOUTHERN MOUNTAIN wild-buckwheat is a rare plant known only from seven areas of very special habitat, called pebble plains, in the San Bernardino Mountains of southern California. All of the sites where the plant grows are threatened. Southern mountain wild-buckwheat was listed by the U.S. Fish and Wildlife Service as a threatened species in 1998; there is no officially approved recovery plan for the species.

Southern mountain wild-buckwheat was originally described for science by Philip Munz and Ivan Johnston in 1924, based on a plant collected at Big Bear Valley in the San Bernardino Mountains. Two other varieties of the species, *Eriogonum kennedyi* var. *kennedyi* and *E. kennedyi* var. *alpigenum* also grow wild in the San Bernardino Mountains. The southern mountain wild-buckwheat (var. *austromontanum*) can be distinguished from them by its longer leaves, long, loosely woolly-haired flowering stems, longer whorls of bracts, and longer fruits.

Pebble plain habitat

The pebble plains where southern mountain wild-buckwheat grows are treeless openings in the surrounding mountain pinyon pine–juniper woodland or conifer forest, located at altitudes from 5,900 to 7,500 feet (1,800–2,300 meters). The plains are remnants of an ancient lake bed dating from the Pleistocene (from about 1,800,000 to 10,000 years ago). They form level or sloping plains with a clay soil that is strewn with pebbles of quartzite. Water soaks into the soil extremely slowly, so the plains have the potential for tremendous runoff during heavy rains. Pebble plains support a unique flora, with many plants endemic. This means that they grow nowhere else. Any damage to the habitat could very seriously threaten the continued survival of southern mountain wild-buckwheat, as well as its companion plants.

There are several specific threats to southern mountain wild-buckwheat. They include the following: destruction and degradation of its habitat by urbanization, recreational development, trampling by people and by animals, the use of off-road vehicles, deliberate vandalism, over-collection of specimens by botanists, grazing by livestock, interference with water drainage in the plains, and competition and hybridization by plants introduced from elsewhere.

Damage to habitat

Urban development has resulted in the destruction of 210 acres (85 hectares) of former habitat in one area near the town of Sugarloaf. Trampling on the pebble plains degrades the habitat by compacting the soil and by introducing seeds of non-native species. The Southern mountain wild-buckwheat grows on lands owned by the U.S. Forest Service, the California Department of Fish and Game, and private owners. Six of the eight known populations and parts of two others are on federally owned lands. Private lands where wild-buckwheat grows are nearly all part of a single pebble plain complex, known as the Big Bear Lake. Most privately owned pebble plain habitat has no protection; however, on a few sites there are voluntary agreements with the landowner.

Protection policies
One of the Forest Service lands where the wild-buckwheat grows is the San Bernardino National Forest. The Forest Service recognizes the plant as a sensitive species and has special policies to protect such plants, including trying to establish them in habitats that are either suitable now or were known to have supported them in the past.

The San Bernardino National Forest has developed a management plan for all the special species of the pebble plains, including southern mountain wild-buckwheat. The Forest Service has already put up fences around all the larger pebble plain localities to protect this buckwheat from off-road vehicle use and trespassing.

However, even if most of the remaining pebble plain habitat in the San Bernardino National Forest could be protected from human disturbance, the total area where this buckwheat still grows may not be large enough to guarantee its long-term survival. For that to be effected, some kind of recovery plan must be put into action.

Steamboat Buckwheat
(Eriogonum ovalifolium var. *williamsiae)*

ESA: Endangered

IUCN: Endangered

Size: A densely matted, perennial herb to 18 in. (46 cm) across, with a woody taproot
Leaves: Clustered into rosettes, with leaf blades oval to kidney-shaped, 5–10 mm, and densely pale and hairy
Flowers: May to June. Erect, hairy flowering stems 4–10 in. (10–25 cm) tall bear heads of 5–8 densely hairy, top-shaped bract whorls; the actual flowers are white, pinkish tan with age, and 2.5–4 mm long
Seeds: Unknown; the seed has been searched for but not yet found. Dispersal is possibly by the wind
Habitat: Open slopes among desert scrub, with a gravelly, sandy-clay soil, formed from the deposits of active hot springs
Range: Known only from the Steamboat Springs geothermal area near Reno, Nevada

IMAGINE A SANDY area in the desert of the American Southwest, with steam drifting across from hot springs and the sharp smell of sulfur hanging in the air. You are standing just a few miles from the city of Reno, Nevada. This special place is the habitat of a very rare mat-forming plant with an extremely limited natural range: it is known only from this one geothermal area near Reno. If you carefully examine the ground, you will notice that the tight, hairy mats of foliage formed by the Steamboat buckwheat plants sometimes become dome-shaped as they gradually grow over accumulated, wind-blown sand.

Recovery plan needed
This highly vulnerable plant was first described for science by American botanist James Reveal in 1981. He named it in honor of Margaret Williams, a founding member of the Northern Nevada Native Plant Society. The most urgent conservation that is now required for Steamboat buckwheat is the protection and maintenance of its dangerously small natural habitat. There are many threats to this habitat not only because it is so small but also because it is so close to a major urban area. The plant was listed by the U.S. Fish and Wildlife Service as an endangered species in 1986, but there is not yet an officially approved recovery plan for the Steamboat buckwheat, which grows naturally only around the steamboat Springs geothermal area next to the quickly expanding urban areas of Reno and Sparks,

N

STEAMBOAT BUCKWHEAT
North America

Nevada. The total extent of the plant's habitat is less than 100 acres (40 hectares), ranging from 4,590 to 4,720 feet (1,400 to 1,440 meters) in altitude. The vegetation is desert scrub, including species such as broom snakeweed (*Gutierrezia sarothrae*), greasewood (*Sarcobatus vermiculatus*), rubber rabbitbrush (*Chrysothamnus nauseosus*), saltgrass (*Distichlis spicata*), and shadscale or spiny saltbush (*Atriplex confertifolia*). This buckwheat has a patchy distribution in its habitat: some patches have only a few individual plants, while others have several thousand. Although the general area is desert scrub, the Steamboat buckwheat tends to grow in very specific areas on open slopes with a gravelly, sandy-clay soil formed from the deposits of the hot

Steamboat buckwheat (*Eriogonum ovalifolium* var. *williamsiae*) prefers soil formed from hot springs deposits.

springs. It tends to colonize this soil type and is the commonest plant there, with few other species present.

As growing conditions improve, with leaching of soluble chemicals from the soil and the gradual development of more soil, other species move in and compete with the buckwheat, which then may decline or completely disappear.

Hot springs

The hot springs deposits of the Steamboat Springs geothermal area are nearly all silica based. Some carbonate deposits are also produced, but these are quickly weathered and dissolved by sulfuric acid, which forms when hydrogen sulfide oxidizes at the ground surface.

Steamboat buckwheat does not receive significant moisture from the actual thermal water, but probably gains enough from rainfall in order to survive.

In fact, this buckwheat may not be able to survive at all in very moist soils.

Threats

A major road bisects the small area where Steamboat buckwheat grows. Construction of the road destroyed a significant part of the plant's habitat, as did building a post office several years ago. Part of the road is now designated for possible realignment, which would cause even more damage. All the habitat lying east of the road is privately owned and threatened by commercial developments; the same applies to much of the habitat west of the road (a large trailer park site is already under construction).

Uncontrolled vehicle traffic and garbage dumping have also disturbed to the plant. Steamboat buckwheat is further threatened by geothermal drilling. Two geothermal projects are now operating on land west of the area where the plant grows. They both use the geothermal aquifer that supplies the hot springs. They could eventually affect the outflow from the springs and then, indirectly, the buckwheat.

Any future recovery action for Steamboat buckwheat must try to control or restrict development, as well as vehicle traffic, on private lands. This could come about by purchasing the best habitat still located on privately owned land.

The habitat owned by the Bureau of Land Management would also need protection from unauthorized vehicle traffic. Additional action could include maintaining the water table and restricting mining activities.

Nick Turland

Wild Asiatic Water Buffalo
(Bubalus bubalis)

IUCN: Endangered

Class: Mammalia
Order: Artiodactyla
Family: Bovidae
Subfamily: Bovinae
Tribe: Bovini
Length: 30–31 in. (76–79 cm)
Shoulder height: 59–75 in. (150–190 cm)
Diet: Grass, aquatic plants
Gestation period: 300–340 days
Longevity: 25 years
Habitat: Open forest, swampy areas, grasslands
Range: India

MOST PEOPLE are familiar with the domestic water buffalo, found over much of Southeast Asia. It has now been introduced to Australia, South America, Europe, and Africa. They are large, gray to black, with curling horns. They are a common beast of burden, and can be seen pulling plows in rice paddies.

These domestic water buffalo are descended from the wild water buffalo, but have been bred in captivity for hundreds of years. This breeding has resulted in a marked difference between the domesticated water buffalo and the wild water buffalo.

A fierce bovine
The wild water buffalo is a larger animal with larger horns. Its temperament is completely different from the domesticated species; it is not tranquil or docile. It is a formidable animal that is considered one of the most dangerous animals in Southeast Asia. When solitary bulls are surprised, they

Unlike domestic cattle, the wild Asiatic water buffalo is not a docile animal. It is considered one of the most dangerous animals in Southeast Asia. Generally, it will not attack a human being unless threatened.

can charge without warning or provocation. A cow with a calf is also a dangerous animal to encounter. These buffalo are strong fighters, and no other wild cattle (not even the larger gaur) are as ferocious.

Crossbreeds
The wild water buffalo has no particular aversion to humans, particularly in areas where they are not persecuted; people can approach them fairly closely before the buffalo will bolt. They will even mix with herds of domestic water buffalo and crossbreed with them. Local farmers, however, do not appreciate these offspring. The hybrids

usually grow to a larger size than their domestic counterparts and are too big for the farmers' yokes and plows. They also tend to inherit the ferocity of their wild parents, which makes them more dangerous to keep around. Because of this, hybrid offspring are often destroyed as soon as they exhibit this temperament.

Herbivorous

Grass eaters in the wild, water buffalo will also eat leaves from aquatic plants. They usually bear one calf a year and are very protective of them. Other than humans, their only other predator is the tiger, but even tigers are cautious about hunting water buffalo, preferring to pursue a calf. When water buffalo sense a tiger's approach, the adults stand between the cat and their young.

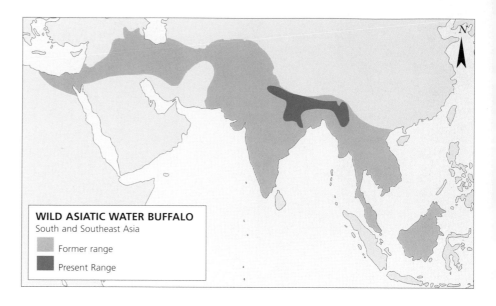

WILD ASIATIC WATER BUFFALO
South and Southeast Asia

Former range

Present Range

Wild water buffalo are now facing decline due to shrinking habitat, and also the animal is a victim of poachers.

Once the wild Asiatic water buffalo had a huge range from China and Southeast Asia into North Africa.

Water buffalo once numbered into the millions, but now are a pitiful few in scattered, isolated populations and are considered endangered. Today, it is thought that no purebred water buffalo exist in captivity.

Warren D. Thomas

Zanzibar Bushbaby

(Galago zanzibaricus)

IUCN: Lower risk

Class: Mammalia
Order: Primates
Family: Lorisidae
Subfamily: Galagoides
Weight: 3.5–10.5 oz.
Length: 13–15.5 in.
Diet: Mostly insects, some fruit
Gestation period: 120 days
Longevity: 14 years in captivity
Habitat: Coastal forest
Range: Zanzibar, Kenya, and Tanzania

THERE ARE at least seven identified species of bushbabies, and they belong to a suborder called Prosimii (prosimians), which includes the lemurs. This means that although they are related to monkeys and apes, bushbabies have more primitive characteristics. Of all the bushbabies, this bushbaby at one time faced the most serious survival threats.

The Zanzibar bushbaby (also known as the dwarf galago) lives in the lowland coastal forests of Tanzania, Zanzibar, and Kenya, and may also occur in Mozambique. Experts are divided in their opinions over the classification of this animal, and it is sometimes included as a subspecies of *Galago senegalensis*. Whatever the case, the Zanzibar bushbaby is a distinct coastal race, smaller than the average bushbaby, with an elongated muzzle and medium-sized ears. Like other bushbabies, it has the ability to move its ears independently of each other, which enables it to locate precisely the whereabouts of an insect moving in the dark. Overall, it is cinnamon in color with no contrasting color on the limbs. However, the head, neck, and a stripe down the back are darker than the rest of the upper parts.

The Zanzibar bushbaby is nocturnal and arboreal. Like other bushbabies, it is quiet and slothful during the day when it rests; it comes to life at night to run and jump with great agility. Its hind legs are nearly twice as long as its forelimbs, which makes the bushbaby a superb

Although the Zanzibar bushbaby was the most endangered of all the bushbabies, it now survives due to a conservation program and measures taken for its protection.

leaper. It also uses its tail for balance. Its neck is extremely supple, able to turn the head in an 180-degree arc, which helps the bushbaby locate its prey with great accuracy. The Zanzibar bushbaby's eyes are very sensitive to light. Each eye has a special reflective layer in its retina that captures extensive light rays and allows for superb night vision.

Zanzibar bushbabies tend to stay below heights of 16 feet (5 meters) in thick undergrowth, and individuals forage alone. They do not form large groups; generally, only one male with one or two adult females and their offspring are observed. They are territorial, with males patrolling their territory and barking at rival males. Female bushbabies tend to be friendly toward related females living in the same area, but will exclude non-related females from their territory.

Insects make up about 70 percent of the Zanzibar bushbaby's diet, but it also eats some fruit and tree sap. Its gestation period is roughly 120 days and it reproduces twice a year from February to March and from September to October, one infant at a time. The mother carries her baby in her mouth by the scruff of its neck. The infant is born with its eyes open, its body covered with ash-gray fur. It is able to cling to objects immediately. At ten days old the bushbaby is still very awkward and unable to leap. At birth it weighs, on average, ½ ounce (14 grams), and becomes fully grown at four months.

The bushbaby's characteristic sound is a cry that sounds very much like that of a human baby (hence its name). However, bushbabies can vocalize in other

ZANZIBAR BUSHBABY
Zanzibar, Kenya, and Tanzania

ways typical of primates, including cackles, clicks, grunts, squeaks, and shrieks.

The main threats to the bushbaby's existence are deforestation and tourist development near its habitat. No real estimates of its population exist, but in the forests of Kenya densities can reach up to 150 animals for every 0.4 square mile (1 square kilometer). However, forest indigenous to the bushbaby's habitat is being cut down and replaced with exotic conifer trees, even in certain reserve areas such as the Shimba Hills National Reserve in Kenya. In addition, the Kenyan government's anti-deforestation policy has yet to show effectiveness in coastal forest areas.

The bushbaby's existence is also threatened by extensive hotel development along the coast of Zanzibar. It is protected by law in Kenya, and it is illegal to keep a bushbaby as a pet. In Malawi it is found in one national park and in at least one forest reserve; it has also been bred in captivity in the Wroclaw Zoo in Poland. It may even be present in other zoos, but because of confusion over its classification, it is difficult to know for certain.

Bushbabies are a protected species, and exportation from their home country is prohibited unless there are exceptional reasons for doing so.

Although bushbabies are now recognized as being at a lower risk of extinction, they are still dependent on conservation for their survival. If there is too much pressure on their small habitat, there is a likelihood that they will again become endangered.

Sarah Dart

White-browed Bushchat

(Saxicola macrorhynca)

IUCN: Vulnerable

Class: Aves
Order: Passeriformes
Family: Muscicapidae
Subfamily: Turdinae
Length: About 6 in. (15 cm)
Weight: Unknown
Clutch size: Unknown
Incubation: Unknown
Diet: Insects
Habitat: Open desert country with scattered shrubs
Range: Northwestern India and Pakistan east of the Indus River

The white-browed bushchat is so named because of its dirty white or buff colored eye line, a characteristic found in the male and the female. In summer the eye line changes to white.

THE 13 BIRDS IN the genus *Saxicola* are variously known as chats, bushchats, and stonechats. Smallish songbirds, they resemble thrushes in physique. Some ornithologists combine the chats and thrushes into a single group, while others divide them into separate but related subfamilies. It is an entirely Old World group.

In the winter, the male bushchat is a dull buff with a brown streak above the tail. Its upperparts are dark brown with white outer feathers, and the underparts are a dull buff with a whitish throat. There is a dirty white or buff eye line. In the summer, the male is a darker brown above and the eye line is a bright white. The female of the species is similar in coloring, but displays white in the wing or tail.

The white-browed bushchat lives in northwestern India and eastern Pakistan, although the species has not been seen in Pakistan in recent years. A few strays have been seen in Afghanistan.

The bushchat prefers open desert country where it perches on top of low shrubs. Usually seen as solitary birds, pairs may also travel together. Nowhere abundant, the white-browed bushchat occurs irregularly across its range. In some places it is quite rare, while in other places it is commonly seen within a localized area.

Details about the white-browed bushchat's natural history remain unknown. It is unlikely that this information will ever be easy to attain. When so little is known about an animal, effective protective action is difficult to establish or enforce. Little can be done to learn more about this rare bird.

Kevin Cook

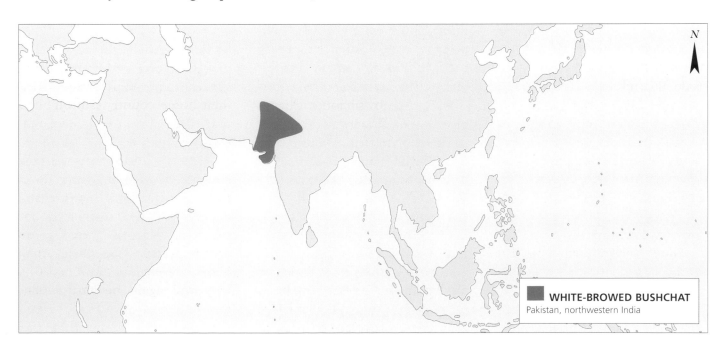

N

WHITE-BROWED BUSHCHAT
Pakistan, northwestern India

Houbara Bustard
(Chlamydotis undulata)

IUCN: Lower risk

Class: Aves
Order: Gruiformes
Family: Otididae
Length: 22–26 in. (55–65 cm), but stands 2 ft. (0.6 m) tall; female slightly smaller
Weight: 2½–5 lb. (1,200–2,400 g)
Clutch size: 2–3 eggs
Incubation: 28 days
Diet: Omnivorous
Habitat: Plant communities, with sandy desert country
Range: Western Mongolia and China to eastern Turkey, through the Middle East; the Canary Islands

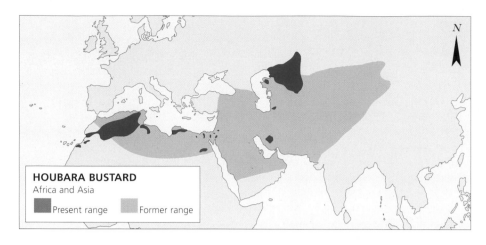

HOUBARA BUSTARD
Africa and Asia
■ Present range
■ Former range

THE HOUBARA BUSTARD belongs to a family of peculiar birds. With their long legs and long necks

The Houbara bustard is a cinnamon-brown color, with irregular dark spots on its upperparts and a dark streak that runs from the cheek to near the shoulder. The head area is off-white, and there is a slight black and white crest near the crown. The underparts of the bird are a dull white with some black barring on the flank.

they look like small cranes. They are a little too stocky to be mistaken for the larger rails and sandpipers. Their terrestrial lifestyle in dry uplands suggests they had a pheasant heritage. However they appear to be a unique species.

Many species have exquisite plumage colored in grays, browns, black, and white, enabling them to hide by crouching and sitting still. Males of several species are adorned with loose plumage, which can be erected and fanned during courtship. The long sturdy feet and legs suit the bustards well for life on the ground. They are wary birds that can see over low vegetation, and they can become swift runners when danger threatens.

Excessive hunting

The Houbara bustard provided a century of sport hunting for those who enjoyed shooting, and it would be naive to believe that shooting has not affected the species. Other bustards, notably the great bustard (*Otis tarda*), were totally eliminated from some parts of their ranges early in the last century because shooting was engaged in without restraint. Shooting affected the Houbara bustard more in some parts of its range than in others, and it most likely compounded the severity of other factors leading to its decline.

Unexplained decline

Human population growth has forced people into areas that were previously inhabited only by Houbara bustards. Some bustard habitat has been eliminated by livestock, land irrigation, and excessive goat grazing.

Because the bird readily feeds on certain crops, farmers in some areas often harass it in order to defend their livelihood.

There are as yet no good explanations for the Houbara bustard's decline in some parts of its range. Although many countries now legally protect the species, as do international treaties, effective protection efforts and conservation programs will ultimately depend on learning more about the bustard's natural history.

Kevin Cook

BUTTERFLIES

Class: Insecta

Order: Lepidoptera

Of all the earth's living creatures, butterflies are among the most beautiful, and they have long been studied and enjoyed by laypeople and naturalists alike. The disappearance of butterflies from an area is likely to be noticed immediately.

Thus it is little wonder that they have begun to appear on endangered species lists in recent years. Many butterfly species are adaptable, even when their habitats are disturbed, so that their disappearance or endangerment, sometimes to the point of extinction, draws attention to potential problems that can impact on the entire ecosystem of an area. Endangered butterflies have served as key species in challenging the construction of major dam and reservoir projects, the spraying of dangerous organophosphate pesticides, the clearing of land for agriculture or for building homes, and even mining activities.

Recently butterflies have become important indicator species of biodiversity present in the rain forests of Jamaica, New Guinea, Brazil, Madagascar, and West Africa. Habitat changes in these areas have often been detected first by the impact on the larger and more obvious species of butterflies.

Butterflies can also serve as a warning for biologists who are interested in the impact of change on thousands of other species such as plants, birds, mammals, reptiles, amphibians—even aquatic organisms.

There are estimated to be slightly more than 18,000 species of butterflies in the world today. Together with about 11 times that number of moth species, butterflies comprise the insect order Lepidoptera.

Butterflies and moths may be distinguished from other groups of insects by the modified hairs or scales that are laid down on their bodies like roof shingles.

Most species have a long, coiled tongue (proboscis) which functions like a soda straw to suck nectar from flowers and other fluids such as sap.

ditions. Worldwide, several hundred species and subspecies of butterflies have been recognized as either rare or endangered by various government bodies and conservation agencies.

Until recently, the major threat to the continued existence of butterfly species occurred in the industrialized nations, where rapid urbanization and pollution caused initial extinctions to occur. Now the major threat is habitat clearing in the less developed countries, where lumbering operations, agriculture, and mining destroy huge tracts of rain forest annually.

The first recorded butterfly extinction was probably a swallowtail in the West Indies, *Papilio (Battus) polydamus antiguus*. This species disappeared on the island of Antigua before any specimens could be preserved and, by 1906, experts noted that other subspecies of this swallowtail were also becoming rare on other islands in the Lesser Antilles. This was due to farming.

The earliest known extinction of a North American butterfly occurred in the San Francisco Bay Area around 1880. This was *Cercyonis sthenele sthenele*, a subspecies called Boisduval's satyr. The second known North American loss was the Wheeler's satyr (*Cercyonis pegala wheeleri*) in the Owens Lake Valley in California between the turn of the century and the late 1920s. Owens Lake was being drained to supply water for the growing city of Los Angeles far to the south. In both of these cases, habitat destruction caused the extinction. Boisduval's satyr was exterminated by the encroachment of the city of San Francisco onto the sand

Fossil records suggest that butterflies first appeared in the Mesozoic Era (over 55 million years ago) at a time when the flowering plants began to diversify. The greatest diversity of butterflies today is in the Central and South American tropics. About 8,000 species occur in tropical America. Tropical Asia (4,000 species) offers the second center of diversity, with Africa (3,300 species) coming in a relatively poor third. The Palearctic regions (1,900 species) of Europe and northern Asia rank next in diversity, while North America (750 species) comes in almost last, with only Australia

(at about 350 species of butterflies) lagging behind. With the tropical islands of Oceania and the Australian region combined, the total is 1,300 species south of tropical Asia.

Because butterflies generally are easily identified, are active during the daytime, and use specific plants for feeding during their caterpillar and adult life stages, they can be readily studied and monitored by scientists. Changes in the population size and structure of particular butterfly colonies reflect the general health of the ecosystem that each inhabits; hence butterflies are an excellent measure of habitat con-

dunes along the coast, through building of houses and stores. Wheeler's satyr was lost due to the drying up of Owens Valley and the loss of its larval food-plant, grasses.

The third known North American loss was the Xerces blue (*Glaucopsyche xerces*), which was last seen in the Presidio of San Francisco on March 23, 1943. In this case, too, the city of San Francisco had destroyed virtually all of the species' original sand dune habitat.

Although no noticeable change occurred in the last remaining population's habitat on the grounds of the Presidio from 1943 to 1944, the butterfly apparently disappeared after its 1943 flight period. Today, the old dunes and foodplants on which

that last population of Xerces blue flew and laid eggs still remain at the Presidio. The fourth North American butterfly extinction occurred in 1983 in the city of Rancho Palos Verdes, a suburb located due southwest of Los Angeles. During the development of a baseball field on the last remaining habitat area, a bulldozer exterminated the last known colony of the Palos Verdes blue (*Glaucopsyche lygdamus palosverdesensis*).

Germany was the first country to legally protect a butterfly when in 1913 it outlawed the capture of the Apollo butterfly (*Parnassius apollo*). In 1938, the city of Pacific Grove, California, protected trees that were used as overwintering roosts by the Monarch butterfly (*Danaus plex-*

The Lange's metalmark (*Apodemia mormo langei*) survives on just a small area of sand dunes on the north side of San Francisco Bay.

ippus). Today, special interest groups are trying to convince the United States Congress to recognize the Monarch butterfly as the national insect. In Mexico, overwintering roosting sites are being protected by an international conservation effort.

Population decline

Since the passage of the Endangered Species Act by the United States in 1973, several butterflies have either been recognized as endangered or threatened species, or are under consideration for such status. In 1976, two Florida swallowtail butterflies, the Schaus swallowtail (*Papilio aristodemus ponceanus*) and the Bahaman swallowtail (*P. andraemon bonhotei*), were the first insects to be recognized nationally as threatened or endangered. Shortly thereafter, six lycaenid butterflies from California were recognized as endangered. All of these have suffered population decline due to habitat destruction or modification.

The Schaus swallowtail in Florida declined to less than 70 adult individuals by 1984. Investigations showed that destruction of their tropical hardwood hammocks in the Florida Keys had contributed to a major decrease in the swallowtails during the preceding 40 years. The hammocks were cleared for housing developments.

From 1972 through 1984, the introduction of two pesticides used for mosquito control caused a sharp decline in the remaining population. Subsequent banning of spraying on parts of northern Key Largo allowed recovery to begin there.

Trouble by the bay

Nearly 10 percent of the human population of the United States of America lives in California, primarily along its scenic coast. The expanding urban areas are causing loss and alteration of habitats of coastal butterflies. So it is not surprising that the first butterflies recognized as endangered species in California live in isolated patches of coastal habitat surrounded by urbanization. Scientific studies have shown that these butterflies share several biological features which actually increase their vulnerability to extinction. For example, they have very specific larval and adult

foodplant requirements. Thus the adults tend to stay very close to their "home" area and do not readily move to other, unaffected habitat. In most cases, the larval foodplants are long-lived plants with year-round growth, but the larvae prefer certain specific plants that are middle-aged rather than juvenile or aging. Furthermore, larvae and adults of three endangered butterflies restrict their feeding to only the flowers of the foodplants.

The San Bruno elfin (*Callophrys mossii bayensis*) and mission blue butterfly (*Icaricia icarioides missionensis*) are limited to a handful of locations on the San Francisco Peninsula. The primary populations of both butterflies are found on San Bruno Mountain, which supports many rare and endangered plants and animals. The Lange's metalmark (*Apodemia mormo langei*) survives on only 75 degraded acres (30 hectares) of sand dunes on the north side of San Francisco Bay.

Molecular studies have shown that other populations of this butterfly need protection, and that the taxonomic status of *langei* is in doubt. Similarly, decline of the El Segundo blue (*Euphilotes battoides allyni*), which lives on sand dune remnants in Los Angeles, has been slowed due to habitat management. Along the Monterey County coast, Smith's blue (*Euphilotes enoptes smithi*) lives in both coastal sand dunes and the rugged coastal mountains.

An unsuccessful story is that of the lotis blue (*Lycaeides idas lotis*) butterfly, which lived in boggy areas near the Pygmy Forest of coastal Mendocino County. Despite recent intensive

searches, it has not been observed since 1983 and is now feared to be extinct.

Several species of large blues or *Maculinea* are distributed from western Europe to China, including the large alcon blue (*M. alcon*), large dusky blue (*M. nausithous*), greater large blue (*M. arionides*), Rebel's large blue (*M. rebeli*), large blue (*M. arion*), and large scarce blue (*M. teleius*). Nearly all of these species are from small, isolated colonies. In addition to their foodplant needs, the successful growth of their caterpillar stage is dependent upon a mutualistic relationship with native ants. Caterpillars overwinter in ant nests for about nine months, where they feed on ant eggs, grubs, and prepupae. Thus, conservation efforts have been focused on maintaining suitable habitat for both the butterfly's foodplants and the local ant species.

Many forms of fritillary butterfly (in the family Nymphalidae) in North America and Europe have greatly declined during the last 200 years due to a variety of human and natural changes in their habitats. These butterflies and their violet larval foodplants of the genus Viola (*Violaceae*) are among the best indicator organisms of native, undisturbed ecological communities. For example, the regal fritillary (*Speyeria idalia*) and its larval foodplant, the blue prairie violet (*Viola pedatifida*), are two of the best indicator species of virgin tall-grass prairie in the central United States from Indiana and Iowa eastward. This native ecosystem has been eliminated in virtually all areas by agriculture, and today the butterfly and violet are mainly confined to the few small patches of virgin prairie that are being preserved by state and private agencies. Many other fritillary species have been affected by heavy grazing of rangelands and meadow habitats, water diversion from springs and valleys, suburban growth and development, introduction of rapidly growing weeds and grasses that have crowded out the native plants, and elimination of natural periodic fires that once maintained the health of native grasslands. The Oregon silverspot (*Speyeria zerene hippolytta*) breeds in the salt spray meadows of northern California and Oregon, but adults disperse into adjacent forests for shelter. In many places where this silverspot was once abundant, its larval foodplant (*Viola adunca*) has been displaced by changes in the vegetation. Rescue efforts are focusing on maintaining habitat conditions that favor the growth and reproduction of the violet foodplant. A close relative, the Myrtle's silverspot (*S. zerene myrteleae*) occurs in coastal grassland habitats immediately north of San Francisco, and was nominated for endangered status in the early 1990s. The umcompahgre fritillary (*Boloria acrocnema*) is an arctic species left behind by the retreating Pleistocene glaciers 10,000 years ago. Today, it is known from only two alpine meadows in the San Juan Mountains of southwestern Colorado. Although its habitat is not likely to be developed or otherwise disturbed by man, recent studies on alpine plants and animals suggest that global warming may be the most imminent threat to its survival. A permanent change in air

temperature of only a few degrees (as from an increased "greenhouse effect" caused by more carbon dioxide in our atmosphere) will cause the death of alpine species that have adjusted to very cold mountain temperatures.

The bay checkerspot (*Euphydryas editha bayensis*) is restricted to serpentine grasslands in the San Francisco-San Jose area of California. Urbanization and drought combined to eliminate more than a dozen populations during the past two decades. Today, only three populations still remain. The checkerspot depends upon plants that grow only on hillsides and hilltops with the right amount of exposure to sunlight. If the plants thrive, the butterfly will, too.

The World Conservation Union (IUCN) recently completed a comprehensive review of the family Papilionidae, which includes the swallowtails, kites, and birdwings. From evidence based on this study, the IUCN recognizes nearly 80 species of swallowtails, particularly those from tropical regions, as rare or endangered species.

Some butterflies occur in very low numbers in natural populations and are not really "endangered." The short-tailed swallowtail (*Papilio indra*) is found in the isolated "island" mountain ranges of the western desert and canyon country of the United States. It exists in local populations of less than 50 individuals, but adults are able to fly many miles in search of mates and foodplants. They also have relatively long adult life spans of up to a month. The pupal stage can stay in suspended animation

for up to five years before the adult emerges. Thus the swallowtails are able to compensate for low population size and survive the drought years or other environmental stress normally found in the desert.

Also, the rugged and isolated habitats inhabited by the various rare *Papilio indra* subspecies are rarely developed or disturbed by any humans.

Brazilian species

The strikingly beautiful swallowtail (*Parides ascanius*) of the coastal swamps near Rio de Janeiro in southeastern Brazil was the first and only insect to date to be placed on the official list of Brazilian animals threatened with extinction. Like the Schaus swallowtail, it has been illustrated in many popular and scientific books on New World butterflies. While the distribution of *P. ascanius* has probably always been restricted and spotty, the inaccessible and inhospitable nature of its swampy and mosquito-infested habitat kept many of its colonies safe from developers and collectors until recently. Today, the growing population of Rio de Janeiro has caused the draining of the coastal and lowland swamps in order to create recreational areas, banana plantations, or pasture.

Several colonies of the butterfly occur in the 12,000-acre (5,000-hectare) Poco das Antas Biological Reserve, which may guarantee its future preservation. Harris' mimic swallowtail (*Graphium lysithous harrisianus*) mimics in its coloration and wing pattern several other species of Parides swallowtails, including *P. ascanius*. Although it was quite common around Rio de Janeiro until the 1940s, today only a single colony is still known to exist.

Other swallowtails

Two other internationally important studies of swallowtail species are also worth noting. The Homerus swallowtail (*Papilio homerus*) is the largest species in this genus. Because of its large size, its unusual beauty, and its limited occurrence on the island of Jamaica, it has always been highly prized by butterfly collectors. The destruction of its habitat for timber and coffee plantations threatens the survival of this swallowtail.

Queen Alexandra's birdwing (*Ornithoptera alexandrae*), the world's largest butterfly with a wingspan of 10 inches (25 centimeters), occurs in an area of less than 36 square miles (100 square kilometers) on the northeastern coast of New Guinea. New colonies have recently been discovered elsewhere in New Guinea. In this range, the butterfly inhabits rain forest tracts with its sole larval foodplant, *Aristolochia schlecteri*.

The butterfly and plant are further restricted to areas with a very sparse ground layer and a thick forest canopy. The two major disruptive influences on

the vegetation of the Popondetta region have been people, and volcanic activity. People have cleared the forest for shifting cultivation and most recently for oil palm plantations, and have used fire to create grasslands for hunting wallabies. The egg-to-adult development time for this tropical swallowtail is very long at about 122 days, increasing the chances that something will discover the egg, larva, or pupa. Adults suffer little predation and may survive in the wild up to three months. They apparently

The mission blue butterfly is an endangered resident on San Bruno Mountain in northern California.

move very little and live in small populations. A maximum of 25 individuals per acre (square kilometer) were found in some locations. The reasons for the limited distribution and low population of *O. alexandrae* are uncertain, but may result from at least three factors: the specialization of the larvae to only one foodplant species, which is itself rare although much more widely distributed than the butterfly; competition with a much commoner species in the same area, another birdwing swallowtail (*Ornithoptera priamus*) and egg parasites, such as Chalcid wasps, that heavily attack eggs of two common birdwings and other swallowtails in New Guinea.

A habitat lost

However, what is most clear is that much of the butterflies' habitat is being rapidly lost to logging of the rain forest and the growing oil palm industry that is centered immediately in the range of Queen Alexandra's birdwing in the Popondetta Plain.

The Division of Wildlife in New Guinea is attempting to obtain control of certain areas of government land that have been rejected for use as oil palm plantations. They are also trying to set up additional wildlife reserves by agreements with other landowners. Once the future of the species is assured, the economic importance of Queen Alexandra's birdwing may be considerable. Worldwide demand by collectors for birdwing species can be satisfied by farming certain species, as has already been demonstrated for the past two decades in New Guinea for non-protected species. Specimens of the world's largest birdwing, *O. alexandrae*, that were collected before the species was protected, sold for $1,800 to $2,000 in 1984, $2,700 for a perfect specimen in 1986, and $5,000 for a perfect pair in 1990.

Thomas C. Emmel and
Richard A. Arnold

The Queen Alexandra's birdwing is the world's largest butterfly with a wing span of more than ten inches (25 centimeters). It occurs in an area of less than 36 square miles (93 square kilometers) in New Guinea.

CACHORRITOS

Class: Actinopterygii

Order: Atheriniformes

Family: Cyprinodontidae

Cachorritos are part of the rather widespread family of killifishes (Cyprinodontidae). Representatives of this family are found in temperate and tropical climates throughout most of the world. In contrast with most freshwater fish, killifishes are able to adapt to environmental extremes. They are found in both saltwater and freshwater, as well as waters having a high mineral content. As a group, they can also tolerate great ranges in temperature. Killifishes bear a strong resemblance to minnows (the Cyprinidae family). Differences between the two include the usually rounded tail and head scales of the killifish, which the minnow does not have.

As the name suggests, killifishes have teeth. The cachorritos species are found in Mexico and are similar to species called "pupfish" in the United States. The Spanish word "cachorrito" refers to a little whelp or pup. Cachorritos are found in closed desert basins and often rely on springs or spring-fed environments. Most have evolved in isolated habitats that have remained relatively unchanged for thousands of years. Over time, gradual changes have occurred in these isolated fish, causing them to develop into a unique species. These small, curious fishes are very colorful.

Most species exhibit differences in color, markings, or body form between males and females, which is called sexual dimorphism. All of the cachorritos are egg layers, and the male fishes often exhibit territorial behavior at breeding time. Most cachorritos tend to spawn in the spring or early summer, releasing eggs and sperm simultaneously on or near aquatic vegetation, although some species seem to prefer to lay their eggs on gravel or mineral deposits.

Some species have even adapted to temporary ponds that contain water only part of the year. Eggs are laid on the pond bottom and survive even when the pond has dried up and all the adult fish have died. Miraculously, the eggs hatch once the seasonal rains return. The mouth of most cachorritos is at the top of their somewhat flattened head, and they mostly feed at the surface of the water. Because of their small size, large numbers of these fish can occupy restricted habitats. Cachorritos are rarely found near the habitat of large predatory fish, and they become vulnerable prey when larger, aggressive species are stocked in waters previously occupied by cachorritos and other small fish.

Cachorrito Boxeador

(Cyprinodon simus)

IUCN: Endangered

Length: 1.2 in. (3 cm)

Reproduction: Egg layer

Habitat: A shallow, slightly saline tropical lake

Range: Laguna Chichancanab, Yucatan Peninsula, Mexico

THE CACHORRITO boxeador (in English, a "vertical-jaw pupfish") is a member of a species flock, which is a group of closely related fish with a common ancestry found coexisting in the same freshwater lake. This small pupfish is found only in Laguna [Lake] Chichancanab near the center of the Yucatan Peninsula. It is found nowhere else on the planet except in this shallow, fluctuating, slightly saline lake.

Due to the extremely small range of the cachorrito boxeador and its scarcity (there are five other pupfish found in its native habitat), its status is considered endangered. This situation is compounded by the recent introduction of non-native tilapia (*Oreochromis sp.*) into Laguna Chichancanab. Native to Africa, tilapia have been widely distributed as a food crop in underdeveloped countries. The impact of tilapia in the Yucatan has not yet been fully assessed, but similar introductions in other tropical and subtropical areas of Central and South America have resulted in rapid and disastrous effects on native fishes.

A boxnose pupfish

The cachorrito boxeador may be distinguished from other pupfish in Laguna Chichancanab by its unique vertical lower jaw. It has a short, narrow head with a small mouth located at the top of its very pronounced square jaw. The small head has large eyes that dominate its rather tiny body.

Differences in color occur between males and females, and between breeding and nonbreeding males. Most males and females are dark brown or black on the back, with irregular dark vertical bars on the sides of the body. Females also have a pronounced dark spot called an ocellus at the base of the dorsal fin on the back. Males are larger and more robust, with dark-colored margins or patches on all fins. In addition, males develop brilliant coloration when spawning. Their bodies become jet-black, highlighted by metallic blue speckles on the back, while the tail becomes bright yellow with a black vertical band. This striking coloration change is only temporary and will disappear after spawning.

The "vertical-jaw pupfish," or cachorrito boxeador, has been observed congregating in large numbers in three to six feet (0.9 to 1.8 meters) of water. This common schooling behavior helps it to more easily find food and to reproduce more effectively. Schooling is even believed to aid swimming, while at the same time it is thought to reduce the risk of being eaten. Schools of cachorritos seem to stay slightly above the bottom of this shallow lake, where they feed for a while and then move slowly on to another area.

The small, narrow mouth at the top of the snout enables these fish to feed in a most unusual manner. They depress their lower jaw to form a sort of suction tube. This enables them to pick small aquatic organisms, called plankters, from the water. One by one, plankters are suctioned into the tiny mouth of the cachorrito boxeador. This method of feeding also helps to explain the prominence of the eye positioned on top of the head.

This pupfish's distinct mouth shape could be adapted as the result of specializing in one particular food. This seems likely in the case of the cachorrito boxeador, because its feeding behavior is different from other pupfish in Laguna Chichancanab, and differs from other cyprinodonts in general.

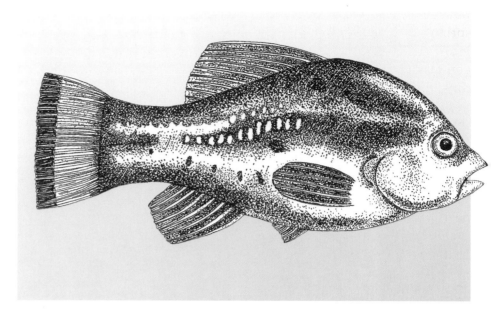

Cyprinodons come in many shapes. This *Cyprinodon latifasciatus* comes from the Mexican state of Coahuila.

Although a few hybrids have been observed in Laguna Chichancanab, it is not known whether or not they are fertile. In any event, these closely related species are able to distinguish members of their own kind. How they do it remains one of the great puzzles of understanding species flocks. Somehow, the time or place of spawning helps keep the species separate and distinct from each other.

Cachorrito Cabezon

(Cyprinodon pachycephalus)

IUCN: Critically endangered

Length: 1½ in. (4 cm)
Reproduction: Egg layer
Habitat: Warmwater spring
Range: Baños de San Diego, Chihuahua, Mexico

LOCATED IN THE Chihuahua Desert of northern Mexico and east of Caudad, Chihuahua is a tiny warm water spring known as Baños de San Diego. This spring is noteworthy for its extremely warm water (110 degrees Fahrenheit, or 44 degrees Celsius) and the remarkable collection of fish, mollusks, and crustaceans that inhabit it. Cachorrito cabezon is found only in this remote desert spring. It is not uncommon for an entire pupfish species to be limited to one small pool or spring.

Long before the Ice Age the climate here was wetter and ancestors of this small cachorrito were, no doubt, more abundant and widely distributed. But the ice receded, leaving the arid desert basins of northern Mexico and the American southwest, and these fish became isolated. Unable to change localities, they were forced to slowly adapt to the changing conditions or perish.

Because of the extremely small size of this desert fish's habitat, and the great demand for water by people, this cachorrito is now an endangered species. The spring which once flowed directly into the Rio Chuviscar has been completely diverted by humans; thus, the fish are completely isolated and dependent upon the spring at Baños de San Diego.

Cachorrito cabezon is the Spanish name for "bighead pupfish." The name is appropriate, as this cyprinodont has the largest head of any of the pupfish or cachorritos. The length of the head takes up nearly a third of its entire body. Its jaws are massive, and the width of the mouth is nearly half the length of the head. Colors are rather subdued on this odd creature. There is a hint of yellow on the head and dark vertical bars on the tail, with only slight differences between the sexes. The fin between the anus and tail (the anal fin) is highly colored, particularly when the cachorrito is ready to spawn.

The extremely high temperature of the water in the spring at Baños de San Diego is an unusual environment for fish in general, but other species of the family Cyprinodontidae are also able to exist in similar warm temperatures. Nonetheless, the cachorrito cabezon is the most unique, as no other freshwater fish lives constantly in such hot water. The water temperature actually prevents other fish found near the outlet of the spring from entering it, but some hybrids have been observed in ponds and

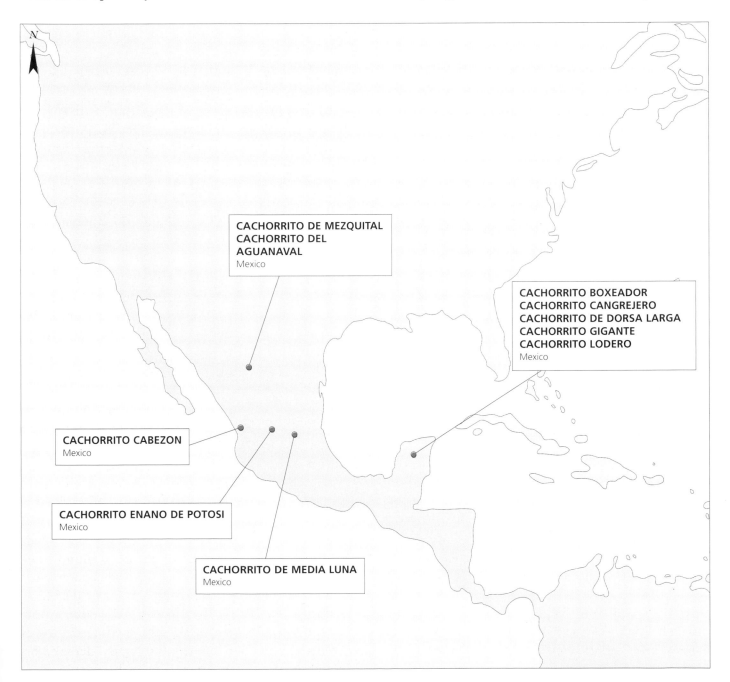

CACHORRITO DE MEZQUITAL
CACHORRITO DEL AGUANAVAL
Mexico

CACHORRITO BOXEADOR
CACHORRITO CANGREJERO
CACHORRITO DE DORSA LARGA
CACHORRITO GIGANTE
CACHORRITO LODERO
Mexico

CACHORRITO CABEZON
Mexico

CACHORRITO ENANO DE POTOSI
Mexico

CACHORRITO DE MEDIA LUNA
Mexico

pools that are below the Baños de San Diego Spring.

Foods of the cachorrito cabezon include a few crustaceans and snails found within the spring, as well as an occasional ant or other insect that happens to fall into the warm water. Pupfish in general are rarely known to eat organisms as large as the snails found at Baños de San Diego. Thus, the enlarged head and mouth of cachorrito cabezon may be related to its somewhat distinct eating habits.

The future for this curious pupfish will depend on the demands for water in this land where water is so scarce. If the residents of the small desert community are sensitive to the presence of this unique cachorrito, precautions can be taken to protect its limited habitat. Attempts to maintain the fish in captivity have met with only moderate success, but captive breeding may contribute somewhat to its security.

Cachorrito Cangrejero
(Cyprinodon labiosus)

IUCN: Endangered

Length: 1½ in. (4 cm)
Reproduction: Egg layer
Habitat: A shallow, slightly saline tropical lake
Range: Laguna Chichancanab, Yucatan Peninsula, Mexico

EASILY DISTINGUISHED from other fish in Laguna Chichancanab (and from all other cyprinodonts, too), this small, slender pupfish has large convoluted lips that are quite distinct. It is one of five closely related fish (or species flock) in Laguna Chichancanab. All these pupfish are considered vulnerable to extinction for two main reasons. First, they are known to exist only in this shallow lake in Mexico's Yucatan Peninsula.

Their limited range makes them susceptible to rapid decline if there are any dramatic changes in their environment.

Second, as with their relatives a recent introduction of a nonnative tilapia (*Oreochromis sp.*) into Laguna Chichancanab may threaten all of the small fish native to this shallow lake. In similar environments throughout Central and South America, nonnative tilapia have had dramatic and unfortunate effects on smaller native fish.

Because cachorritos did not evolve in the presence of a predator such as tilapia, they have little or no defenses against them. Cachorritos become easy prey for the larger, more aggressive new member of their community; in many cases the result is the disappearance of many, if not all, native species.

The cachorrito cangrejero is one of the most peculiar of all the pupfish. It has large fleshy lips that resemble those of a sucker (family Catostomidae) except that they point upward. In some individuals, the lips are so pronounced that the fish is unable to completely close its mouth. There is no difference between the mouth of the male and female, but some differences can be observed in coloration, particularly when the males are reproductively active.

Both sexes are dark brown or black on the dorsal or back side. This dark coloration blends into a number of vertical bands on the side of the fish. The underside is mostly silver or white. When males become reproductively active, they become much darker and develop numerous metallic

Cyprinodon alverezi is a pupfish that shares a small pond in the town of El Potosi in Mexico with another, more rare species, the Cachorrito enano de Potosi.

blue spots on the back. The tail fin develops horizontal yellow stripes, which are trimmed by a black vertical band at the tip of the tail. As in many fish, this dramatic coloration of the males is associated with spawning, and is only temporary.

Like the other cachorritos of Laguna Chichancanab, the "thicklipped pupfish" has numerous pharyngeal (comb-like) teeth in the throat region, which are used to crush and grind food into smaller particles. Pharyngeal teeth are vitally important because the diet of the cachorrito cangrejero includes snails and small crustaceans.

Most pupfish are known as "opportunistic feeders," meaning they generally eat what is available, when it is available. Such is the case for the cachorrito cangrejero. It is usually found near the margins of Laguna Chichancanab, where it stays in loose groups with other pupfish. It spends much of its time at or near the bottom, consuming large quantities of detritus (dead organic matter, bacteria, and microscopic organisms located at the bottom of a lake). Its unusual lips are used for food gathering, but no specialized food habits have been observed.

Because they are often observed in close association with other species of cachorritos in Laguna Chichancanab, it is somewhat of a mystery how each species is able to recognize its own kind. In general, they are all capable of reproducing throughout the year. Spawning is usually accompanied with guarding of territories by the males, followed by a courtship ritual that culminates in release of sperm and

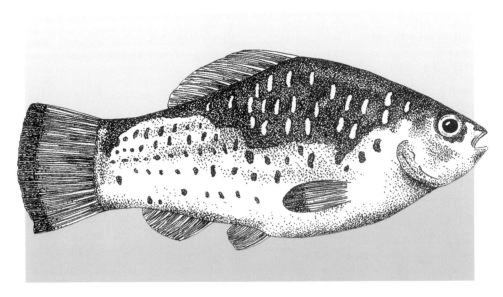

eggs over aquatic vegetation. Only time will tell if the cyprinodont will survive the demands on its environment in the Yucatan, and the impact of non-native predators.

Cachorrito Enano de Potosi

(Megupsilon aporus)

IUCN: Extinct in the wild

Length: 1½ in. (4 cm)
Reproduction: Egg layer
Habitat: A small, spring-fed pond
Range: El Potosi, Nuevo Leon, Mexico

THE CACHORRITO enano de Potosi has a tiny native range. It only exists in one spring-fed pond, near the town of El Potosi in Mexico. The public spring has been drying up in recent years. Combined with a long drought and an increasing human population, this small but important

The cachorrito de mezquital is one of a group of pupfish that are now geographically isolated.

water supply is in huge demand. Also, an advanced irrigation complex has been constructed with a deep well pumping system. Pumping groundwater from the area around El Potosi has caused the water level in this small pond to drop, and there are fears that the spring that feeds this pond may dry up entirely.

Needless to say, without water this small pupfish has no chance of survival in its native home. To add to its dilemma, large mouth bass (*Micropterus salmoides*) have been introduced into the pond. These large fish are voracious predators that are able to consume many pupfish in just a single day. The small cachorritos have not historically had to cope with such heavy predation and have little or no defense against the bass. The combination of declining water levels and reduction in numbers from the non-native bass paint a gloomy picture for the future. It is considered extremely endangered if not extinct.

Special characteristics

This small cachorrito clearly resembles other pupfish and cachorritos, but close examination has revealed some important differences. These differing characteristics include various dissimilar body parts, a unique number of chromosomes, and peculiar behavior of the males during courtship. Such differences have prompted scientists to give this cachorrito a new and exclusive name: *Megupsilon*.

The males of this species extend their lower and upper jaws when they are attempting to spawn. This behavior has been called "jaw-nudge," and it is believed this behavior helps the female cachorrito to identify appropriate partners. This is important because another species of pupfish (*Cyprinodon alverezi*) is also found in this small pond in central Mexico. The unique behavior prevents hybridization, or reproduction between two different species, from occurring in the wild.

The cachorrito enano de Potosi prefers the shallow edges of the pond that are often thick with aquatic plants and algae. It will utilize many types of food, but the adults seem to eat more animal matter than most other pupfish species.

Captivity

Because of the difficult situation this cachorrito now faces, attempts have been made to keep this pupfish in aquariums. Mexican biologists, however, have had very limited success in bringing about reproduction in captivity. Given the ever-declining state of the pond at El Potosi, the negative effects of the presence of large mouth bass, and the failure to successfully reproduce in captivity, the cachorrito enano de Potosi may unfortunately find itself on the list of recently extinct species in the near future.

Cachorrito Gigante

(Cyprinodon maya)

IUCN: Endangered

Length: 4 in. (10 cm)
Reproduction: Egg layer
Habitat: A shallow, slightly saline tropical lake
Range: Laguna Chichancanab, Yucatan Peninsula, Mexico

ONE OF THE largest of all the cachorritos and of all pupfishes, the cachorrito gigante is another member of the "species flock" of Laguna Chichancanab. A species flock is a group of closely related aquatic invertebrates or fishes that are believed to have a common ancestor. These cachorritos have been found in many of the older lakes in the world. Fish that comprise species flocks usually show subtle differences in the shape of the head and mouth. The cachorrito gigante is a good example, as it differs from other cachorritos not only by its larger size but also by its long wide head and broad mouth.

The cachorrito gigante has been isolated in this relatively small basin on the Yucatan Peninsula for thousands of years. No large predatory fish was able to find its way into these waters. Unfortunately, the recent introduction of tilapia (*Oreochromis* sp.) may have a devastating impact on this cachorrito and the other fish of Laguna Chichancanab. Because the native fishes of this lake were not exposed to predators such as tilapia, they had no reason to develop the defensive behavior that would protect them from being eaten. The cachorrito gigante is a sitting duck for the larger, very aggressive tilapia; it is feared that in time this fish may disappear from Laguna Chichancanab.

The cachorrito gigante is nearly twice as large as the typical pupfish. It also has a very robust head and body with rather large eyes positioned at the top of the head. The basic body color is a silvery tan, becoming brown toward the tail. Darker vertical brown bars provide stripes along the side of the body. Differences between the males and females are much more subtle than in other cachorritos, but when the males are ready to court a potential mate, they become brighter and develop metallic blue speckles on the head and back. Females have a dark round spot at the base of the fin on their back (called an ocellus), and both sexes have a dark brown band at the tip of the tail.

Varied diet

The large size of this pupfish allows it to eat larger aquatic organisms than the other cachorritos in Laguna Chichancanab. In general, pupfish consume a wide variety of foods, but most of their diet consists of detritus (decaying organic matter at the bottom of a lake or pond). This cachorrito prefers snails, small crustaceans, and even other fish. In fact, this is the only cachorrito that has been observed eating adult fish. It is not unusual for eggs or small immature fish to be consumed, but the cachorrito gigante with its larger size and mouth is likely to consume all sizes of mosquitofish and small cachorritos in Laguna Chichancanab.

Although the cachorrito gigante does interact with the other species in the lake during its daily activity, there is little hybridization, as it rarely attempts to mate with any of the other closely related cachorritos.

Cachorrito Lodero

(Cyprinodon beltrani)

IUCN: Endangered

Length: 1½ in. (4 cm)
Reproduction: Egg layer
Habitat: A shallow, slightly saline tropical lake
Range: Laguna Chichancanab, Yucatan Peninsula, Mexico

OF THE FIVE closely related cachorritos that can be found exclusively in Laguna Chichancanab, the cachorrito lodero is the most similar to a typical pupfish in general appearance. Its home is in the north-central portion of Mexico's Yucatan Peninsula. Laguna Chichancanab is actually a series of eight permanent lakes that interconnect during periods of high rainfall. It is situated in the center of a closed basin; that is, streams in the immediate area flow into this series of lakes, but there is no outlet to the ocean. Because of this unusual interconnecting arrangement of lakes, Laguna Chichancanab is subject to seasonal and long-term changes in water level.

There are five species of cachorritos that make up a small but interesting species flock. A species flock is a group of closely related organisms, believed to be descended from a common ancestor, that inhabit the same general area. Species flocks are most commonly observed in large, relatively old lakes, and examples are found throughout the world, most notably in Africa's Lake Victoria and Lake Tanganyika, as well as in southern Siberia (Lake Baikal).

Laguna Chichancanab is modest in comparison with those famous lakes, and there are far fewer species of fish present, but there are striking similarities nonetheless. In Laguna Chichancanab, the cachorrito lodero appears to have a normal mouth and head, especially compared to the cachorrito boxeador (*Cyprinodon simus*) and the cachorrito cangrejero (*Cyprinodon labiosus*). One explanation for the occurrence of these species flocks is that the different species have become specialized in their feeding habits. This allows each species to take advantage of a different food source and thus avoid extreme competition.

The cachorrito lodero, or blackfin pupfish, is a small but colorful cyprinodont. Males and females can be distinguished during spawning. The males become darker on the body when their black vertical bands grow in size. Their fins display an increase in pigmentation, dominated by the bright head and back. Females may be identified by the round, dark spot near the base of the fin on their back, and their colors are much less intense than the males.

The cachorrito lodero has lived in this same basin for thousands of years. It has coexisted with the other cachorritos and one small mosquitofish (*Gambusias exradiata*). It is believed that historically there were no larger predatory fish in Laguna Chichancanab. But now this remarkable group of fishes is considered quite vulnerable to extinction. The reason for this threat is the tilapia (*Oreochromis sp.*), a fish common throughout the world as a food source for people. Either deliberately or by accident, they are released into waters outside of an aquaculture facility. This is what occurred in Mexico, as tilapia are now found in Laguna Chichancanab. Being larger and more aggressive than the cachorritos, the non-native tilapia are a threat to the cachorritos' long-term survival.

Cachorrito de Dorsal Larga

(Cyprinodon verecundus)

IUCN: Critically endangered

Length: 1½ in. (4 cm)
Reproduction: Egg layer
Habitat: A shallow, slightly saline tropical lake
Range: Laguna Chichancanab, Yucatan Peninsula, Mexico

OF THE FIVE species of cachorritos known from Laguna Chichancanab, a closed basin in the middle of Mexico's Yucatan

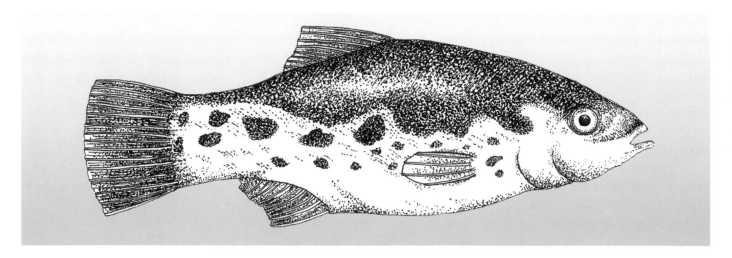

Female Cachorrito del Aguanaval

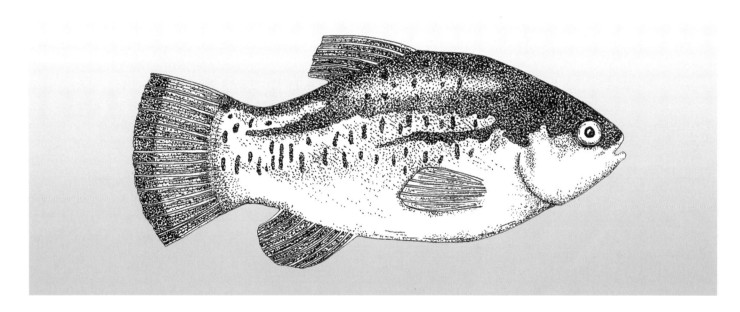

Male Cachorrito del Aguanaval

Peninsula, the cachorrito de dorsal larga is the rarest and most difficult to observe. It is part of a species, which is a group of closely related fish with a common ancestry, occurring in the same freshwater lake.

It was the last of the species of cachorritos to be discovered, due to its habit of remaining close to the bottom of the lake and because it is found only at relatively few locations within the lake. The main threat to this small cachorrito (aside from the restricted nature of its home range), is predation from tilapia (*Oreochromis sp.*). Tilapia have been introduced to Laguna Chichancanab by humans, and represent a distinct threat to the long-term survival of all the cachorritos in this lake. As a result, the cachorrito de dorsal larga is now considered to be vulnerable to extinction.

The name "dorsal larga" refers to the relatively large fin on the back of the fish. In fact, all of the fins are a bit larger than a typical pupfish, as are the eyes. The mouth tends to be located at the

The Cachorrito del Aguanaval, like all the fishes of Mexico, faces destruction of its habitat in a land where water is needed for agriculture and human consumption.

bottom of the snout, which is also different from most cachorritos, whose mouths are generally at the top of the snout.

Since the cachorrito de dorsal larga is nearly always found on the bottom of the lake on or near gravel, the position of the mouth is most likely the result of specialized feeding on organisms that inhabit this bottom gravel.

The color of this pupfish is yellowish tan, with five vertical brown bars along the side of the body. Males generally show quite a bit of variation in intensity of color. This is usually associated with different levels of reproductive or territorial activity.

During courtship they tend to be nearly all black and display a scattering of shiny blue speckles on the back and head. Femalesof this species display a prominent dark round spot at the base of the fin on their backs.

Due to the rarity of the cachorrito de dorsal larga, it has not been observed while spawning. It is presumed, however, that it prefers to deposit its eggs on the hard-surfaced areas of the bottom rather than amid aquatic plants. This fish has a preference for hard-surfaced bottom areas. This may explain its overall rarity in Laguna Chichancanab, as most of the lake bottom is covered with soft layers of decaying organic material or char, which is an aquatic plant. The cachorrito de dorsa larga uses its large fins to clear and stir up the bottom gravel with broad sweeping motions, thereby exposing tiny aquatic organisms that inhabit the small spaces between the rocks. This specialized feeding behavior could be the reason why the fins on the cachorrito de dorsal larga are so much bigger than those of other cachorritos.

This rare and elusive pupfish is an important component of the unique species flock of Laguna Chichancanab.

Hopefully it will be able to elude the potentially severe threat posed by tilapia so we may learn more about its unusual habits and life history.

Cachorrito del Aguanaval
(Cyprinodon nazas)

IUCN: Lower risk

Length: 1½ in. (4 cm)
Reproduction: Egg layer
Habitat: Small streams and rivers, ponds and lakes
Range: Basin of Rio Nazas and Basin of Santiaguillo

LIKE MANY MEMBERS of the pupfish family, the cachorrito del Aguanaval resides in a closed desert basin with no external outlet. All of the small, predominantly spring-fed rivers and streams in the basin of the Rio Nazas (which includes the Rio Aguanaval) flow into Laguna Mayran, a shallow lake near the small community of El Palmito in the state of Durango, Mexico. To the south another basin ending in Laguna Santiaguillo contains a diminishing population of these fish. The pupfish in the Santiaguillo basin are similar to those in the Nazas River, but there are enough differences to consider the Santiaguillo pupfish to be a sub-species of cachorrito del Aguanaval.

Precarious existence
This cachorrito faces problems common to many species of fish throughout Mexico. It lives in small, fluctuating aquatic habitats in a land where water is scarce and each drop is precious. The range of the cachorrito has been greatly diminished by the diversion of water for human consumption and agriculture. When streams are diverted they are often polluted as a result of human activities. The combination of decreased range and drastic change in water quality is compounded in the case of the cachorrito del Aguanaval by the introduction of large aggressive fish such as bass (*Micropterus*). Bass have eliminated these pupfish from Laguna Mayran, and are also affecting those in tributaries of the Rio Nazas.

Attractive appearance
The cachorrito del Aguanaval is a colorful, attractive fish. The dorsal fin on the back is bright yellow to yellow-orange. The yellow tail fin has a black vertical bar at the tip of the tail. Males and females look different, especially the body shape. Males are more rounded, while females are thinner from top to bottom. Females are less colorful, especially when they are near spawning males, and they have the typical large round spot at the base of the dorsal fin, although this is less pronounced than in other species of cachorritos.

Cachorrito de Media Luna
(Cualac tessellatus)

IUCN: Endangered

Length: 1½ in. (4 cm)
Reproduction: Egg layer
Habitat: Small upland creeks
Range: Panuco drainage, central Mexico

THE CACHORRITO de media luna is found in a small reach of upland creeks in the Mexican state of San Luis Potosi. This region of central Mexico has been subject to a long drought in recent years that has had a negative impact on this cachorrito.

Restricted range

To support agricultural activities in this rather poor region, nearly all of the creeks that represent the native range of this fish have been diverted for irrigation. This creates a big problem for the cachorrito de media luna because its range is restricted to just a few spring-fed creeks. Extensive groundwater pumping for agriculture has further reduced flows from the sources of these already small upland creeks. The quality of the water in this area has been degraded by agricultural runoff and pollution from other human activities. Adding to this gloomy picture is the recent introductions of non-native smallmouth bass (*Micropterus dolomieu*) into these small creeks, which have placed the cachorrito at risk.

The half moon pupfish

This colorful pupfish is much like other cachorritos in its general body shape and appearance, yet scientists have observed keen differences. Because of this, they have given the fish a name that is unique to cachorritos: *Cualac*. Males and females are readily identified by the amount of yellow coloration on the fins. The yellow shows when males show territorial or courtship behavior.

Some attempts to raise this fish in captivity have been made, but with only limited success. As a result, the cachorrito de media luna is among the rarest and most endangered of this group of Mexican pupfishes.

Cachorrito de Mezquital
(Cyprinodon meeki)

> **IUCN:** Critically endangered

Length: 1¾ in. (4.5 cm)
Reproduction: Egg layer
Habitat: Small spring-fed streams and tributaries
Range: Rio de Tunal and Rio de Sauceda, Durango, Mexico

THE SCIENTIFIC NAME of this vanishing cachorrito was named for Seth Eugene Meek, a naturalist who explored much of Mexico in the early 1900s, discovering and describing many fish in what was then a remote and inaccessible landscape.

Old stock

The cachorrito de Mezquital is believed to have originated from ancestral stocks that occupied the region now known as the Chihuahuan desert. It is one of a group of closely related pupfish that are now geographically isolated in small drainages or closed basins with no external outlet.

The cachorrito de Mezquital is found in two tributaries of the Rio Mezquital near Durango City in the state of Durango, Mexico. The Rio de Tunal and Rio de Sauceda are small spring-fed streams in what is known as the Pacific Slope Drainage, part of the Sierra Madre Occidental Mountains.

Like many streams in Mexico these are relatively short and carry little water. They are subject to seasonal periods of extremely low water flow, and

recent diversions of much of this water for agriculture has worsened the situation.

The cachorrito de Mezquital is a typical pupfish in terms of body shape. It is, however, rather dull in coloration when compared to most members of the same genus (*Cyprinodon*).

The dorsal fin on the back is dark and lacks the yellow coloration that is often present in other cachorritos. This cachorrito has a narrow, vertical bar at the tip of the tail.

Distinctive shape

Although males and females are very similar in body shape, the females may be easily identified by the numerous fine spots over the entire body, and a larger round spot (*ocellus*) that can be seen on both the dorsal fin and the anal fin (between the anus and the tail). The bodies of the female and the male are also slightly more rounded than those of other pupfishes.

Shrinking habitat

Pollution associated with human habitation in or around Durango City has greatly reduced the available habitat of the cachorrito de Mezquital.

Predators

To add to the problems of deteriorating water quality and loss of available water, the cachorrito de Mezquital has to cope with perhaps an even greater threat: the presence of bass (*Micropterus*) in its springs and streams. As a result of its ever-diminishing range and the predation by bass, this once relatively abundant pupfish has become quite rare.

Donald S. Proebstel

CACTI

Phylum: Anthophyta
(flowering plants)
Order: Caryophyllales
Family: Cactaceae
Subfamily: Cactoideae
Tribe: Cacteae
Genus: Sclerocactus

The genus *Sclerocactus* includes 19 species of small, globular cacti native to the southwestern United States and adjacent Mexico. The Lloyd's Mariposa and Wright fishhook cacti both belong to this genus. *Sclerocactus* is very much sought after by specialist growers of cacti and other succulent plants because of their rarity and the challenge of cultivating them successfully (they have a reputation of being difficult to grow). The genus is related to *Pediocactus*, which has six species, all native to the southwestern United States and similarly attractive to collectors.

The horticultural market is not the only threat to these cacti. Other negative factors include mining, oil and gas drilling, potential industrial use of habitat, recreational use of off-road vehicles, and grazing by livestock.

Blaine Pincushion

*(Sclerocactus blainei =
Sclerocactus spinosior* ssp. *blainei)*

IUCN: Endangered

Class: Dicotyledones
Stem: 1.5–6 in. (3–15 cm) tall, green to dark green, ovoid or cylindrical, solitary or a few clumped together
Spines: Dense, usually in clusters, with 3–6 central spines (1–3 are irregularly or strongly hooked, some
may be strongly flattened and ribbonlike), and 6–12 radial spines
Flowers: April to May. Bell to funnel shaped, violet-pink or reddish purple petals with reddish brown midribs
Pollination: By insect
Habitat: Great Basin shrub lands
Range: Nye County, Nevada

IN THE BASIN AND Range country of western North America, off the beaten path, past ghost towns and abandoned mining camps lies the home of an enigmatic cactus. Hidden among clumps of galleta or surrounded by the branches of shadscale and the pungent scent of sagebrush, Blaine pincushion remained unknown to botanists until the mid 1980s.

Its flowers open in the warm afternoon sun of spring, revealing sprays of red-violet that surround several hundred bright yellow anthers. Small solitary bees, beetles, and bee flies gather among the anthers, feeding on the protein-rich pollen or probing the deep recesses of the flower for nectar. As summer arrives, small cylindrical fruits develop at the summit of the stems, amid the tangle of spines. Apparently unattractive to birds and rodents, the fruits dry and split open, still attached to the maternal plant. The large, dark seeds fall from the fruit and lie scattered at the base of the plant, transported only by the scouring winds and rains of the Great Basin desert.

When first described by S. L. Welsh and K. H. Thorne, *Sclerocactus blainei* was known to occur at only three locations, in a relatively unexplored region of Nevada. Very few plants were known to occur at each of these sites. Cattle grazing, common in the intermountain western United States, was considered to be a serious threat. Cattle are known to trample small cacti such as Blaine pincushion. In addition, mining activities seemed to be a potential threat to the small populations.

Perhaps the greatest concern to wildlife managers has been the threat of illegal collection of plants. Often, when a new species of cactus is described, there is great interest shown by some cactus enthusiasts in obtaining it for collections.

Complex species

The genus *Sclerocactus* has been of particular interest to cactus collectors and has been coveted by them for many years. Together, these concerns prompted conservationists and land managers to consider this species for protection. Unfortunately, very little was known about Blaine pincushion. The little that was known about its distribution and morphology was very perplexing. Blaine pincushion is very similar to, and believed to be closely related to, *Sclerocactus*

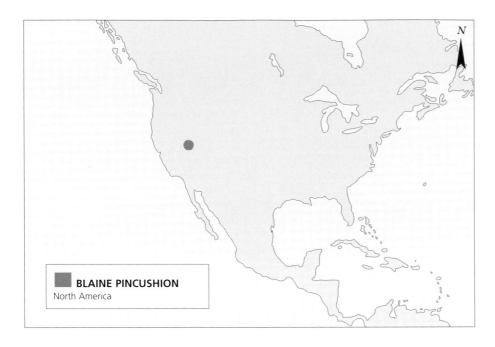

BLAINE PINCUSHION
North America

spinosior, a species restricted to the deserts of western Utah. Two of the known populations of Blaine pincushion were also found in this region, but the third was to the southwest, in the Mojave Desert of California. This is an unusual distribution. Morphologically, the population to the south differs from the ones in the north in several respects. For example, the fruits of the northern populations split open along one to three vertical slits, but the population to the south-west opened irregularly along the base of the fruit. Similarly, plants in the northern populations possessed about four central spines. However, individuals in the population to the southwest had as many as seven central spines. Was this a single, variable species, or were there two species involved? Subsequent investigations have revealed a complex picture that only now is beginning to make sense.

One of the first important contributions to our understanding of Blaine pincushion involved insight on the ability of popula-tions of this species to interbreed, or cross, with other populations and other species. The ability of different populations to exchange genetic material is an important criterion in determining species boundaries. It follows that mem-bers of the same species can freely exchange genes. However, in some groups of plants, differ-ent species can, through hybridization, also exchange genes. As a result, groups of pop-ulations that can interbreed are either of the same species or members of species that are capable of hybridizing.

One or four species?

Crossing studies revealed that all three populations of *Sclerocactus blainei* can exchange genes with each other and also with *Sclero-cactus pubispinus* (Great Basin fishhook cactus), *Sclerocactus sch-lesseri* (Schlesser pincushion), and *Sclerocactus spinosior* (Desert Valley fishhook cactus). This could indicate that there are four species that are capable of hybridizing or, alternatively, that there is only one species. The dif-ficulty is knowing which hypothe-sis is correct. Botanists have interpreted the interbreeding evi-dence differently. However all recent treatments of *Sclerocactus* hypothesize that the southwestern population of *Sclerocactus blainei* is a different species, known as *Sclerocactus nyensis*. Further, all include *Sclerocactus schlesseri* within (as a synonym of) *Sclero-cactus blainei*, suggesting that there is not really a fundamental difference between the two.

DNA study

A recent comparative study of DNA sequences from the chloro-plast genome of species of *Sclerocactus* provide new insight into this problem. These data provide evidence that *Sclerocactus blainei*—but not the southwestern population, *Sclerocactus nyensis*—and *Sclerocactus pubispinus*, *Sclerocactus schlesseri*, and *Sclero-cactus spinosior* share several mutations unique in the genus. This at once provides evidence for the common ancestry of *Scle-rocactus blainei*, *Sclerocactus pubispinus*, *Sclerocactus schlesseri*, and *Sclerocactus spinosior*, and of the independence (species status) of *Sclerocactus nyensis*. Field stud-ies verify that Blaine pincushion, given the current interpretation, is indeed locally common but scattered over a wide area.

There appears to be no major threats to the taxon as a whole, therefore protection seems to be unwarranted. Such is not the case for *Sclerocactus nyensis*, a species that has been restricted to a habitat of an actively mined, gold-bearing geologic formation. It has also been surrounded by taxonomic confusion.

J. Mark Porter

Hatchet Cactus (Peyotillo)

(Pelecyphora aselliformis)

IUCN: Rare

Stems: Single or multiple spherical stems, often flattened on top, ¾–2 in. (2–5 cm) across, dull grayish green in color

Spines: White or gray arranged in groups of 40 to 60, joined together at the base in two comblike rows

Flowers: Bell or funnel shaped, purplish pink

Habitat: Desert grassland vegetation on limestone hills

Range: San Luis Potosi, Mexico

This view of the Hatchet cactus (*Pelecyphora aselliformis*) shows the distinctive wood louse-shaped spines.

HATCHET CACTUS
Mexico

THE HATCHET CACTUS is a strange little cactus, covered in flattened spines that look like wood lice. In the wild, these appear only slightly above ground level among the rocks and grassy vegetation. The hatchet cactus is very popular with cactus collectors and has been heavily collected in its native habitat. Despite a national ban on exports from Mexico, many wild plants were sent out of the country until the listing of *Pelecyphora aselliformis* in Appendix I of the Convention on International Trade in Endangered Species of Wild Fauna and Flora (CITES) in 1984. Since that time more nursery-grown plants raised from seed have become available.

Pelecyphora aselliformis is found only in the state of San Luis Potosi in the Chihuahuan desert region of Central Mexico. Several localities for the species are known in areas of low, rounded hills with outcrops of flat limestone. Other succulent plants that grow in the grasslands are agaves and yuccas, along with various other cacti.

Collecting from the wild remains a threat to *Pelecyphora*

aselliformis. The other main threats are road building, house construction, and the mining of limestone. Agriculture is not a significant threat because the rocky highlands where the species occurs are too poor for cultivation. Grazing of animals takes place but does not seem to be harmful, and it may help the low-growing cactus by allowing more light to reach the ground. Much of the land where *Pelecyphora aselliformis* grows is privately owned and is likely to remain as grazing land.

The widening of a very busy major road destroyed some of the habitat of *Pelecyphora aselliformis* in the early 1990s. Fortunately in 1992 about 1,000 plants were rescued by Cante A.C., a cactus conservation organization. Permission was granted by the appropriate authorities and the plants were taken to the botanic garden run by Cante A.C. in San Miguel de Allende.

Mexico has the richest cactus flora of any country in the world and the highest number of endemic and endangered species. *Pelecyphora aselliformis* is just one of many cacti that are in need of conservation in the country. Legal protection has been in place for over 50 years, but it has not prevented cacti from being smuggled out of the country. Cactus enthusiasts around the world can help by not buying wild plants and by growing species like this one from seed.

Sara Oldfield

Knowlton Cactus
(Pediocactus knowltonii)

ESA: Endangered

IUCN: Endangered

Stem: ½–1½ in. (1–4 cm) tall, bright green, globose to ovoid, often barely protruding from the soil
Spines: Not at all dense or obscuring the stem, in clusters, with 18–32 very short unhooked spines, radially arranged
Flowers: April through early May. Bell to funnel shaped, pink petals with pale margins
Pollination: By insect
Flowers: Habitat: Pinyon-Juniper woodlands
Range: San Juan County, New Mexico

A SOLITARY, gravel-covered hill, clothed in pinyon pine and mountain juniper, is the home of Knowlton cactus. Few species are naturally restricted to areas as small as 330 feet (100 meters) by 80 feet (25 meters). However, this is the approximate size of the hill, and *Pediocactus knowltonii* is known only from this single site. It seems reasonable to assume that a single hill in a wooded wilderness would be unlikely to fall victim to human disturbance. After all, there are many hills in this region of the United States, and most of them appear to be undisturbed. However, this particular hill has not been so fortunate. Not once or twice, but repeatedly, the location has been

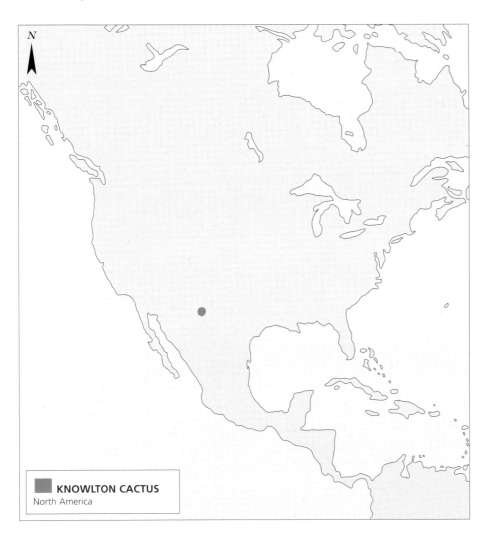

KNOWLTON CACTUS
North America

Knowlton cactus (*Pediocactus knowltonii*) has a striking appearance. The spines radiate outward from the stem in clusters, and the pink flower, which is often bell-shaped, emerges from the spines.

disturbed. Even the very discovery of Knowlton cactus was the result of a severe impact upon the only population of this species.

Discovery

This miniature cactus was discovered during the construction of a road into the wilderness. The operator of the bulldozer, F. G. Knowlton, happened to notice the quarter-dollar-sized stems as the bulldozer blade cut along the edge of the hill. Mr. Knowlton sent plants to a recognized expert in Cactaceae, Dr. L. Benson; however, a decade passed before the species was described in scientific literature. Although the construction destroyed several hundred plants, it was estimated that the remaining population numbered in the thousands. Because of the high degree of endemism, this species was recognized as being extremely rare

and its survival as being in jeopardy, even at the time it was first described. This resulted in an overzealous conservation effort that did more harm than good.

Well-intentioned conservationists attempted to save Knowlton cactus from inundation during the construction of a major dam along the San Juan River. During a series of field trips, a large number of plants were removed from the type locality. These plants were transplanted in gravel-covered areas at slightly higher elevations in the area. Unfortunately, the locations of most of the transplant sites were not well documented, nor was the number of plants transplanted at each site. The few sites that were rediscovered displayed no reproductive success. Over subsequent years of monitoring, these experimental populations ultimately failed. Retrospectively, the natural population fared far better than all of the experimental populations combined. Even so, the salvage mission reduced the population to only a few hundred. Ironically, the natural population was never in any danger of flooding.

The attempted salvage effort had another unwanted impact. The precise location of this very rare species was revealed to cactus collectors.

Collector's item

Because of its great rarity, Knowlton cactus was highly prized in personal collections. Once the location of Knowlton cactus was known, the hill was nearly denuded of every cactus plant. To make matters worse, oil was discovered beneath the population. The eastern side of the hill was scraped and leveled for a well site. To this day, an active oil well remains as evidence of the disturbance to the plant.

Knowlton cactus has a history characterized by threats from humans. Long before recorded history in the area, the solitary hill that is home to this species was also home to the Anasazi, builders of the cliff dwellings of Mesa Verde. The top of the small hill bears testament to the impact of human activity. Native vegetation, including the pinyon trees, have been removed, perhaps for planting crops.

Today big sage has moved into this area and Knowlton cactus does not occur. There, the red-brown soil is littered with shattered pieces of pottery and chips of stone. Indeed, the southern end of the hill has the ruins of a multi-roomed dwelling.

Somehow, the tiny cactus has managed to persist even while its home served also as a home for humans. Coupled with the history of severe impacts is also a history of extreme resilience. This cactus species, restricted to a single hill, so far has appeared to recover from each of these disturbances.

Today several hundred plants survive at the hill location. Currently protected by national and international laws, with the hill under the jurisdiction of The Nature Conservancy, and with the population no longer in decline, it seems that Knowlton cactus may finally be on its way to recovery. However, every inspection of the location reveals evidence that there has been further illegal collection of this imperiled species.

J. Mark Porter

Lloyd's Mariposa Cactus

(Sclerocactus mariposensis)

IUCN: Vulnerable

Stem: Globular, up to 4 in. (10 cm) tall, blue-green, with small conical protrusions (tubercles), each tipped by a cluster of spines

Spines: Slender, each tubercle with 2–4 central spines, 5–20 mm long, and 25–35 spreading, radial spines, 5–10 mm long

Flowers: Early March. Greenish and reddish purple midribs and pink margins; inner petal-like bracts that are pink or yellowish tan with white margins; the central stigma is green with 5–8 lobes

Seeds: Fruits are yellowish green, globular or oblong, to 10 mm long, drying and splitting open on one side to reveal small black seeds, and appears late April. Seed dispersal is probably by gravity, raindrop spatters, and ants

Habitat: Rock crevices and patches of limestone chips on gentle slopes in arid, open desert shrub lands

Range: Central Coahuila in northern Mexico and adjacent areas of Texas (mainly Big Bend National Park)

LLOYD'S MARIPOSA cactus is greatly valued by collectors of succulent plants. This is probably because it is difficult to propagate and rather rare in cultivation. Whole plants as well as seeds are traded and, as with most cacti, it has been seriously over-collected in the wild. Because of its very limited distribution, Lloyd's mariposa cactus is seriously threatened by such collecting, and several populations have been wiped out in this way. Other species have also suffered, and large tracts of land have been scoured of almost all cacti. Areas where past collecting was heavy can be identified by the near absence of older plants. Fortunately, the populations in Big Bend National Park in Texas still have many large specimens, although a large specimen of this naturally dwarf plant may be only 4 inches (10 centimeters) tall. Little collecting has occurred in this area because it is difficult to reach and because collecting is illegal within the park.

From 1994 to 1997, all the Lloyd's mariposa cactus seeds exported from the United States were from cultivated plants. The main importers were Europeans and Japanese. Changing trade practices may benefit the species.

The systematic cactus collecting of the past has been quite damaging. Professional collectors abandoned cacti in large piles to be sorted later for sale. As a result, many of the plants rotted or died of sunburn while lying in the pile or in transit. Plants ended up in supermarkets, stores, and curio shops, where they were bought by individuals who may have had good intentions, but who may have been ignorant of their special requirements in cultivation.

In some of the areas that were very severely collected, Lloyd's mariposa cactus now appears to have returned. Seedlings that were small enough to escape attention or to not be worth collecting have now grown sufficiently large to be noticed. Even so, the populations have not yet returned to normal.

Widespread sites

All together, Lloyd's mariposa cactus is known from about 30 sites in three parts of the Big Bend Region of Texas. One area is in the southeastern corner of Brewster County and is mostly private land owned by the Lajitas Museum and Desert Garden. Another area is in the northeastern portion of Big Bend National Park. The third area is in the eastern part of Brewster County, north of the Black Gap Wildlife Management Area, and is owned by ranchers. Lloyd's mariposa cactus also grows in the state of Coahuila, Mexico, near Cuatro Ciénegas and Monclova.

Lloyd's mariposa cactus is part of the Chihuahuan Desert flora. It grows on arid, gravelly, limestone soils on gentle slopes at altitudes from about 2,460 to 3,440 feet (750 to 1,050 meters) in open shrub lands of lechuguilla (*Agave lechuguilla*) and smooth sotol (*Dasylirion leiophyllum*). The individual plants are widely scattered, but occasionally they are found in denser concentrations in this habitat.

The cactus grows only in areas with a very stable ground surface. It prefers either rock crevices or pavements of limestone chips. When growing in full sun in patches of limestone chips, the reflection from the pale rock raises the heat and light radiation around the cacti to an extremely high level.

Collecting is not the only problem for Lloyd's mariposa cactus. Additional threats include habitat destruction through the building of resort homes, mercury mining activities, use of off-road vehicles, and livestock grazing. The populations in Big Bend National Park are threatened by camping, hiking, and maintenance of roads and trails.

Lloyd's mariposa cactus was listed on Appendix I of Convention on International Trade in Endangered Species of Wild Fauna and Flora (CITES) in 1983. It was also listed as a threatened species by the U.S. Fish and Wildlife Service (U.S.F.W.S.) in 1979. The cactus is also on the protected plant list of the state of Texas. There is an officially approved (U.S.F.W.S.) recovery plan for Lloyd's mariposa cactus. The plan or objective is for the species to be taken off the threatened list. For this to happen, there must be at least three sites where the species is protected, containing a total of 20,000 plants. One site should be on private land in northeastern Brewster County, Texas, one in Big Bend National Park, and one in Mexico. Each site should initially contain at least 1,000 plants and should contain enough suitable habitat to allow the cactus population to expand.

Nick Turland

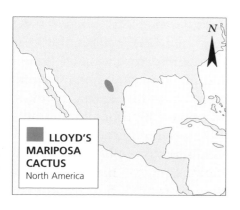

LLOYD'S MARIPOSA CACTUS
North America

Mesa Verde Cactus

(Sclerocactus mesae-verdae)

ESA: Threatened

IUCN: Vulnerable

Stem: 2–13 in. (3–18 cm) tall, pale green, with a waxy appearance, globose to ovoid
Spines: Not at all dense or obscuring the stem, in clusters, with 1–4 central spines (none of them are hooked; only rarely do the clusters have one hooked spine) and 7–14 radial spines
Flowers: April to May. Bell to funnel shaped, with cream-colored petals, or very rarely pink with darker midribs
Pollination: By bees
Habitat: Saltbush desert shrub lands
Range: Montezuma County, Colorado, and San Juan County, New Mexico

THE ADOBE CLAY HILL county of the Anasazi is a bleak and nearly lunar landscape. The saline, barren slopes boast few species of plants. Mat saltbush (*Atriplex corrugata*) and James frankenia (*Frankenia jamesii*) are two of the few low-growing, tufted perennial shrubs; but they offer shade only to the rodents and rattlesnakes.

With less than 8 inches (20 centimeters) of precipitation annually and summer temperatures soaring to 110 degrees Fahrenheit (43 degrees Centigrade), this appears a cruel

Mesa verde cactus lives in harsh, barren conditions with the threat of habitat intrusion by development and roaming livestock.

environment. It seems unlikely that many plants would choose to live here, let alone humans. This is the Navajo Indian Reservation of New Mexico, home of the Diné peoples. The local residents say that the harsh habitat is matched by a stark beauty and surprising diversity. Scattered like the rounded hogans that occasionally mark the hills around the town of Shiprock, low, rounded stems of the Mesa Verde cactus can infrequently be seen on clay hills.

Scented flowers

With short spines pressed against the waxy green stem, the plant could easily be mistaken for a small rock and be overlooked. Following the spring rains, the pale flowers open with a faint but decidedly perfumed scent. The flowers are known to attract a myriad of small insects, but the most common visitors are small bees: *Halictus*, *Tetralonia*, and *Andrena*. These are the primary pollinators of the Mesa Verde cactus. Although the species has been shown to be capable of self-

fertilization, it appears that reproduction is the result of cross-fertilization rather than selfing. Such a reproductive system may insure that some pollination takes place, even during years when pollinators are not abundant. Restricted to the badlands of northwestern New Mexico and southwestern Colorado, populations of the Mesa Verde cactus are never very large. On any given slope, perhaps only a dozen plants will be found. However, there is a large number of these small populations. In fact, it is likely that most of the smaller populations of this species are linked to some degree by ongoing gene flow. Such more or less integrated population systems are referred to as metapopulations. Mesa Verde cactus may be composed of only three or four such metapopulations, but the metapopulations are very large.

Threats

The basis for protection of this species rests largely on the threats to the existing populations. Threats to the survival of Mesa Verde cactus can be found not only around the cities and small towns of the region, but

also in the areas that appear isolated. One of the largest concentrations of plants can be found around the city of Shiprock. This is an actively growing hub of the Navajo Nation, and as the city expands, development results in the loss of habitat and consequently the Mesa Verde cactus. Because this species has been under federal protection for many years, it is well known to developers and construction companies, who have on occasion destroyed populations to avoid being slowed down by the Endangered Species Act. Much of the construction activities of the region are farther from the towns, associated with oil and gas exploration. New roads, seismic studies, well sites, and pipelines form a spider web of human impact in the habitat of *Sclerocactus mesae-verdae*. The total impact of development upon this species has never been assessed, but development is only a part of the threats.

One important source of income for the Diné is livestock. In spite of the bleak landscape, sheep, goats, and even cattle use the habitat of Mesa Verde cactus as open range land. This cactus is occasionally uprooted or more commonly trampled by the grazing animals. The animals also increase the rates of erosion of the soft clay, which impacts the cactus. Similar disturbance (trampling, uprooting, and erosion) results from the recreational use of off-road vehicles such as motorcycles. The use of these vehicles is becoming increasingly common in the habitat of Mesa Verde cactus.

In addition to the dangers mentioned above, the taking of

plants from the wild by cactus collectors has continued unabated for over 50 years. Field investigations have uncovered evidence of illegal taking of seed and plants. Collectors are so bold that they have even poached specimens from study plots that are being used to develop an understanding of population demographics of this cactus. One collector actually published the number of different collections he had made of this species in a book, even though the plant was protected by the ESA and by the Convention on International Trade in Endangered Species of Wild Fauna and Flora (CITES).

Humans pose the greatest risk to Mesa Verde cactus, but there are natural threats as well. Parasitic fungi are common in some populations, and frequently infection by these fungi results in the death of the cactus. Infestation by the larvae of a native beetle also results in high mortality.

Although most rodents do not appear to be attracted to Mesa Verde cactus, occasionally the entire top of a stem will be found to have been devoured by some small mammal.

The Mesa Verde cactus is a prime example of one type of plant rarity. It is a species that is narrowly restricted in geographic distribution but locally common.

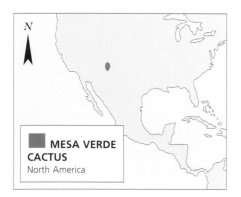

MESA VERDE CACTUS
North America

Most species with similar characteristics are not afforded protection. However, Mesa Verde cactus seems plagued by natural and human-caused threats that, if unchecked, could easily push this species nearer to extinction.

J. Mark Porter

Peebles Navajo Cactus

(Pediocactus peeblesianus var. peeblesianus)

ESA: Endangered

IUCN: Endangered

Height: Up to 2 in. (5 cm)
Stems: Single stemmed, 1 in. (2.5 cm) tall and ¾ in. (2 cm) in diameter
Flowers: Spring. Yellow to yellow-green up to 1¼ in. (3 cm) wide
Pollination: By insect
Habitat: Well-drained soils on sunny slopes or flat hilltops
Range: Navajo County, Arizona

TWO VARIETIES OF *Pediocactus peeblesianus* exist: *Pediocactus peeblesianus* var. *fickeiseniae* and *Pediocactus peeblesianus* var. *peeblesianus*. Both are endemic to Arizona, but the majority of this article will consider *Pediocactus peeblesianus* var. *peeblesianus*.

The Peebles Navajo cactus is, as its name suggests, endemic to Navajo County, Arizona. There are only five known populations, which comprise some 1,000 individuals in total. Even though this plant is endangered, where it does occur it is found to be common. These populations are

found in the low hills of the Great Basin grassland biotic community at an elevation of some 5,500 feet (1,680 meters). This cactus prefers a well-drained gravelly soil. As far as it is known the historical range of the Peebles Navajo cactus is the same as the current range. It seems that the plant is well adapted to its environment and it is only the direct action of people that is leading to a gradual loss in its numbers. Two populations are on public land owned by the Bureau of Land Management, and the remaining three populations are on private land. The potential habitat for this species is estimated to be some 4½ square miles (11.5 square kilometers), but the most recent searches have found the cactus on only 15 to 20 percent of this land.

Causes of decline
As with many endangered plants, the greatest threat to this species is habitat destruction. Suitable habitat is gradually being destroyed by the building of a coal-powered electricity generating station, gravel extraction, road construction, and the recreational use of off-road vehicles. Population numbers declined

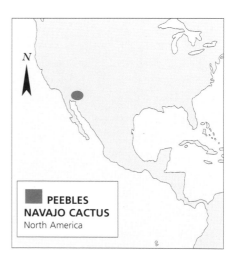

PEEBLES NAVAJO CACTUS
North America

rapidly in the 1970s and 1980s because of this habitat loss, and it is believed that if positive action is not taken soon the plant will become extinct in the wild. Population numbers are also declining due to illegal plant collection. Recent sites have been set up for monitoring plants, and since 1985 two sites have doubled in numbers and two others have tripled. It is hoped that this trend will also be followed in the unmonitored sites.

Pediocactus peeblesianus var. *peeblesianus* will remain under threat for the foreseeable future. Its very small distribution makes its populations very vulnerable to a single natural event. The low numbers represent a depletion in genetic variability, which does not bode well for the reproductive future of this species.

Recovery plans

Future recovery plans include the establishment of reserves along with artificial propagation

The Peebles Navajo cactus has adapted to its rocky environment, but the plant is now declining due to habitat destruction and illegal collection.

to reintroduce the species to suitable habitat, as well as to reduce the pressure from collectors. Unfortunately the genus *Pediocactus* is very difficult to cultivate. The endangered status of *Pediocactus peeblesianus* var. *peeblesianus* will not be altered until the population size is in excess of 10,000 individuals. Extensive research is being done in Europe and Japan to find the most suitable methods for propagation of this species.

Pediocactus peeblesianus var. *fickeiseniae* is in a similar threatened state. It also is referred to as the Peebles Navajo cactus. This variety can be found in scattered populations stretching along the canyon rims of the Little Colorado and Colorado Rivers. It also favors a gravel-based soil. This variety is known from 11 different populations, none of which has shown an increase in size in recent years. In fact one population, in North Canyon, has been heavily vandalized.

Threats also include collection, trampling and grazing, road construction, and mineral extraction. The land where it occurs is

owned and managed by the Bureau of Land Management.

Like all other members of the genus *Pediocactus*, cultivation is not impossible but it is very difficult. This taxon is regarded as vulnerable to extinction because of its slightly higher numbers and wider distribution.

San Rafael Cactus

(Pediocactus despainii)

ESA: Endangered

IUCN: Endangered

Height: Less than 4 in. (10 cm)
Stem: 2½ in. (6 cm) tall and 4 in. (10 cm) wide, barrel shaped
Spines: Clusters covering the stem
Flowers: Spring. Up to 1 in. (2.5 cm) across, peach to yellow color with a bronze bloom
Pollination: By insect
Habitat: Hills, benches, and flats of Colorado semiarid regions
Range: Utah

THE SAN RAFAEL CACTUS is a dwarf plant that is a relict member of a once widely distributed genus. This species is known only from Emery County, Utah. There are only two known populations, which are some 25 miles (40 kilometers) apart. Each population comprises approximately 2,500 to 3,000 individuals.

Threats

Unfortunately the greatest threat to this species is illegal collection. Many cactus collectors are taking this species from the wild to add to their collections. As the plant becomes rarer, the price it will command among collectors of cacti rises.

Half of the remaining San Rafael cactus populations are on land that is leased for exploration for fossil fuels (oil and gas) and minerals (chiefly gypsum). Active exploration for these resources destroys the habitat of plants such as the San Rafael cactus.

One of the two populations of the San Rafael cactus is next to a campsite, which imposes a level of threat from recreational use of the area. This level of damage can be brought about by hikers and the use of recreational off-road

Because of its particular growth and habitat requirements, the San Rafael cactus is difficult to cultivate.

vehicles. Like many plants of this sort of habitat, cattle grazing is also a threat to the species.

Savanna-like habitat

The San Rafael Cactus is found in semiarid regions that have characteristic scrub vegetation. It grows in association with pinyon pines, juniper, and assorted shrubs and herbs. This is known as a savanna-like habitat.

Reintroduction of this species from cultivated examples is likely to be a long-term project. The genus *Pediocactus* is notoriously difficult to grow in cultivation, particularly from rootstock. Growth from seeds is slightly easier although this is still very difficult. Further research is needed to learn about the growth and habitat requirements of this species.

Ilegal collection

This plant also suffers when its seeds are collected. Due to their fragile nature, the often rough seed collection by illegal collectors ends up killing the plants. These cacti are usually fairly short-lived in the wild: an individual plant may only live for one or two seasons. This means that most of the new plants every year come from new growth from seeds. Death of plants or their removal or the removal of their seeds leads to a very precarious situation for the continued survival of this species.

It is illegal to remove this species from federal lands; it is also illegal to trade or move this species in any way or form. The sites are readily accessible, however, and as a consequence illegal collecting does still occur.

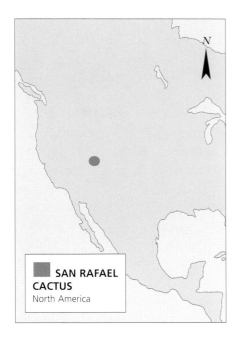

SAN RAFAEL CACTUS
North America

Many collectors of cacti illegally trade in this species. There is a move afoot among collectors to ensure they have the full set of the genus *Pediocactus*. The San Rafael cactus is one of the rarest members of this group. Trade is generally confined to whole plants due to the difficulty of growing this plant from seed.

Legal seed exportation

A number of seeds have been legally exported from the United States; this is chiefly to Europe and Japan for research into their growth requirements. Work is still being carried out in this field.

This species is under threat because of its reduced numbers and its reliance on only two sites. It is hoped that increased knowledge will lead to adequate protection and recovery methods.

By the year 2000 it was still impossible to grow sufficient plants in cultivation to allow reintroduction into the wild. Greater care must be taken at the two remaining population sites to ensure survival. The total number of 6,000 individuals is a good

population size from which to recover, and there is still plenty of natural diversity within the gene bank. The threat is based on the fact that the two populations are very close to each other, so a relatively small natural disaster would be capable of destroying the plants at both sites. Further work is required to guarantee the continued survival of this species.

Gordon Rutter

Schlesser Pincushion

(Sclerocactus schlesseri = Sclerocactus spinosior)

IUCN: Endangered

Height: 1½–4 in. (4–10 cm)
Flowers: April to May. Pink to purple, tubular, ¾–1½ in. (2–4 cm) long and ½–1 in. (1.5–2.5 cm) in diameter
Pollination: By insect
Fruits: Shiny light red to pink
Habitat: Highland desert
Range: Nevada

SCHLESSER PINCUSHION is one species in a genus of about six species from the southwestern United States. The generic name, *Sclerocactus*, is a Greek word meaning *hard cactus*.

Sclerocactus schlesseri (*sclerocactus spinosior* ssp. *blainei*) is a slow growing, long-lived perennial. The plant consists of a spherical green stem with undulating ribs, reaching a height of 1½ to 4 inches (4 to 10 centimeters) and a diameter of 1 to 2½ inches (2.5 to 6 centimeters). The roots are fibrous and spread near the sur-

face of the ground. Areoles typically contain a papery white central spine that twists around the body of the plant and can reach a length of 2¾ inches (7 centimeters), and up to five reddish brown or white hooked or twisted central spines from ¾ to 1½ inches (2 to 4 centimeters) long. From 7 to 12 smaller radial spines also occur, reaching a length of 4 to 18 millimeters. Spination can be dense, obscuring the body of the plant. Schlesser pincushion has six to eight yellow stigma lobes and a smooth style. It dehisces irregularly. The asymmetrical seeds are black and warty.

Taxonomy

The nomenclature of *Sclerocactus* is very confusing, and different numbers and combinations of species occur in almost every flora or account. Also, at various times some *Sclerocactus* species have been moved in and out of the genus *Echinocactus*. This makes population data unclear, and it is difficult to compare various taxa from one publication to the next. It also makes accurate assessment of distributions, population size, and conservation status complicated.

The taxon that has been called *Sclerocactus schlesseri* has a narrow distribution in Nevada and is almost completely absent from the literature under that name.

Confused classification

In a 1995 treatment of the genus *Sclerocactus*, Fritz Hochstatter places *Sclerocactus schlesseri* in *Sclerocactus spinosior* ssp. *blainei* (Blaine pincushion). To add further confusion, this taxon has also been called *Sclerocactus blainei* Welsh and Thorne. IUCN–The World Conservation Union, however, currently lists *Sclerocactus schlesseri* (Schlesser pincushion) and *Sclerocactus blainei* (Blaine pincushion) as separate species, both of which are endangered.

Breeding system

Like many cacti, Schlesser pincushion has relatively large brightly colored flowers that produce enough pollen and nectar to make them attractive to foraging insects. Research has not been done on ratios of outcrossing to inbreeding, and information is not available on insect visitation. However, because of insect interest in pollen and nectar it seems likely that this species makes use of insect-facilitated outcrossing.

Seeds of Schlesser pincushion can remain dormant for several years, until the ideal circumstances arise for germination. This species occurs only in Lincoln County, Nevada. It occurs at 4,270–5,900 feet (1,300–1,800 meters) in small scattered populations and sometimes as single isolated individuals

Habitat

This species occurs in highland desert in Nevada, in a shrub-grass community. Associated vegetation includes sagebrush, greasewood, and other desert shrubs, agave, and yucca, and sometimes sparse pine forest. Sometimes other genera of cactus such as *Echinocereus, Echinocactus, Ferocactus, Mammillaria,* and *Opuntia* share these habitats. *Sclerocactus schlesseri*

SCHLESSER PINCUSHION
North America

usually grows where the ground is rocky, though it sometimes grows in fine red or gray sand. *Sclerocactus* can occur on various strata, including limestone, granite, and basalt.

The type specimen of *Sclerocactus schlesseri* was collected from a tertiary lacustrine deposit. However, while no substrate preferences are recorded for *Sclerocactus schlesseri* (*Sclerocactus spinosior* ssp. *blainei*), *Sclerocactus spinosior* ssp. *spinosior* seems to prefer limestone soils that are rich in calcium.

The flowers of Schlesser pincushion produce pollen and nectar that attract insects, possibly leading to outcrossing.

Since Schlesser pincushion occurs in few populations of scattered individuals, it is vulnerable to destruction by chance events such as rock slides or human disturbance. Like all cactus it is also threatened by illegal collections, which are often fueled by enthusiastic hobbyists.

Christina Oliver

Winkler Cactus

(Pediocactus winkleri)

ESA: Threatened

IUCN: Endangered

Height: 2¾ in. (7 cm)
Stems: Up to 2¾ in. (7 cm) long with a maximum diameter of 1 in. (2.5 cm)
Spines: Up to 4 mm long
Flowers: May to June. Produced apically and up to 1 in. (2.5 cm) wide, which appears large for this plant. Peach-colored with a reddish brown midstripe
Pollination: By insect
Habitat: Fine, alkaline soil derived from shale on south facing slopes at a height of 5,300 ft. (1,600 m)
Range Colorado Plateau, Utah

WINKLER CACTUS IS endemic to the lower hills of the Colorado Plateau in southern Utah. It grows in fine, alkaline soils that are derived from shale: this is chiefly as part of the Dakota formation. This plant occurs as part of the drought-tolerant vegetation on south-facing slopes.

There are currently four known colonies of Winkler cacti,

and these are spread from Notom in Wayne County to Last Chance Creek in southwestern Emery County, Utah. Essentially all of the plants are on government land—as part of either the Bureau of Land Management or Capitol Reef National Park. This range coincides with the range of the related and equally endangered San Rafael cactus, which has similar growth requirements.

Populations

The four populations of Winkler cactus comprise some 20,000 individuals that occur on pockets of land widely separated and varying in size from 1/2 to 8 acres (1 to 20 hectares). This shows a marked change from the surveys of 1993, where six populations of 3,500 plants were recorded, and 1998, when 5,800 plants were recorded. The current estimate, at the start of the 21st century, of 20,000 individuals is based on recent surveys and takes into account the amount of potential habitat that is available.

The reason the number of populations changed from six to four is merely a paper exercise. Some populations are counted as

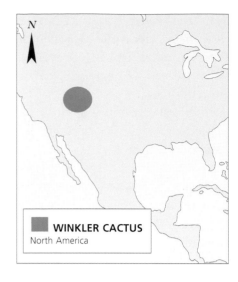

WINKLER CACTUS
North America

one, where previously they were regarded as two. It is possible that the cactus numbers had been underestimated because this species usually remains underground during periods of drought.

Causes of decline

Winkler cactus is threatened by the action of collectors for the illegal plant trade. In fact, the Notom population recently suffered a decline of some 80 percent due to plant collection.

Winkler cactus, growing on the left in the photograph, suffers from being collectable. It thrives on shale slopes but is difficult to grow in cultivation.

The sites where this plant grows are easily accessible to collectors and are well known. There is a strong desire among some collectors to possess a full set of the whole genus *Pediocactus*, all of which are rare. Off-road vehicle usage has also contributed to the decline of this species. Grazing and mining also threaten the plant. Some of the Bureau of Land Management land is leased to companies for the extraction of minerals.

The *Pediocactus* genus is one of the most difficult to grow in cultivation. Because it is not impossible to grow, a number of companies sell plants and seed. It is possible that some plants are taken from the wild by some unscrupulous companies to replace stock which is sold. The plants themselves are relatively short-lived, and continuation of plants within an area depends heavily upon production of new seed every season. Removal of plants breaks this chain of production and very rapidly leads to loss of plants in that area. If seed is collected from wild populations, this can also be seen to threaten the future of Winkler cactus within an area. Winkler cactus is very fragile, so when seed is collected it is not uncommon for the growing center of the cactus to be fatally damaged.

Some of the land on which this species occurs is owned and managed by government bodies. These bodies are charged with ensuring that any activities on these lands do not damage the endangered species there. Some of the land is leased out to companies who carry out potentially damaging activities such as mining and cattle grazing.

This species is not in immediate danger of extinction because of its relatively large numbers. However, all of the sites are relatively close to each other. Continued research, protection, and monitoring are required. A reliable and easy method of cultivation is still to be found. Cultivation will alleviate the pressure from commercial collectors and also allow the reintroduction of plants into suitable habitats.

Gordon Rutter

Wright Fishhook Cactus

(Sclerocactus wrightiae)

ESA: Endangered

IUCN : Endangered

Stem: A small, globular cactus, 2–3 in. (5–7.5 cm) wide, with small, conical protrusions (tubercles), each tipped by a cluster of spines
Spines: Slender, each tubercle with 4 central spines (the main one hooked), 12–19 mm long; and 8–10 spreading, radial spines, 5–12 mm long
Flowers: Usually two, each ¾ in. (2 cm) long; up to 12 outer bracts, 3–6 mm long, with lavender midribs and pale margins. About 12 inner, petal-like bracts 4.5–6 mm long, nearly white; the pollen-bearing anthers are yellow
Seeds: In barrel-shaped fruits, 9–12 mm long
Habitat: Desert hills with alkaline soils
Range: Southern end of the San Rafael Swell, Utah

WRIGHT FISHHOOK cactus was first described for science by Lyman Benson in 1966 and named in honor of Mrs. Dorde Wright of Salt Lake City, Utah, who discovered the plant in 1961. This rare cactus is known from a total area about 50 miles (80 kilometers) across: a desert trough at 4,750–6,070 feet (1,450–1,850 meters) in altitude around the southern end of the San Rafael Swell in Utah. The habitat of this cactus can vary from saltbush clay flats to sandy desert grasslands.

The barren soils support widely spaced shrubs and perennial herbs, such as Castle Valley clover (*Atriplex cuneata*), mat saltbush (*Atriplex corrugata*); and shadscale or spiny saltbush (*Atriplex confertifolia*); bunch grasses, such as galleta (*Hilaria jamesii*); or sparse woodlands of true or doubleleaf pinyon pine (*Pinus edulis*) and Utah juniper (*Juniperus osteosperma*).

The soils vary from clays to sandy silts to fine sands with or without gypsum. The ground surface is usually strewn with gravel, pebbles, and boulders of sandstone or basalt.

At most of the population sites of Wright fishhook cactus,

WRIGHT FISHHOOK CACTUS
North America

the soil has a surface crust of small non-flowering plants such as liverworts, lichens, and algae. This organic ground surface, and also the rock litter can hold rainwater within the soil. It can also provide safe niches for seed germination and seedling establishment. It is significant that the cactus is rare or absent where the surface crust has been destroyed or has not developed.

A thorough population count has not yet been done for Wright fishhook cactus. The populations tend to consist of groups of individual plants, each group clustered within a few square feet, with many square feet or even acres between them. This patchy distribution may be the result of poor seed dispersal. However, where suitable habitat exists, these populations can extend over quite large areas.

Wright fishhook cactus is prized by collectors of succulent plants. The plants are traded either whole or as seeds. Like other members of the genus *Sclerocactus*, this species has a reputation for being difficult to cultivate.

Wright fishhook cactus was first listed as endangered by the U.S. Fish and Wildlife Service in 1979. The species was also listed in Appendix I of the Convention on International Trade in Endangered Species of Wild Fauna and Flora (CITES) in 1983. During this period, both amateur and commercial collecting were the main threats to the survival of the species in the wild. However, the patchy distribution of the cactus probably helped it to escape near extirpation. Commercial collecting would take up more time and therefore be less profitable for

this cactus than for a more densely distributed species.

Fortunately, the seeds from the cactus that have been exported from the United States in recent years have been produced in cultivation, rather than collected from the wild.

Other threats

In addition to the problem of collecting, Wright fishhook cactus may be threatened by mineral exploration, off-road vehicle traffic, and livestock grazing. There is also the potential for energy developments and industrial use of habitat in the area. Off-road vehicles and livestock not only cause direct damage to plants, but they disrupt the organic crust on the ground surface and so prevent the establishment of seedling cacti.

In 1979, the plant was known from about five sites and was nowhere common. These areas

Wright fishhook cactus (*Sclerocactus wrightiae*) displays the hooked spines that give it its name.

are now under the jurisdiction of the state of Utah.

Wright fishhook cactus is now known from numerous sites, and there is a federal recovery plan that has been officially approved. The plan's objective is to achieve two self-sustaining populations, in two areas, with a total of at least 10,000 plants. This will allow the cactus to be reclassified as threatened.

Wright fishhook cactus will be taken off the federal list of threatened and endangered species altogether when at least one additional self-sustaining population of at least 10,000 plants is achieved.

These populations must, of course, be protected from illegal plant and seed collecting.

Nick Turland

Cahow
(Pterodroma cahow)

ESA: Endangered

IUCN: Endangered

Class: Aves
Order: Procellariiformes
Family: Procellariidae
Length: 14–18 in. (36–46 cm)
Weight: Unknown
Clutch size: 1 egg
Incubation: 51–54 days
Diet: Squids and shrimps, possibly small fish and other crustaceans
Habitat: Pelagic; comes ashore only to breed
Range: Breeds only on a few small islets of Bermuda; wanders western North Atlantic Ocean from Greater Antilles northward, probably to 35-40° N, but exact distribution at sea poorly known; not seen from Atlantic Coast of North America

NO BIRD SO FULLY demonstrates the human impact on wildlife than does the cahow. Its story remains one of the most remarkable tales of survival of any endangered species.

The story begins in 1603 when a crew of Spanish sailors took refuge from a storm. Their sanctuary was a small cluster of islands 580 miles off the coast of North Carolina. They survived the storm, but were then terrorized by great numbers of unknown, shrieking creatures descending upon them in the night. The creatures were not spirits or demons, but cahows attracted to the lanterns aboard the ship. The sailors recovered from their fright, eventually capturing the birds for food.

In 1609 Great Britain settled on a group of islands they called Bermuda. Cahows at that time occupied most of the islands (this has been verified by recovery of bones and fossils). The winter of 1614 proved hard on the settlers. Food being scarce, they turned to the cahow as an edible fowl and slaughtered it on a grand scale. By 1616 the carnage was nearly complete, and the colonial governor spoke against further killing of cahows. In 1621 an official proclamation was issued which protected the cahow during its nesting season. The generous act came too late. The cahow disappeared from Bermuda and wasn't seen again for 294 years.

The return

A cahow was found in 1916, and further sightings began to occur. A deliberate search in 1951 located about three dozen birds and less than a dozen nests. Rediscovering a species presumed to be extinct for three centuries was a wonder to naturalists. However, the full plight of the cahow became apparent in succeeding years as the nests were monitored.

All the nests were located on small islets that were free of cats, dogs, pigs and, for the most part, rats. The burrow-nesting cahows were defenseless against such exotic predators. Additionally, the larger islands held more people and suffered heavier losses, primarily because of the native plants being cleared to create agricultural land. Severe erosion left several islands with thin soil

The cahow was believed to be extinct after it was used as food by 17th-century colonial settlers of the Bermuda islands. It was later rediscovered in the 20th century.

or none at all. Without soil for digging nest burrows, the cahows were forced to seek alternatives. They began using crevices in the rocky islets. Although this seemed a reasonable adaptation for the birds, it proved unfortunate. A slightly larger bird, the white-tailed tropicbird (*Phaethon lepturus*), also nests in these crevices, and became the cahow's rival.

The upperpart of the cahow is uniformly a dark, brownish black except for a white or grayish white band across the rump. The bird's underpart is mostly a dull white to silvery gray, with outermost flight feathers a darker, brownish gray. The forehead is white extending back as a white line over the eye; the cheek is dirty white. The cahow's beak is black and its legs pale.

Cahows begin breeding before the tropicbirds do. They return beginning in late October to the same nest sites they used

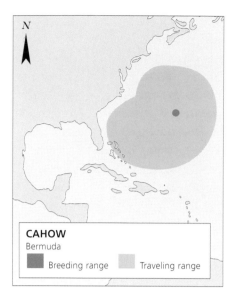

CAHOW
Bermuda

Breeding range   Traveling range

the previous year. Using various types of greenery, they construct new nests, and both birds occupy the nest burrow during the day. In December, cahows vacate the site for about two weeks while they feed at sea. They return in early January to lay a single egg, a clutch-size typical of birds that feed at sea and nest on islands. The parents take turns incubating, one bird often remaining at the nest for two weeks without leaving. They survive this by using fat stored in their bodies.

When the egg hatches in late February, the parents take turns staying with the chick for just a few days. Before the chick's first week ends, the parents abandon it altogether during the day and return only at night to feed it. Several nights may pass with no feeding visits at all. When they reach about ten days to two weeks of age, the white-tailed tropicbirds return to begin their breeding cycle. Because the cahow chicks are unattended in the burrows and crevices, the tropicbirds can enter and kill them. In some years the cahows fail to raise any chicks to fledgling

age. It is ironic that white-tailed tropicbirds and cahows coexisted on Bermuda for thousands of years before people arrived.

Coexistence to competition

The cahows have well developed legs and feet and can walk in a fashion similar to gulls or ducks. Tropicbirds have extremely small, poorly developed feet. So tropicbirds locate nesting sites by flying, while cahows find nesting burrows by walking. Each species, then, finds different nest sites. Human activity on Bermuda disrupted their coexistence and made the two birds competitors. Because tropicbirds pirate the nesting burrows by day, the adult cahows are not around to defend their chicks.

A further problem for the cahow's nesting grounds was the floodlighting at a nearby American military installation. The bright lights disrupted the bird's normal nocturnal behavior, especially during its courtship season.

As a final blow, the cahows suffered chemical poisoning. Tests of their eggshells during the 1960s showed the birds were accumulating DDT. This pesticide interferes with a bird's calcium metabolism, so when a female lays an egg, less calcium is deposited in the eggshell. The thinner shells are more fragile and easily broken, and they lose essential moisture too rapidly through tiny pores. If an egg survives without breaking, the chick may, nevertheless, die in the shell of dehydration. Besides DDT poisoning, the cahows were vulnerable to oil spills. As the birds swim and dive for food, they can get coated with crude petroleum spilled at sea. Heavy exposure to

oil can be lethal to the cahow. Several actions have been taken to recover the cahow. Some of them have been taken deliberately to help the cahow, and some have been more indirect. The United States banned the general use of DDT in the 1970s, and other pesticides similar to DDT were banned soon after. With smaller amounts of DDT entering the marine food chains, the cahow suffered less contamination and began laying healthier eggs. The American naval base also dimmed its floodlighting to reduce interfering with nesting cahows. The Bermuda government has designated several islets as sanctuaries and restricts human access to them. Rats are regularly eliminated from these sanctuaries, as well. Perhaps the most innovative action has been the building of artificial nest burrows strictly for the cahows. Tropicbirds are slightly larger than cahows, so a special collar inserted into burrow entrances prevents the tropicbirds from getting inside.

The cahow has responded slowly to human assistance. By 1985 the population had only grown to 35 pairs.

Still, chick survival has improved, and residues from harmful chemicals have declined since the pesticide bans. A national pride has now emerged for this bird that was once eaten to near extinction, plagued by habitat destruction and exotic predators, endangered by natural competition for nesting space, and threatened by chemical contamination of its food and water. The cahow may at last be beating the odds.

Kevin Cook

CAIMANS

Class: Reptilia

Order: Crocodylia

Family: Alligatoridae

The word caiman is a common term for reptiles of the genera *Caiman*, *Melanosuchus*, and *Paleosuchus*. A part of the Crocodylia order, these animals are carnivorous reptiles with relatively long life spans. They have elongated bodies and short, stocky legs. Armored skin covers the whole body with large, strong plates. Caimans may live in fresh or brackish waters in Central and South America. Although these animals move most efficiently in water, they can maneuver on land to catch prey.

Like other families in this order, the caiman has forelegs that end in five digits that are separated, while the four digits of the hind legs are connected by webbing. The webbing does not play a role in moving the animal in the water—this is accomplished instead by snake-like, back-and-forth movements of the whole body or achieved by strokes with the tail.

Melanosuchus niger, the black caiman, is considered to be endangered by the IUCN.

Black Caiman

(Melanosuchus niger)

ESA: Endangered

IUCN: Endangered

Length: Up to 20 ft. (6 m)

Clutch size: 30–60 eggs

Diet: Small fish, amphibians, insects, crustaceans, snails; some mammals

Habitat: Freshwater

Range: Restricted to Amazon Basin; found in French Guiana, Guyana, Peru, Bolivia, Brazil, Colombia, and Ecuador

THE BLACK CAIMAN is the only member of the genus *Melanosuchus*. It is the largest species of the new world Crocodylia, including American alligators. The adult is black in color, but the young often have yellowish spots and stripes. It inhabits fresh waters, particularly quiet backwaters or large bends in rivers, lakes, and lagoons. This caiman can also be found in creeks and swamps on the Amazon delta islands of Marajo, Mexiana, and Caviana, and along the Rio Branco. The black caiman has been found in the Amazon River itself, even in areas with strong currents, but it appears to avoid rivers with rocky banks.

Like other crocodilians, the black caiman is carnivorous. The young of the species feed on small fish, amphibians, insects, crustaceans, and snails, while the adults consume a wide variety of prey, ranging from fish to small mammals to reptiles, including other caiman. Fish supply the majority of the black caiman's diet in the dry season, particularly in the lower Amazon basin, when this food source becomes concentrated in the shrinking depths of pools and lagoons, offering a convenient prey.

Pest control

The black caiman was once the largest of the abundant predators in tropical South America. Today its importance to the environment has been demonstrated with the steady decline of its populations. Many animals that were destructive to crops were prey of the caiman, which kept their populations in check. For example, in Bolivia the number of piranhas has increased as there have become fewer caiman to prey upon them. The piranhas are known to attack livestock in flooded grasslands during wet seasons. In addition, the black caiman's excrement provided an important nutrient for lakes and swamps. This nutrient was used by a wide variety of plankton and invertebrate insects. These organisms, in turn, provided food for fish hatchlings. As their food source dwindled many valuable fish species have declined because of a lower survival rate for their offspring.

Little is known about the breeding habits of the black caiman. It is a mound-nesting species, constructing 2½-foot (0.75-meter) tall nests made of vegetation. The female remains near the nest, often lying on top if it is exposed to the sun. She will protect it vigorously against potential predators. Incubation takes five to six weeks, or longer in shaded forest sites.

The black caiman was formerly widespread throughout its range and was abundant in several areas. Its size and unwary nature probably made it the most conspicuous of all crocodilians in the Amazonian basin.

Today, there are no populations of the density that were encountered in the nineteenth century, and the total population is probably about one percent of what it was at that time. With the exception of a few hardy populations in the Kaw region of French Guiana, eastern Ecuador and parts of Peru, the species is severely depleted throughout the Amazon basin.

Hide hunting

This species was once renowned for its large size. Because of its high-quality belly skin it was heavily exploited by the leather industry. As with most crocodylia, hunting for its hide has been the major reason for the depletion of the black caiman population. Other factors in its decline include loss of habitat to logging, agriculture, and cattle ranching. The animal has also been killed as a pest in cattle ranching areas. Often, several hundred caimans would be killed in a matter of days during the dry season when lower water levels would leave them particularly exposed. On the island of Marajo in the mouth of the Amazon, for example, annual caiman hunts have been held that have almost eradicated the species in the area.

Hunting of this caiman was at its height in the middle decades of the 20th century, and by the 1950s and 1960s it was difficult to find this increasingly rare animal. For example, the black caiman was extremely abundant in Colombia when hide hunting started in the 1940s. More than 66,000 hides were exported in 1970 and 1972 alone. Today, the species is virtually extinct in that country. In Brazil, the species was once the mainstay of the hide industry, but by 1982 less than 1,000 hides per year were collected. Unfortunately, the black caiman is often hunted when it is still too young to breed, causing further damage to the population. Today, wild black caimans and their skins are banned from international trade under the Convention on International Trade in Endangered Species of Wild Fauna and Flora (CITES).

Conservation

Black caimans are protected throughout much of their range but enforcement is often poor.

The black caiman was once abundant in the Amazon basin. It is the largest species of New World crocodilian and once played an important role in pest control throughout the region. Today this reptile is rare and considered endangered throughout its range, primarily because of uncontrolled hide hunting and destruction of its habitat.

BLACK CAIMAN
South America

BROADNOSED CAIMAN
South America

Commercial hunting still poses a problem in some areas, but not just for hides. In the upper Amazon of Brazil, for example, most hunting is for the meat, which is reportedly used as bait to trap edible tortoises. The fat of black caimans is also in demand for medicinal purposes.

The largest group of caimans found within a protected area is in Manu National Park of Peru; small numbers also occur in the Parque Nacional de Amazonia in Brazil. Because of the large size of the black caiman, captive breeding is difficult.

As of 1991, three zoos in the United States had begun breeding programs for the species: the Oklahoma City Zoo, the Metro Zoo of Miami, Florida, and the New York Zoological Park. Ecuador has also started an experimental breeding program, while Bolivia has released captive-bred animals at the Beni Biological Station.

Broadnosed Caiman

(Caiman latirostris)

ESA: Endangered

Length: 5–6½ ft. (1.5-2m)
Clutch size: Variable, 20–90 eggs have been reported in different locales
Diet: Aquatic insects, snails, crustaceans, and small- to medium-sized vertebrates
Habitat: Marshes, lagoons, streams and rivers; frequently found in brackish or salt water
Range: Southeastern South America, including Argentina, Bolivia, Brazil, Paraguay, and Uruguay

THE DARK OLIVE-COLORED broadnosed caiman is called the *jacare de papo amerelo* in Brazil and the *yacare overo* in Argentina. It is found in southeastern South America, including the countries of Argentina, Bolivia, Brazil, Paraguay, and Uruguay.

A relatively small crocodilian, the broadnosed caiman is known to be highly aquatic. It maneuvers especially well in water and is seldom found far from shore. In a population in Rio Iguazu in Argentina, the species is seen to leave the water to bask for only about 30 minutes in the early morning during the summer, although in spring and autumn it may bask for up to four hours. In winter, the animal will emerge only on sunny, warm days. The species appears to tolerate cold temperatures better than other species of crocodilians, and manages to survive in cooler regions.

The broadnosed caiman nests at different times throughout its range. It is a mound-nesting species, and nests may be constructed on river islands or in nearby jungles in a wet year. The female collects decaying vegetation and builds a mound of about 1½ feet (0.45 meters) high. The clutch size is extremely variable—from 20 to 90 eggs may be deposited in the nest (the highest number may have been from two females sharing the same nest). Eggs are elliptical in shape and hard-shelled. The incubation period is from 63 to 70 days, or longer if the temperature is slightly below optimum. In captivity, the male has been observed assisting his mate in the early stages of nesting, an unusual trait in crocodylia. As incubation progresses, the female becomes more aggressive and will not leave the nest except to feed. Hatchlings begin to make low noises, indicating it is time for them to emerge from their eggs.

At this time, the female breaks open the nest and carries hatchlings in her mouth to the water. The hatchlings cluster together near the nest in their first year, and both parents remain close by to protect them from predators.

A shy crocodilian

The broadnosed caiman is considered one of the most wary of crocodilians, an important factor in its continued survival. However, populations of the reptile are declining quickly throughout its range, and the reptile is considered extinct in some locations. As with the black caiman, the threat to the species has resulted from heavy hide hunting, and although it is protected throughout most of its range, poaching is difficult to control. Both the black caiman and the broadnosed caiman have highly prized hides compared to other caiman because of their extremely soft-texture and pliable quality.

Habitat loss

Habitat loss due to development including drainage schemes, river channeling, forest clearance, and the construction of hydroelectric dams have also created many problems for the broadnosed caiman. In Argentina, ranching and land for agriculture have taken away much of the animal's natural habitat. Drainage and fertilizer runoff threaten caiman populations in Uruguay, and habitats in Brazil receive significant pollution from industrial centers.

Poached to extinction

In Argentina this caiman is protected by a total ban on hunting and commercial exploitation. Unfortunately, as is often the case, this legislation is difficult to enforce, and poaching continues uncontrolled. The broadnosed caiman is locally extinct in many parts of the country where it was once found. In Brazil, the broadnosed caiman was said to be very near to extinction in the 1970s but it is still reasonably abundant in certain areas.

Breeding programs

Better enforcement procedures, together with additional sanctuaries, are needed to maintain the species in viable numbers. In addition, further biological and population data on existing groups must be collected.

Like most caimans, the potential for captive breeding is good. Argentina is currently experimenting with a breeding program, and similar experimental operations have been run in Brazil and Paraguay since as early as 1969.

Elizabeth Sirimarco

See also Alligators, Crocodiles, and Gharials.

The broadnosed caiman is a highly aquatic crocodilian that maneuvers especially well in water. It is seldom seen far away from shore. Most individuals bask for only short periods, and nesting occurs most frequently on river islands.

Wild Bactrian Camel

(Camelus bactrianus)

ESA: Endangered

IUCN: Endangered

Class: Mammalia
Order: Artiodactyla
Family: Camelidae
Weight: 990–1,540 lb. (450–700 kg)
Shoulder height: 71–90 in. (180–230 cm)
Diet: Grass
Gestation period: 360–410 days
Longevity: 40 years
Habitat: Grasslands
Range: China, and Mongolia

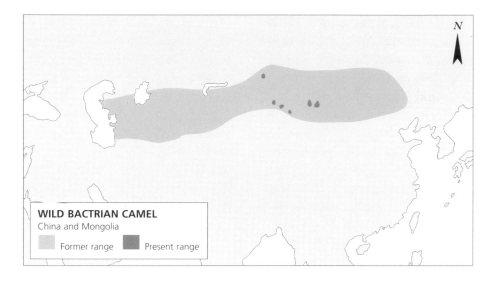

WILD BACTRIAN CAMEL
China and Mongolia

Former range   Present range

THE BACTRIAN CAMEL, or two-humped, camel of central Asia is one of two species of camels found in Africa and Asia. The other is the dromedary, or one-humped, camel.

Camels originated in North America 40 to 45 million years ago and died out during the Pleistocene period, but before they vanished they spread to South America and Asia. The camels that went to South America evolved into camelids such as the llama, vicuna, guanaco, and alpaca. The Asian camels became the bactrian and dromedary camels. Wild camels and the domesticated forms are both

The wild bactrian camel is different from the domesticated form in that it is lighter in color and has smaller humps. The word bactrian means two-humped; the other form of camel is the dromedary, or one-humped camel.

supremely adapted for the harsh desert environment where they are often found. They can close their eyes and their nostrils so that they are not affected by blowing sand and dust. They can store water intercellularly, which allows them to function and work for about five days without water. At the end of that time they either drink, or they are no longer capable of working. If left without water, they can stand or

lie in one place for another ten days to two weeks before dying. Camels can go for long periods of time with very little food. Virtually all of the fat in the camel's body is in the humps. When they are deprived of food for long periods of time, the humps shrink as they utilize their body fat. This unusual characteristic has a second benefit. Since body fat is an effective insulator, the humps can act as a radiator to get

rid of unwanted body heat. These characteristics are common to both wild and domestic camels. For the wild camels, they are essential for survival; for domestic forms, it has given them the nickname: "ships of the desert."

The bactrian camel prefers cold weather, and although they can stand hot central Asian summers, they can also tolerate very low temperatures in winter time, and grow heavy coats.

Wild camels differ from the domesticated form in that they are lighter and have smaller humps. They are quite wary and difficult to approach in the wild.

Bactrian camels are found in the rolling grasslands and steppes of China and parts of Mongolia. They are usually found in small herds of five to eight individuals. Sometimes these groups come together and form herds of up to 40 camels. They have broad padded feet to help them walk over sand and rough terrain.

It is likely that the bactrian camel was domesticated in around 2500 B.C.E. The bactrian camel of today numbers only about 1,100 in the wild, including 500 to 600 camels in Mongolia. About 500 are to be found in western China.

The number of camels in Mongolia may be small, but there are other livestock. Mongolia has one of the highest ratios of livestock to people in the world, and herding is the primary way of earning a living in this arid, landlocked region.

The bactrian camel's primary reason for decline has been heavy poaching, not only for its hide and meat, but to prevent it competing with domesticated animals for vegetation and water holes. Because it competes with domesticated animals for limited food and water resources, the nomadic peoples of the Asian steppes dislike the camel.

Captive camels

Wild bactrian camels are protected over their whole range. However, that protection is not always enforced. Most of the camels in captivity are the domesticated form, but there are a few wild forms in captivity, probably in a few Chinese zoos. Little attention is given to their management and breeding, so there is no secure captive population. A captive breeding program has been established at great Gobi National Park in Mongolia.

Warren D. Thomas

Audubon's Crested Caracara

(Polyborus plancus audubonii)

ESA: Threatened

Class: Aves
Order: Falconiformes
Family: Falconidae
Length: 20–25 in. (51–63.5 cm),
Wingspan: 45–50 in.
Weight: 1½–2½ lb. (0.7–1.1 kg),
Clutch size: 2–4 eggs
Incubation: 28–32 days
Diet: Carrion and live prey
Habitat: Prairies, open country
Range: South America, Mexico and Cuba

THE CARACARAS HAVE not captured public attention as have other birds of prey, but despite being relatively unknown, they are a fascinating group. One caracara (pronounced CARE-uh, CARE-uh) species or another inhabits portions of Central America and all of South America. Experts dispute the exact number of caracara species in existence, but generally agree on six to ten. Only one species, the crested caracara, occurs in the United States, and only in small numbers in a few states. As a species, the crested caracara occurs from Tierra del Fuego in South America through Central America and into North America. Currently, only two subspecies of the caracara have been recognized, *Polyborus plancus plancus* south of the Amazon, and *Polyborus plancus cheriway* north of the Amazon. Traditionally, four distinct subspecies occupy this vast territory. Audubon's crested caracara (*Polyborus plancus auduboni*) inhabits the northern portion of this range, including the Kissimmee Prairie of central Florida, the islands of Cuba and the Isle of Pines, the extreme southwestern portion of Louisiana into Texas and the Mexican border country of Arizona. The crested caracara reaches into northernmost Baja, southward through Mexico, and also extends its range into western Panama.

Distinctive appearance

The crested caracara is dark brownish black above and on the lower breast and belly. The tail is banded white and brownish black producing a grayish look, with a dark band at the tip. The bird's wings are all dark except

Audubon's crested caracara is a predatory bird. Because of this, the caracara and other birds of prey have been attacked by rural peoples who kill the birds to protect their livestock.

for banded white patches at the base of the outer flight feathers that are visible when the bird flies. The upper breast and lower throat of the caracara are a dingy white, sometimes even slightly buff, and banded with brownish black. A pattern extends slightly to the lower hind neck and upper back; this collared effect is furthered by a white chin, upper throat, cheek, and the side of its neck, extending around to the nape. There is bare red skin around the eye extending to the beak. The upper forehead and crown are brownish black, with a

small but conspicuous crest or tuft at the rear of the head, giving an almost square or angular look to the large head. The beak is very large and bluish-gray in color. The very long legs of this bird are yellow with long feet and well developed toes that have flattened claws, unlike the talons of other falcons and hawks. Another bird, the Guadalupe caracara (*Polyborus lutosus*), was originally described as a separate species but may have, in fact, been a fifth subspecies of the crested caracara. Its exact status will always be debated, however, for the bird became extinct 25 years after its discovery.

The Guadalupe caracara was known to Mexican people who tended goats on Guadalupe

Island, but the bird was not known to ornithologists until 1875. At that time it seemed quite abundant on the rugged island 200 miles off the Baja Coast. By the late 1880s it was found to be scarce. In 1900 a collector spotted 11 birds, and shot nine of them. The Guadalupe caracara was never seen alive again. Only 32 specimens were preserved in scientific collections, but specimens alone cannot yield the evidence to determine a bird's status as a species or a subspecies.

Caracaras readily eat carrion, and when goat herders saw a caracara feeding on a dead goat, they were convinced that the goat must have been killed by the caracara. So the Guadalupe caracara perished because it was believed it threatened their livestock; the goat herders took every opportunity to poison and shoot the birds. The degree to which the Guadalupe caracara actually harmed their goats is unknown. Ironically, commercial goat herding and the canning of goat meat disappeared as an industry, but the feral goats survived and these exotic mammals replaced the native bird on Guadalupe.

Audubon's crested caracara did not suffer the wrath of island goatherds, but it was in decline as early as the first decades of this century. Typically a species occurs less abundantly at the edges of its range, and the crested caracara is at the limits of its range in North America. South American subspecies occur at higher elevations and at more extreme latitudes than the North American subspecies. Considering the caracara's decided preference for open country—

whether dry or wet—one would think America's Great Plains would have suited this bird very well, but the caracara never became an inhabitant of the American prairie.

The caracara disappeared from New Mexico decades ago and is rarely seen in Arizona anymore. Many years have passed since it was last seen in Louisiana. Its presence in Texas seems more stable in some areas than in others.

Declining population

Political conditions in Cuba have prevented any verification of the caracara population there, and the Florida population has steadily declined. The Florida, Cuba, and Isle of Pine birds are truly isolated because Audubon's crested caracara does not migrate. Pairs mate for life, but individuals will replace a lost mate. Pairs remain on their terri-

The collared effect and bare red skin around the eye are just two of the distinctive features of the caracara.

tories year-round, so separate populations do not mix. Despite being the national bird of Mexico, the crested caracara is dwindling there, as well.

What's the trouble?

Habitat loss seems to account for much of the bird's troubles. The crested caracara once ranged over most of the Florida Peninsula, from the Georgia state line to the Florida Keys. Now it is seldom seen as far north as Orlando or south of Lake Okeechobee. Conversion of the land to citrus orchards and other row crops, including pine plantations, and an expanding human population that is always building new places to live, work, and play, have degraded the caracara's habitat. In 1987 Florida's caracara population was estimated at 500 birds, down from about 1,500 in 1900. Similar problems pressure the caracara in Mexico and other Central American countries, but human use of the land is not the only reason for the bird's declining numbers.

AUDUBON'S CRESTED CARACARA
South America, Mexico, Cuba

Persecuted predator

Besides its taste for carrion, Audubon's crested caracara is predatory, and rural peoples still guard their livestock carefully. Shooting and poisoning claim many caracaras each year. Although capable of preying on smaller livestock such as lambs, Audubon's crested caracara is neither as large as an eagle nor as agile as a hawk, and it consumes enormous numbers of large insects, reptiles, and rodents, which are easier to capture than sheep and goats. It often finds its prey by strutting around open ground. It also often sits at the top of fence posts and perches on power poles, even though it is a perfectly competent flier.

No specific recovery actions have been proposed on behalf of this caracara, although populations in some places are being monitored. This fascinating bird may become more interesting to the public as its status slides nearer to endangerment.

Kevin Cook

CATFISHES

Class: Actinopterygii

Order: Siluriformes

Family: Clariidae (cave catfish)

Schilbidae (giant catfish)

Mochokidae

(Incomati rock catlet)

The name "catfish" conjures up an image of a cat with whiskers. The most distinguishing features of this ancient group of fishes are the cat-like barbels, or "whiskers," that all catfish species exhibit. Barbels are not hairs, but sensitive organs containing taste buds and other sensors that collect chemical cues from their surroundings. Despite this connection to the house cat, catfishes generally are not considered very handsome or lovable. In fact, these bottom dwellers are thought of by many as slimy and disgusting. However, catfishes have been enormously successful in adapting to a wide range of environments, and colonize all of the continents except Antarctica.

Catfishes are not only diverse in their distribution but also in their various forms and are categorized under several scientific genera. For example, the three species listed below occupy different continents and each belongs to a separate genus. Other catfishes found in this volume include the blindcats and cavefishes. They generally occupy warm water environments and can tolerate high temperatures, low levels of oxygen, and other conditions, both natural and man-made. When introduced to exotic areas, they can thrive to the point where they become pests. The exotic walking catfish (*Clarias betrachus*) of Florida is an example of a species that has adapted to a new environment.

Native to Asia, the walking catfish was introduced to Florida and has displaced some of the less aggressive native fishes. This fish is appropriately named. When state officials tried to poison some of the walking catfish, they simply swam to the surface and walked on the land (while breathing air). They moved to untreated waters, leaving the native fishes to die. Despite their adaptability, some catfishes are now in danger of extinction.

Cave Catfish

(Clarias cavernicola)

IUCN: Critically endangered

Length: 6 in. (15 cm)
Reproduction: Egg layer
Habitat: Underground waterways
Range: Aigamas Cave, Namibia

WATER IS A LIMITED resource in most of southern Africa, and in the African country of Namibia it is a primary reason for concern over the fate of one of the most unique fishes of the world, the cave catfish. The cave catfish's only remaining stronghold is the Aigamas Cave.

Unfortunately, this meager range is under human attack. As the demand for water increases, the water table within Aigamas Cave continues to fall. If this trend is not reversed, the cave catfish will be left high and dry and will probably become extinct. A second threat exists from the introduction of non-native fish species into the Aigamas Cave system. Other more aggressive species such as the sharptooth catfish (*Clarias gariepinus*) could do great harm to the fragile balance that exists between the cave catfish and its environment.

African cave dweller

Caves offer conditions that are very different from those at the surface. Cave-dwelling animals live in total darkness in an energy-poor environment. Caves cannot sustain green plants that capture sunlight and turn it into food for other plants and animals. Because of their distance from the surface and the lack of life-giving sunlight, subterranean fishes depend completely on the movement of food items from the surface to their underground domain. In addition to the absence of light, caves are very stable in temperature. Temperatures vary little, if at all, and usually correspond with the average yearly temperature at the surface. Because of their ability to adapt to such conditions, fish can develop a metabolism that becomes less tolerant of environmental changes—a feature that may limit their ability to expand their range if it is threatened.

Like all members of the family Clariidae, the cave catfish is capable of breathing air for significant periods of time and "walking" across land by pulling itself along with its stout front pectoral fins.

In common with other underground fishes such as the blindcats, this African variety lacks pigmentation, has highly developed senses of taste and touch, and has little use for eyes.

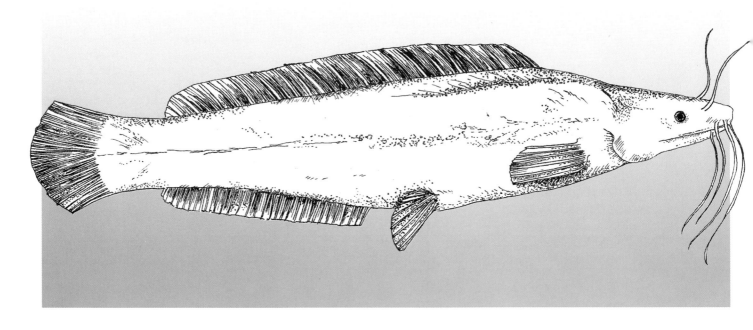

Giant Catfish

(Pangasianodon gigas)

ESA: Endangered

IUCN: Endangered

Length: 8 ft. (250 cm)
Reproduction: Egg layer
Habitat: River pools
Range: Mekong River, Thailand, and Vietnam

ARGUABLY THE LARGEST freshwater fish in the world, the giant catfish is sought as a food fish by local human populations. It is also being considered for use in aquaculture, the raising of aquatic organisms in a controlled environment. True to its name, the giant catfish commonly reaches over eight feet (2.4 meters) in length and can weigh 300 pounds (136 kilograms); some specimens weigh in at over 500 pounds (227 kilograms). This fish is banned from interna-

tional commercial trade under the Convention on International Trade in Endangered Species of Wild Fauna and Flora (CITES). In the 1980s, 300,000 captive-bred giant catfish were released into the Mekong, Chao Phraya and other natural waters in Thailand. The Thailand Fisheries Department has since continued research on how to improve breeding methods and increase the growth rates of these fish bred in captivity.

Lost potential

Its size makes the giant catfish a desirable food item. During its spawning run up the Mekong River, the intensity of fishing by humans is very high. This is unfortunate, because for each sexually mature female fish caught before it spawns, the potential for additional tens of thousands of offspring is lost. Without a doubt, capturing the giant catfish during its spawning period has contributed to its current endangered status. If biologists are successful in raising

The walking catfish, which is able to breathe air and "walk" on land, is an excellent example of evolutionary adaptability.

the giant catfish in captivity for food, it may manage to avoid extinction.

Vegetarian diet

Because of its size and typical catfish appearance, this scaleless monster looks like a vicious predator. However the adult giant catfish is a strict vegetarian and lacks teeth to hold and crush animal prey.

Compared to other catfishes, the giant catfish has a much larger dorsal fin on its back in relation to its overall body size, and the fin has a longer protective spine. The giant catfish also has a blunt snout with a mouth that is positioned forward, instead of the lower-positioned mouth of bottom-feeding catfishes. Fish biologists do not always agree on the classification of this catfish; it is sometimes seen listed as belonging to a family called Pangasiidae.

CAVE CATFISH
Africa

GIANT CATFISH
Asia

Incomati Rock Catlet

(Chiloglanus bifurcus)

IUCN: Critically Endangered

Length: 3 in. (8 cm)
Reproduction: Egg layer
Habitat: Fast-flowing streams
Range: Incomati River, South Africa

THE INCOMATI ROCK catlet lives only within the borders of South Africa in the Transvaal region. It is a member of a group of about 170 fishes called squeakers (Mochokidae), because of the squeaking sound they make when caught by fishermen. The Incomati River is in an area that is undergoing rapid development. While the numbers of Incomati rock catlets are still fairly healthy, the range is small; only the upper reaches of this river system are used by this fish.

Dams cause decline

The primary threat to this species is the construction of dams, which alter the downstream flow and water quality. The catlet requires warm, fast-flowing water. Dams are disruptive to river-dwelling fish such as the catlet. When water from dams is released, colder water from the base flows into their habitat. Dams disrupt temperature patterns and also "smooth out" the seasonal peaks and valleys in water flow that many river fishes use as cues to spawn. Dams also limit fish movement up and down a river system. Miles of river both above and below the dam are useless as a habitat to the rock catlet. Another threat is from a paper mill. In the event of a chemical spill or pollution catastrophe, many of the remaining fish could be wiped out. It is no wonder, then, that the Incomati rock catlet is critically endangered.

William E. Manci

See also Blindcats and Cavefishes.

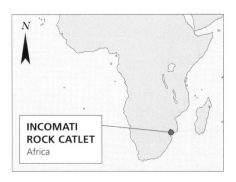

INCOMATI ROCK CATLET
Africa

CATS

Class: Mammalia

Order: Carnivora

Family: Felidae

Cats are among the most highly intelligent of animals. Because their skeletons and nervous systems are adapted for hunting and killing prey, and eating warm-blooded animals, they are superior to other carnivores in their ability to overpower and kill agile and strong prey.

The size of cats varies from a 3½-pound (1.5-kilogram) species to a 600-pound (272-kilogram) tiger. The weight and thickness of the coat also varies, depending on the climate where the animal lives. Color varies from a whitish gray to all shades of buff and golden brown to a deep orange-brown. Many animals, like the lion, have almost no markings while others have stripes, spots, or other distinguishing patterns.

As with domestic cats, wild cats have curved, retractable claws. When they walk, the claws pull back into the claw case formed by the skin of the toe. The claws rarely touch the ground, but a muscle in the lower portion of the foot can contract at will, enabling the cat to climb or to grip the terrain if necessary. The contracted claw holds onto prey tightly, making it difficult for the victim to escape once it has been captured. The cat can grip small objects with its claws, enabling it to use the paw almost like a hand. Cats can remove the worn, outer layer of the claws by scratching against rough objects, such as tree trunks. The next layer is sharply pointed, and this process ensures that the cat's claws are never blunt.

The cat's teeth are the most specialized of the carnivores and are adapted to killing and consuming its prey. The upper teeth are long and almost straight; the lower teeth are hooked, helping the cat hold the prey animal firmly. The cat can kill even large prey with a single bite. Usually it attacks at the neck or throat of its victim. The cat's action severs the spinal cord, instantaneously rendering the animal defenseless. It may also suffocate its prey. The cat is one of the few carnivores that can attack and overpower larger or heavier animals without the help of other members of its pack. Smaller cats, however, tend to feed on prey that is small even in relation to their own size. While large cats capture an animal of a size that they can feed on for several days, the smaller ones must catch many mice or other similar prey in order to have a "full stomach."

Hunting requires acute senses so that the cat can detect its prey, some camouflage to prevent being spotted by the prey, and good maneuverability to chase down the prey and catch it.

The cat has an incredible sense of hearing. For example, a cat can hear a rodent as it is about leave its hole, catching it even before it is visible. Also, the flattened face, short nose, and relatively short, rounded head of the cat allows good binocular vision. The animal's eyesight is as good as, if not better than, a human being's, though its color vision is not well developed. A layer of reflecting tissue behind the light-sensitive cells of the retina sends incoming light back so that it reflects through the retina twice, helping the cat to see well in very dim light, hence it is a crepuscular or nocturnal hunter (hunts at dusk or night). The pupils contract and dilate more visibly than those of other animals. In daylight, the cat's pupil looks like a mere slit or pin-point, while in darkness the pupil dilates to almost the full size of the eye.

The contraction and dilation also indicates the cat's interest in a sound or a sudden movement. The cat's whiskers fulfil two functions. At night the whiskers ensure that the cat locates and avoids any obstacles in its path, while a shorter set of whiskers guides the cat to the best area to bite once its prey has been held down. To hunt successfully, the cat must not be visible to its prey, and the cat will hide in long grass or vegetation. Together with this cover, the markings on the cat's coat, which are typically dark stripes or spots on a lighter ground, will help to break up the cat's shape and make it difficult for prey to notice the threat from the predator.

The classification of mammals is based largely on the skull and teeth of the animal. Members of the cat family, though differing widely in size, color and other factors, have similar skulls and teeth. The cheetah is the most different animal of the cat family, but among other cats, the features of individuals and the features of groups are distributed in contradictory ways. This suggests that the species belonging to a group of related forms were derived from a common ancestor, but began diversifying. This has made classifying cats difficult, and no true classification has been universally accepted.

A British zoologist has developed an expansive system that includes 16 genera differentiated by specific features, grouped into three subfamilies.

Another system, by contrast, includes only three genera and no subfamilies. Because of the conflicting classifications and the uncertainty of the evolutionary path of the cat family, the relationship between different species of cats can be very difficult to determine with certainty.

Due to their status, all species of cats are banned or regulated in international trade under the Convention on International Trade in Endangered Species of Wild Fauna and Flora (CITES).

This entry includes many members of the genus *Felis*. For additional information about other species consult the index under cats.

Flat-headed Cat
(Prionailurus planiceps)

ESA: Endangered

IUCN: Vulnerable

Weight: 3¼–4¾ lb. (1.5–2.2 kg)
Body length: 16–19½ in. (41–50 cm)
Tail length: 5–6 in. (13–15 cm)
Diet: Frogs, fish, crustaceans.
Gestation period: Unknown
Habitat: Damp or riverine regions
Range: Southern Thailand through Malaysia to Borneo and Sumatra

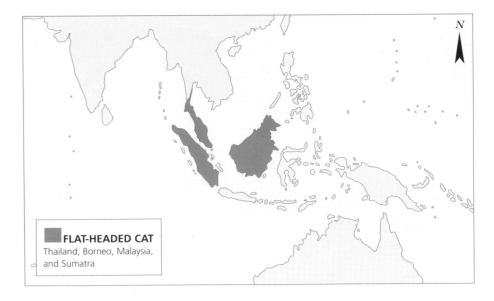

FLAT-HEADED CAT
Thailand, Borneo, Malaysia, and Sumatra

THE FLAT-HEADED cat is probably not common anywhere in its range. While the flat-headed cat is fully protected throughout most of its range, it is significantly threatened by water pollution contaminating its prey. It is a shy and elusive animal, making it very difficult to define its precise distribution or the size of the current population. It appears to be adapted to special environmental conditions and probably has the smallest range of the mainland Asian cats.

The species is dark brown with a silvery tinge. The only markings appear on the head, with the exception of brown-to-blackish spots on the throat, belly, and inner portion of the legs. The chest and chin are white spotted with brown, and the head is a reddish brown. Below the eyes are two narrow, dark lines that run across each cheek. A yellow line runs from each eye to the ear. Its body is cylindrical in shape, and the limbs and tail are short. The head is quite different from other felids, with its long snout and narrow, flat skull. It is also the only cat, with the exception of the cheetah and the Iriomote cat, whose claws cannot be fully retracted. The claws can be lifted so they do not rub against the ground, but the sheaths that cover them in other species are short and cover only one-third of each claw.

The first upper premolar is particularly noticeable in this cat because it is longer than in other species, quite sharp, and very powerful. This cat is thought to feed on a variety of water prey, including fish and frogs from along riverbanks, and its well-developed teeth appear to help the cat to capture slippery prey. A kitten observed in captivity seemed to enjoy taking fish and frogs from water, but ignored live birds. It also appeared to enjoy playing in the water.

Very little is known about the traits and habitat of the flat-headed cat. It seems to be nocturnal, and lives in forests near to rivers, swamps and flooded regions where it it can find various kinds of water prey.

Iriomote Cat
(Prionailurus bengalensis iriomotensis)

ESA: Endangered

IUCN: Endangered

Weight: About 6½–18 lb. (3–8 kg)
Shoulder height: 8 in. (20 cm)
Body length: 23½ in. (60 cm)
Tail length: 7¾ in. (20 cm)
Diet: Small rodents, birds, probably fishes, frogs, and crabs
Gestation period: Approximately 60–70 days
Habitat: Lowland, subtropical rain forest
Range: The island of Iriomote, the westernmost island of the Japanese Ryukyu islands

THE IRIOMOTE CAT, perhaps the rarest of all cats, was first scientifically described in 1966. The species is found only on the island of Iriomote. The island is 180 square miles (292 square kilometers) in size, located about 120 miles (195 kilometers) east of Taiwan. The Iriomote cat is

The unusual shape of the flat-headed cat's skull gives it an appearance that is unique among felids. This shy and elusive cat apparently has the smallest range of the mainland Asian cats.

relatively small, similar in size to a domestic cat. It has a rather elongated body, with short legs and tail, and the ears are rounded. The fur is dark brown or grayish brown with black-brown spots that run in lengthwise rows. Five to seven lines run from the back of the neck to the shoulders. The Iriomote cat's claws are only partially developed and, therefore, do not retract completely.

The Iriomote cat has only been known to scientists since 1967. Researchers consider the Iriomote cat to be the most primitive of living cats, and it presents an interesting case for the study of the feline evolution. Some theories suggest that it may be an ancestor of the New World felid. While the original species exists on Iriomote, some members may have crossed the Aleutian island bridge, migrating to the Americas and undergoing evolutionary changes over time.

Scientists have studied the ecology of the Iriomote cat since 1983. Today, they estimate that about 100 cats exist, a substantial increase from estimates of only 40 existing cats in the 1970s. Because the Iriomote cat is scientifically important, it would seem logical that government and wildlife organizations would take special care of this endangered species. Yet in spite of efforts from the Japanese, and international attempts to protect the cat, little has been done on the island of Iriomote to help to increase the population of this rare cat.

The cat has been protected as a Special National Monument of Japan since 1977. After the cat was discovered on Iriomote, a national park was established, but soon it was decreased to a third of its original size. It is now limited to areas in higher elevations that do not offer the cat its proper habitat because its prey animals exist in the lowlands, river, and stream valleys. Consequently, the density of Iriomote cats in the park region is low. Higher densities do exist around the coastal area of the island and the forest edge. Unfortunately, these areas generally fall outside the national park. Lowland areas are claimed for growing rice, among other purposes. Although Iriomote island has changed less than other areas in Japan, the cat is quickly losing its habitat to agricultural development. There is a chance that this rare cat, together with other endangered fauna native to the island, will be lost forever. The Iriomote Island forest system must be preserved and captive breeding projects started to help rebuild the cat's populations and to learn more about its ecology.

Very little is known about the Iriomote cat's habits. Because none exist in captivity, it has been difficult to study. It leads a solitary life in trees and rock caves. Though it can and does climb trees, it is predominantly a ground animal, like other species of the genus. This cat appears to be both nocturnal and territorial, and its home range does not exceed two square miles. Optimistically, Scientists believe that the Iriomote cat has a chance of survival even though it is in a particularly vulnerable position. Threats to this cat include competition from feral cats and getting trapped in snares set for wild boars. While the Iriomote cat is fully protected, it faces major threats as a result of forest clearance caused by agricultural and cattle-raising projects. In addition, Iriomote Island itself is increasingly being promoted as a tourist destination, with the Iriomote cat a major source of attraction. Without some careful planning, developments to accommodate the tourism industry could have a further detrimental impact on the Iriomote cat.

Little Spotted Cat

(Leopardus tigrinus)

LITTLE SPOTTED CAT
South America

ESA: Endangered

IUCN: Lower risk

Weight: 3¾–6 lb. (1.75–2.75 kg)
Body length: 16–22 in. (55–77 cm)
Tail length: 9¾–15½ in. (25–40 cm)
Diet: Birds, small mammals
Gestation period: 55–60 days
Habitat: Subtropical forests
Range: Central America to northern Argentina

THE LITTLE SPOTTED cat is also referred to as the oncilla. While the species is often classified as part of the genus *Felis*, others classify it among the sub-genus of ocelots (*leopardus*), which is comprised of five species. The breakdown of the genus into species is still in doubt, and all these cats have been given different common names at different times. In addition, they have often been confused with each other, and different species were often given the same name.

The little spotted cat is typical of South American small cats. Both the ocelots and regional bush cats are probably derived from the same species.

The little spotted cat is about the size of a domestic cat, slender with a slim head and moderate-sized, round ears. Its coat is yellowish red to grayish yellow, with rosette-like spots in lengthwise rows. The tail has 10 or eleven bands or rings, but is never spotted, and ends in a black tip. About one-fifth of all individuals are melanistic (nearly all black), or they are all black.

Typical of most Latin American felids, the little spotted cat remains unstudied in the wild and its habits are virtually unknown. Observations in captivity suggest that the little spotted cat captures and feeds on birds. It appears to be less solitary than other small cats, and it is possible that mating pairs stay together permanently.

The gestation period in captivity is 74 to 76 days, and litters are usually of one or two young. The kittens of the little spotted cat are slow developers, opening their eyes at 17 days and taking solid food at 55 days. The species is an able climber and is often

Marbled Cat
(Felis marmorata)

ESA: Endangered

IUCN: Data deficient

Weight: 4½–11 lb. (2–5 kg)
Shoulder height: 15–16 in. (38–41 cm)
Body length: 18–24 in. (45–61cm)
Tail length: 18–21 in. (47–55 cm)
Diet: Small mammals, birds,
Gestation period: Unknown
Habitat: Rain forests
Range: Nepal to Assam and northern Myanmar, Indonesia, Borneo, Java, and Sumatra

As with many of the cat species, there is some question about the classification of the little spotted cat. Some biologists consider it part of the genus *Felis*, while others place it in a subgenus called *leopardus*.

found in trees, although it mainly inhabits forest floors.

Four of the five species of these cats were subjected to severe pressure by the fur industry, which has had a devastating effect on their populations. The species has also been captured for the pet trade. It is assumed that the little spotted cat is a naturally rare animal. Therefore, any stress on its population can have a devastating effect. Reports indicate that it is increasingly rare in most areas of its range. The principle threats to the cat are uncontrolled hunting and habitat destruction.

In 1971, 28,000 pelts were counted in Brazilian warehouses alone. The pelts of the little spotted cat are less valuable than those of the ocelot, but the latter was hunted from accessible areas. As fewer ocelots were available, the pressure on the little spotted cat became greater. At least 3,170 little spotted cats, both live animals and skins, were imported into the United States in 1970. After that, the animal was listed as endangered and importation was banned. Unfortunately, in the early 1980s, it became the leading spotted cat in international fur trade, with the number of skins in trade reaching nearly 84,500 in 1983.

No information exists about population size or the number of offspring that can be expected in a given year. It is protected in many countries throughout its range, although trade of its fur continues. The species probably occurs in several national parks and reserves as well, but it is rare in zoos; only a few have been bred successfully in captivity.

The future of the little spotted cat, as with the other ocelot-like cats, continues to be dim, despite international efforts to protect it. The animal is naturally rare, and the constant threat of the fur trade, together with loss of the cat's habitat to agriculture and logging, is a pressure that must be resisted. It has now been classified as Lower risk by the IUCN.

THE MARBLED CAT is still relatively widespread, but it is a little-known species. It is rare throughout its range, and populations are declining because of the loss of its forest habitat. It is similar in size to a domestic cat and has a strong build with long legs. It is brownish gray to bright yellow in color, often changing to gray shades on the limbs. It is named for the patterns on the sides of the body—large, irregular dark blotches, each outlined in black. There are solid black dots on the limbs and underparts of the cat. The long, bushy tail is spotted with a black tip, and overall its fur is thick and soft. The ears are short and rounded.

The marbled cat spends a great deal of its life in trees and is an extremely able climber. It is a forest dweller and appears to be nocturnal. Its prey is likely to be squirrels and rats, though the diet may include lizards and frogs.

Little is known about the marbled cat's habits in the wild. It has been bred with some success at only one institution, the Greater Los Angeles Zoo. Unfortunately, it is difficult to obtain and keep in captivity. Ten cats were bred at the zoo, but none survived. The program started with a single pair, and in 1982 a new male was introduced. Unfortunately, after his first kitten was born, the new male died. The program never had a large enough gene pool to run an effective breeding program. In other words, because the animals in the group were related, common genetic problems would be magnified and compounded in the offspring. In general, the small wild cats are difficult to breed in captivity, although some species have shown promise.

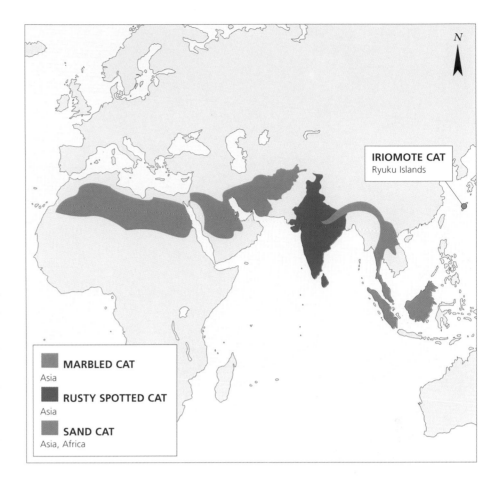

N

IRIOMOTE CAT
Ryuku Islands

MARBLED CAT
Asia

RUSTY SPOTTED CAT
Asia

SAND CAT
Asia, Africa

Pakistan Sand Cat

(Felis margarita scheffeli)

ESA: Endangered

IUCN: Lower risk

Weight: 4½–5½ lb. (2–2.5 kg)
Length: 17–22 in. (45–57 cm)
Tail length: 11–13½ in. (28–35 cm)
Diet: Rodents, occasionally small mammals or reptiles
Gestation period: 59–63 days
Habitat: Arid region
Range: N. Africa, SW. Asia

MANY WILD CATS are particularly well-adapted to life in the more arid regions of the world. The sand cat is one of these. For example, the soles of this cat's feet are covered with dense hairs that are adapted to help it progress easily over loose, sandy soil. There are several subspecies of sand cats; but the Pakistan sand cat faces the most uncertain future of the group.

Sandy-colored

Sand cats are a sandy-yellow color that is common among desert cats. A reddish streak runs across each cheek to the corner of the eye, and the tail has two or three rings above its black tip. The species has short legs, and the ears are set low on the head.

The sand cat is primarily a nocturnal animal, although it is often active at dusk. It spends its days in shallow burrows.

The animal is able to live without the necassity of drinking free water, another unusual attribute that helps it survive in a desert environment. The cat's prey consists of rodents and occasionally hares, birds, or small reptiles. The sand cat may have two litters annually, because kittens have been found in both spring and autumn.

Late discovery

The Pakistan sand cat was discovered much later than its relatives; it was not until 1966 that the cat was described by scientists. It is a rare cat and its decline in populaion was thought to be the result of uncontrolled exploitation by commercial animal dealers.

While hunting of the sand cat is now prohibited in Pakistan and throughout much of its range, a lack of knowledge about its biology makes assessments of any threats and endangerment difficult to predict accurately.

Rusty Spotted Cat

(Felis rubiginosus)

IUCN: Data deficient

Weight: 2¼–4½ lb. (1–2 kg)
Body length: 13½–18¾ in. (41–48 cm)
Tail length: 6–9 in. (15-23 cm)
Diet: Birds, small mammals
Gestation period: Unknown
Habitat: Dense forests, scrub, grassland, and open country
Range: India and Sri Lanka

THE TINY RUSTY spotted cat is perhaps the smallest species in the world. While the cat is normally seen only in the south of India, it was recently reported in Kashmir (India's northern mountains), as well as in the northeast of India. The strange distribution of the cat makes it difficult to study. It is nocturnal, lives in dense forests, and is difficult to find. The cat is named for the reddish brown spots on its back and flanks that grow smaller and paler toward the tail. It has four lengthwise stripes that extend across the nape and withers. The basic fur color is grayish brown. It has a small tail, reaching only to its heel or just above.

The rusty spotted cat is not as rare as others, and villagers have seen the cat. The Indian cat population prefers scrub, grassland, and open country. In Sri Lanka, it occurs in humid mountain forests. Scientists have learned little about the animal's feeding habits or behavior, but studies are underway. In 1990, the first

Sand cats are highly adapted to living in harsh desert environments. For example, it appears that they do not need free water in order to survive.

photographs of the species in the wild were taken in the Gir Lion Sanctuary in western India.

Protected species

The sighting at Gir Lion Sanctuary prompted a survey to assess the cat's status and ecology.

The Indian population of this cat is protected to prevent international commerce, and the Sri Lankan group is monitored closely. The species is rare in captivity, but there are captive specimens in Frankfurt, Germany, and in Sri Lanka.

In the wild, the rusty spotted cat suffers from encroachment and degradation of its habitat.

Elizabeth Sirimarco

CAVEFISHES

Class: Actinopterygii

Order: Percopsiformes

Family: Amblyopsidae

Most people think of fish as being outdoor creatures. Since many caves contain water in the form of underground pools and streams, it is not surprising to find fish living there. Indeed, many fishes have evolved exclusively underground in the absence of light and other qualities of life that we take for granted above ground.

Caves offer conditions that are very different from those at the surface. Cave-dwelling animals live in total darkness, where there is no sunlight to sustain green plants—plants which would normally provide food. Because of their isolation from the surface and the lack of life-giving sunlight, underground or subterranean fishes depend completely on the flow of food from the surface to their underground world. Caves also have temperatures that vary little, if at all, corresponding with the average yearly temperature at the surface.

To adapt to their unusual environment, cave-dwelling fishes have developed unique physical characteristics. One is their lack of eyes. Eyes would not only be useless, but could be damaged in the darkness. As a replacement for eyes, the exterior of these fishes is packed with other sensory organs; touch, taste, and smell are extremely important.

Another unusual trait of cave dwellers is the lack of skin pigmentation; all of these fishes are white and pink, (also called albino). Camouflage as a means to avoid predators, and for protection from the damaging rays of the sun is not required in a cave environment. A third adaptation is a slower metabolism, allowing fishes to survive in a habitat where food is scarce. Cavefishes also tend to have larger fins for more efficient swimming. Last but not least, cave-dwelling fishes are able to store fat more efficiently during times of plenty.

Bats play an important role in the lives of these fishes. Since bats are creatures of both the outside and subterranean world, bats act like transport mechanisms that support fish populations in caves. Bat guano (waste products) and dead bats are key sources of food for cave fishes. Aquatic plankton, crayfish, and salamanders provide significant food sources. Cannibalism is not uncommon when a plentiful food supply leads to spawning success. This behavior limits overpopulation, but may threaten the survival of the species.

Alabama Cavefish

(Speoplatyrhinus poulsoni)

ESA: Endangered

IUCN: Critically endangered

Length: 2½ in. (6 cm)

Reproduction: Egg layer

Habitat: Underground waters

Range: Florence, Alabama

WITHOUT A DOUBT, the Alabama cavefish is one of the rarest fishes on earth; only nine specimens have ever been taken from their natural home in Key Cave near Florence, Alabama. The principle threat to this cavefish is agricultural runoff and pollution of the groundwater supply to the cave. Water analysis has revealed little in the way of an immediate threat to the well-being of this fish, but industrial and commercial development in the Key Cave area could add to the water pollution problem. The Alabama cavefish population in Key Cave is fewer than 100 individuals, and no more than 10 cavefish have ever been observed on a single visit.

Like all other cavefish, this small fish is blind, and has no skin pigmentation. The skin is loaded with rows of sensory canals that detect motion and vibration. This indicates that the fish probably relies more heavily on touch, rather than on smell or taste, to capture food. Breeding probably occurs from February through April and is triggered when underground water flow increases during spring rains and runoff. The Alabama cavefish breeds on a more regular cycle than other cave-dwelling fishes such as the blindcats, which spawn only when adequate food is available.

When the Alabama cavefish was first found in Key Cave in 1967, fishery biologists believed that other populations of this species would be found in other nearby caves. Instead, they found the more common southern cavefish. This fish is aggressive and has a higher reproductive capacity. Scientists concluded that the southern cavefish was out-competing the Alabama cavefish for habitat and food.

Efforts to save the Alabama cavefish from extinction must include preservation of Key Cave and its threatened water

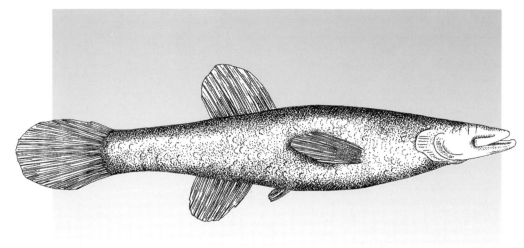

The northern cavefish is the largest of its family. Like all cavefish, it is colorless, an adaptation that helps it thrive in its environment.

can reduce the amount of water that moves through the underground cave systems and increase silt deposits in these areas. Both are disruptive and could further diminish the chances for survival of cave inhabitants.

resources. The Tennessee Valley Authority is the owner of the two entrances to Key Cave, and has erected a fence to minimize human disturbance. However, other measures will need to be undertaken as well. Because opportunities to study this fish are so rare, little is known about it, and many conclusions are based only on speculation.

Northern Cavefish

(Amblyopsis spelaea)

IUCN: Vulnerable

Length: 4 in. (10 cm)
Reproduction: Egg layer
Habitat: Underground waters
Range: Indiana and Kentucky

THE LARGEST POPULATION of this highly specialized fish is in Orange County in southern Indiana, but others can be found as far south as Mammoth Cave in Kentucky. As with the Alabama cavefish, water pollution poses the greatest threat to the well-

being of this species. Water-filled sinkholes above ground feed the underground water system that supports the northern cavefish. These are under attack by polluters and garbage dumpers. Unwittingly, these humans are threatening not only underground wildlife, but also their own drinking water supply.

In the interest of both people and animals like the northern cavefish, many of these sinkholes have been identified and targeted for preservation. Unfortunately, these areas are not immune to the effects of careless waste disposal and pollution.

The northern cavefish is the largest of the endangered cavefishes; this means it is also the largest of its family. This meat-eater does eat other fish, but relies heavily on other smaller aquatic animals. In addition to being longer than other cavefish, the snout and body of this colorless species tends to be more streamlined. It has the characteristic large fins of all cavefishes.

In addition to pollution, this cavefish is also threatened by the diversion of water for human use and flood control projects. This

Ozark Cavefish

(Amblyopsis rosae)

ESA: Threatened

IUCN: Vulnerable

Length: 2½ in. (6.4 cm)
Reproduction: Egg layer
Habitat: Underground waters and streams
Range: Missouri, Oklahoma, Arkansas

OF THE THREE cavefishes that deserve attention as threatened species, the Ozark cavefish is the least in jeopardy. However, it is also the most well-studied, and the problems that plague other cavefishes are common to this species as well. Changes in its habitat caused by pollution, diverted water, and cave flooding by reservoirs are the principal threats to this fish. Cave vandalism and collectors for the aquarium trade also take their toll on the populations.

This tiny cave dweller is a bit different from other cavefishes in that it prefers areas of moving water over gravel or other rubble.

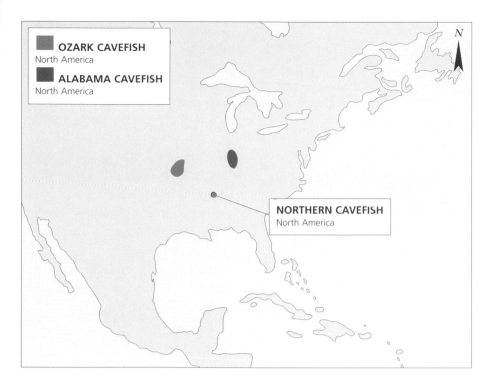

The Ozark cavefish is the least jeopardized of endangered cavefishes, but it does face the same perils as its relatives in caves in other states.

Moving water creates "noise" that can disrupt a fish's ability to sense movement of prey. It is unclear how the Ozark cavefish filters out noise in order to capture its prey.

This species resembles the northern cavefish in appearance, having the characteristic white and pink skin, large fins, and sensory canals on the head and body, but it is somewhat smaller. Cave pollution from the runoff of pesticides is common in rural areas, and caves near urban areas are assaulted by septic tank waste and street runoff that contains chemicals that can move through a cave system for hundreds of miles, and have a devastating effect on fish. The ultimate effect of runoff pollution is fairly clear. A survey of caves in southwestern Missouri showed a dramatic drop in the number of sites that were currently occupied by the Ozark cavefish compared to populations in years past.

Cavefish populations in Arkansas and Oklahoma are less in danger, but they too must endure the same pressures as their Missouri relatives.

Oklahoma populations are fairly small and therefore more susceptible to harm. If appropriate steps are taken to reduce pollution and waste dumping within its range, and to better manage the available water resources, prospects for the recovery of the Ozark cavefish are still fairly good.

William E. Manci

See also Cachorritos and Catfishes

This threatened cavefish (*Phreatichtys andruzzi*) is from Somalia, eastern Africa. It has the same distinctive features as its relatives in the United States.

CHAMOIS

Class: Mammalia

Order: Artiodactyla

Family: Bovidae

Subfamily: Caprinae

Tribe: Rupicaprini

The chamois are one of the most agile of all the alpine-dwelling animals. These animals live at relatively high altitudes, and during late spring and summer they often spend their time above the tree line, eating the grasses and low vegetation that occurs there. During this time of the year they are quite sociable and are seen in sizeable groups.

Chamois have been introduced successfully in South America and especially New Zealand. The captive population of chamois in North America is almost entirely derived from the New Zealand introduction.

Apennine (Abruzzo) Chamois

(Rupicapra pyrenaica ornata)

ESA: Endangered

IUCN: Endangered

Chartreuse Chamois

(Rupicapra rupicapra cartusiana)

IUCN: Critically endangered

Weight: 44–110 lb. (20–50 kg)

Shoulder height: 27½–35½ in. (70–90 cm)

Diet: Grasses, leaves, shoots

Gestation period: 170–180 days

Longevity: 15 years

Habitat: Mountain terrain

Range: French Alps

CHAMOIS MOVE FROM one precipitous rocky ledge to another with unbelievable agility and balance. In summertime their coat is often a fawn brown with dark flashings on their face; in winter their hair grows much longer and they become quite dark with some light markings showing around the chin and underneath their neck and abdomen.

In winter chamois move from the upper to the lower altitudes and into the tree line. At that time they tend to break up into much smaller groups. This is a survival strategy that works well because with little food available, staying in a large group would mean some could starve.

The females stay with their herd for their whole life and stay with their parent group. The males stay with the parent group until they are sexually mature (at about two or three years old) and the breeding season begins. Then the adult male chamois, which tend to be more solitary and nomadic, will wander in and drive the young males away. The most aggressive and strongest males then take over the parent herd.

If a female is rejected because of population pressures, or if she loses a battle for dominance, she will wander away. Fortunately, there are plenty of peripheral males beyond the range of the dominant males to insure that she does not miss a year being fertilized. Female chamois bear young in May and June on secluded rocky ledges; the young follow their mother within hours.

Fierce battles

Battles for dominance among chamois are sometimes very aggressive. They display threats by raising the hair on their backs to make them look larger. The opposing male will do the same unless he is intimidated and decides not to fight.

Hooked horns

When the males do fight, they hook with their horns. Their horns are short with a very marked hook on the end. With these they can do a lot of damage to each other. Fortunately, with their heavy coats and tough hides they are well protected. In some fights they can be terribly vicious and literally rip each other open. When a chamois is losing, one way it shows submission is to lie flat on the ground with its neck extended. This calms the aggressor to where he no longer attacks the loser of the contest, but it is not as vulnerable a position for the loser as it may seem. Because his horns are so dramatically curved on the ends, the dominant chamois can't inflict as much damage to an animal on the ground as it could if the animal were standing up.

Once chamois were found throughout much of the mountainous regions of Europe, including the Pyrenees in Spain, the French Alps, the Apennines of Italy, and even as far east as the Caucasus in Asia. The two most endangered species are the Apennine chamois and the Chartreuse chamois, also known as the French chamois.

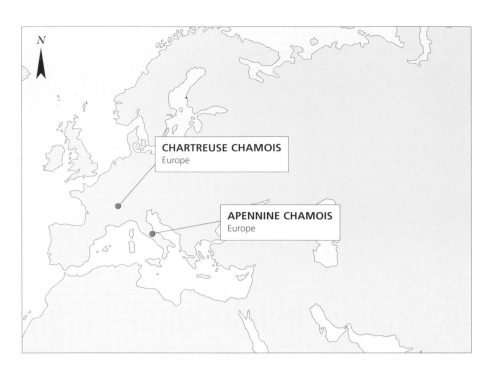

CHARTREUSE CHAMOIS
Europe

APENNINE CHAMOIS
Europe

The Apennine chamois

The Apennine chamois is found in Abruzzo National Park. Hunting and sheep herding took its toll on this chamois' range, leaving it all but extinct in the wild. There are now several hundred thousand chamois in Europe, but only about 400 Apennine chamois remain in the wild. About 150 Chartreuse chamois survive in the French Alps. Its narrow range and poaching, has reduced its numbers drastically. However both chamois are now under strict protection and their numbers have stabilized.

Warren D. Thomas

CHARALS

Class: Actinopterygii

Order: Atheriniformes

Family: Atherinidae

The charals, or silversides, are schooling fishes that live in marine, coastal, and freshwater environments in both temperate and tropical parts of Mexico. Because of their small-to-moderate size, they are preyed upon by other larger fishes that inhabit the same areas. Even people harvest charals as a source of high-quality protein. Some charal species are so valued as a food source for people that they are reproduced using aquaculture techniques, the raising of aquatic plants and animals in a controlled environment, usually for food. This technique can assist the recovery of a threatened or endangered fish. By producing the species in hatcheries and then releasing them into the wild, the threatened species has an opportunity to recover from threats to its population.

Charal de Achichica

(Poblana alchichica)

IUCN: Critically endangered

Charal de Quechulac

Charal de la Preciosa

(Poblana letholepis)

IUCN: Endangered

Length: 10 in. (25 cm)
Reproduction: Egg layer
Habitat: Lake water and inshore
Range: Lake Alchichica, Mexico

THESE THREE SPECIES of the genus *Poblana* all occupy a very small range in the Mexican state of Puebla. For example, the charal de Alchichica is found only in Lake Alchichica.

The charal is a silvery-colored fish with a slender body and a pointed snout, with a slightly upturned mouth and lower jaw. A prominent and well defined horizontal stripe runs from just behind the head to the base of the tail. The body is well-scaled from behind the head to the base of the tail, and the fins are relatively small and pointed. It has two dorsal fins on the back, but the forward fin is extremely small and probably does not contribute to stability in the water. However, the anal fin is quite long and nearly as large as the tail fin. All fins except the pectoral fins (just behind the gills) show some dark pigmentation.

Information on the breeding habits of this fish is not widely available, but it is known that it prefers small aquatic invertebrates as its primary food source.

The small range of the charal is only one of its problems. For example, the charal de Alchichica must endure attacks from fishes such as largemouth bass (*Micropterus salmoides*), and destruction and alteration of its preferred habitat by people. Both the charal de Quechulac and the charal de Preciosa face habitat destruction as well. All three species are now regarded as endangered, and an uncertain future lies ahead.

Charal del Valle de Mexico
(Chirostoma regani)

IUCN: Data deficient

Length: 10 in. (25 cm)
Reproduction: Egg layer
Habitat: Warm lakes and streams
Range: Central Mexico

THE CHARAL DEL VALLE de Mexico is a freshwater variety of the Mexican charal or silversides. It is so named because, like many other native fishes, this charal is found within the valley that runs through the nation's capital, Mexico City. Once abundant throughout many states in central Mexico, this species has been decimated by the introduction of the non-native and predatory largemouth bass (*Micropterus salmoides*). Not even the schooling behavior of this charal, which normally helps discourage efficient predation, has afforded much in the way of safety. Largemouth bass thrive in the warm waters of central Mexico, and have been responsible for the total elimination of endangered poeciliid and goodeid fishes, as well as charals from many area lakes and reservoirs.

Like the other charals, this fish has a silvery-colored, slender body and a pointed snout, with a slightly upturned mouth and lower jaw. A prominent and well-defined horizontal stripe runs from just behind the head to the base of the tail. The mouth contains two or three bands of teeth that are used to hold small prey. The body is well-scaled from behind the head to the base of the tail, but the fins are relatively small and pointed. It has two dorsal fins on the back, but the forward fin is extremely small and probably does aid its stability in the water. However, the anal fin is quite long and nearly as large as the tail fin. All fins except the pectoral fins (situated just behind the gills) show some dark pigmentation.

Charal sanctuary
Information on the feeding and breeding habits of this fish is scarce. Lake Juanacatlan in the state of Jalisco, the most remote site containing the charal del valle de Mexico, appears to be free of bass as well as other predators. More sites like this one are needed to save this charal. The lack of appropriate sites is one of the primary threats to its continued survival. Continued encroachment by people into the charal's natural range, particularly in the Valley of Mexico City, most certainly will have a negative effect on this fish as well.

William E. Manci

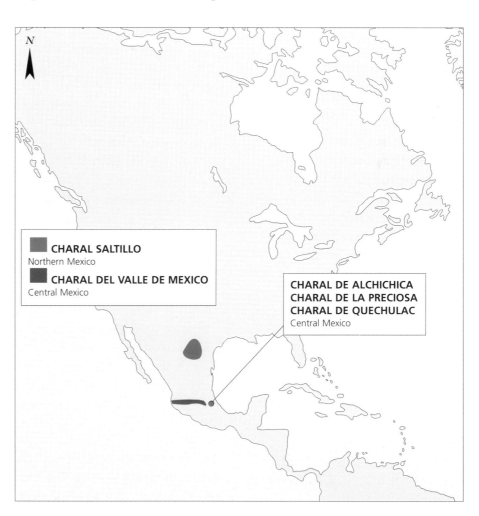

CHARAL SALTILLO
Northern Mexico

CHARAL DEL VALLE DE MEXICO
Central Mexico

CHARAL DE ALCHICHICA
CHARAL DE LA PRECIOSA
CHARAL DE QUECHULAC
Central Mexico

Cheetah
(Acinonyx jubatus)

ESA: Endangered

IUCN: Vulnerable

Class: Mammalia
Order: Carnivora
Family: Felidae
Subfamily: Acinonychinae
Weight: 77–159 lb. (32–72 kg)
Shoulder height: 27–34 in. (70–90 cm)
Body length: 46¾–58½ in. (120–150 cm)
Tail length: 23–31 in. (60–80 cm)
Diet: Gazelles and other small- to medium-sized hoofed animals
Gestation period: 90-95 days
Habitat: Grass and bush steppes, but will occasionally retreat to mountain areas
Range: Africa south of the Sahara, Afghanistan, and Iran

THE CHEETAH IS the only living representative of its genus and differs considerably from other cats. The species appears to have split from the common cat lineage earlier than others. Because it has many characteristics found only in this cat, it has been assigned to its own subfamily. The cheetah has a small, arched head with a short nose and neck, joined to a slender body on long, thin legs. The body shape is highly adapted to the cheetah's role as the fastest mammal. It can reach a running speed of up to 70 miles (112 kilometers) per hour, but such high speeds can only be maintained by the cheetah for a few hundred yards.

The ground color of the cheetah's coarse coat is a tawny to pale buff or grayish-white; the underparts are paler, often white. It is marked with round black spots set close together, and there is a black stripe that extends from the anterior corner of the eye to the mouth. The last third of the tail has a series of black rings. The neck has slightly longer fur, forming a short mane that is more pronounced in the young of the species. The paws of the cheetah are quite narrow in comparison to those of other cats, and its blunt claws are only partially retractable. This cat makes a number of different sounds, ranging from purrs of contentment to a loud yelp that can be heard from more than a mile away.

An adaptable animal

The cheetah can survive in a wide variety of habitats, which explains why its former range was so vast. It lives in areas from semidesert regions to open grasslands to thick bush. This cat is most active during the day, seeking shelter in dense vegetation. An adult male may wander as far as 4½ miles (7 kilometers) in a single day, while a female with cubs will move only 2¼ miles (3.7 kilometers). The cheetah often climbs trees, even playing in them for a time.

Unlike most cats, the cheetah does not ambush its prey. It stalks an animal and then charges from a close distance, usually about 200 or 300 feet (60 to 90 meters) away. It is seldom successful in attacks from a further distance and can only continue to chase its prey for about 500 yards (460 meters). For this reason, most hunts fail, and the cheetah must spend a great deal of its time hunting. When an animal is overtaken, the cat will usually knock it down with the force of its charge, and then suffocate it. After a successful hunt, the cheetah must rest for 20 or 30 minutes before starting its meal. Animals like gazelles or impalas make up the bulk of the diet. A female with cubs will kill such an animal every day, while a lone individual can go up to five days without hunting. Because the cheetah has to work so hard for its food, human changes to the environment can be especially devastating.

Relatively social

The home range of the cheetah is about 50 to 80 square miles (53 to 85 square kilometers). It travels alone or in small groups, which are usually made up of a female with cubs or two to four related adult males. These groups of males will defend their territory against others, aiding in access to prey and mates. Unlike lions, which travel in groups, cheetahs do not appear to work together when hunting. Although cheetahs are generally friendly to others of their kind, groups avoid each other. They will "mark" an area by urinating on objects in the area. The scent alerts other animals that they have entered another group or individual's territory. Occasionally, males will fight over a female in heat.

Reproduction

Births occur from January to August in East Africa, from November to January in Namibia, and from November to March in Zambia. Females give

birth about every 17 months, but if her young are lost, the mother may mate and bear another litter more quickly. The cubs weigh about 5¼ to 10½ ounces (150 to 300 grams) at birth, and are weaned between three and six months of age.

At about six weeks they begin to follow their mother, and families may shift their place of shelter on a daily basis. The cubs leave the mother at 15 to 17 months and will attain sexual maturity shortly afterward.

The cheetah is not strong in relation to its size. Leopards and lions will kill the animal if they can catch it, and the young are threatened by hyenas and other carnivores, as well as by large birds of prey. This has played a role in the relatively small popu-

lations of cheetahs. Animals it depends on for prey have steadily declined in numbers during this century, which has in turn hurt the cheetah. But these are not the most significant threat to the animal. Human beings and the loss of natural habitat are most threatening to the cheetah.

Cheetahs have been taken from the wild for a number of purposes, and this has contributed to their decline. For more than 4,000 years, people have used the animal to assist in hunting. If it was successful in the hunt, it was rewarded with a portion of the kill. Because the cheetah tires quickly, it was easy to recapture if it tried to escape. Tame cheetahs are usually playful and affectionate. The cheetah has also been the victim of excessive

The cheetah is the only living representative of its genus and is quite different from other cats. Because there are many characteristics found only in this cat, it has been assigned to its own subfamily: Acinonychinae. One of the most remarkable features of this animal is its ability to run at speeds of up to 70 miles (112 kilometers) per hour.

hunting. Its interestingly marked coat was popular with the fur trade, and it was often killed because of the danger it posed to livestock. Studies show that today there is an increasingly low level of genetic variation between cheetah individuals, and this may be very damaging to the species in the future. The lack of a sizable gene pool, both in the wild and in captivity, causes a number of problems—including high infant mortality rates, disease suscepti-

bility due to a weakened immune system, and difficulty in reproduction.

Humans and the cheetah

The cheetah appears to have a more difficult time adapting to the presence of humans than other cats do. As its natural habitat has become increasingly altered by the activities of people, the cheetah population has declined steadily. The Asiatic subspecies (*Acinonyx jubatus venaticus*) is now listed as critically endangered, although African populations are considered to be endangered. The Asiatic cheetah once ranged from southwest Asia to India, but it is now found only in Iran and Afghanistan where an estimated 200 individuals are thought to exist. In that country, the animal was believed to be extinct for decades, but was rediscovered there recently. In Iran, the cheetah once lived in grass and bush steppe areas, which are its preferred habitat; today, it has moved into mountainous regions in the southeastern part of the country, where it hunts wild sheep with much success.

In India, the cheetah became extinct when its principal source of food became more and more difficult to find. Some authorities believe, however, that the cheetah may never have been a native of India, but had been imported there from Africa. The number of individuals in Africa was estimated most recently at 9,000 to 12,000, with the largest populations believed to occur in the east African countries of Kenya and Tanzania and several countries in

The cheetah was once common over most of Africa and the near East into Indian and Iran, but today it is found only south of the Sahara desert in Africa and possibly in Iran. The cheetah in Africa is endangered, while the Asiatic cheetah is critically endangered.

southern Africa. A survey has been under way to better determine the cheetah's population numbers. The cheetah is protected throughout most of its range. It is also banned from international trade under CITES (Convention on International Trade in Endangered Species of Wild Fauna and Flora), although limited exports of hunting trophies are permitted from Namibia, Zambia and Zimbabwe, where populations are considered more stable. Cheetahs do not tend to do well in protected areas where other large predators like lions or hyenas exist because there is strong competition for prey. Because of this, many cheetahs live in unprotected areas. As more African land is used for agriculture, the cheetah has begun competing with man for food. In Namibia, 95 percent of the cheetahs live on private ranchland. Most livestock loss is blamed on the cat, and ranchers kill animals found on their land. They are only required to obtain a permit for killing a cheetah they have trapped. However, only a small percentage of cheetah deaths in this country

are due to human predation; most are from natural deaths like illness or broken legs, or attacks by other predators.

Today there are estimated to be more than 600 cheetahs in captivity, the great majority of which have been born while in captivity, according to the International Species Information System (ISIS). In addition, many cheetahs are held in zoos that do not register their collections with ISIS. The large number of captive-born cheetah has meant that the cheetah has become self-sustaining in captivity, although

safeguarding the wild population remains important.

In Namibia, nature conservation officials suggest there are large areas in the country that may in fact be suitable for cheetah reintroduction programs. These areas have few or no humans, few large predators, and plenty of prey—all requirements for a safe habitat. Although reintroduction programs have not been successful in the past, it is believed that a well-managed, long-term effort would produce better results.

Elizabeth Sirimarco

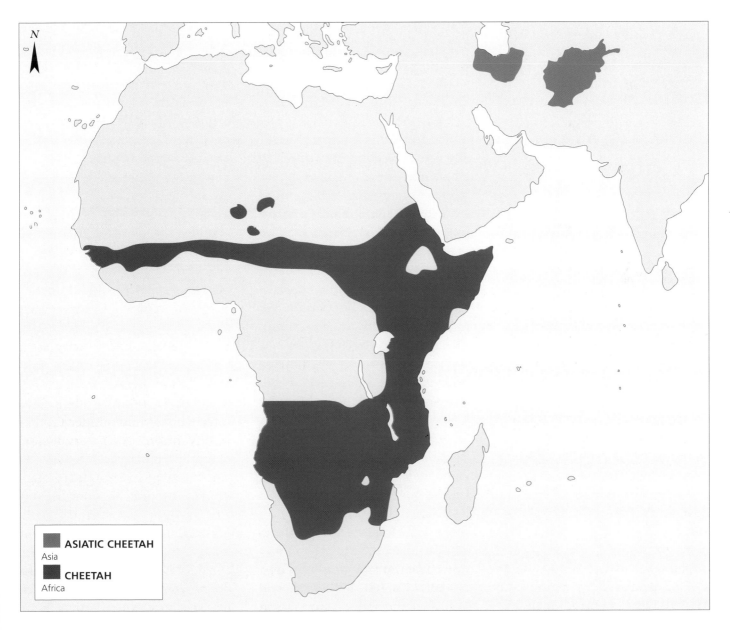

ASIATIC CHEETAH
Asia

CHEETAH
Africa

CHIMPANZEES

Class: Mammalia

Order: Primates

Family: Pongidae

The chimpanzees are part of the group known as the great apes—their closest relatives are the gorilla and the orangutan.

Their strong similarities to human beings have made the antics of these particular apes appealing to young and old. Chimps have been the subject of many scientific studies, and have been sent up in spacecraft to stand in for humans.

The common chimpanzee, (*Pan troglodytes*), is found in a wide variety of forest habitats stretching across Equatorial Africa and reaching as far south as Tanzania. The pygmy chimpanzee or bonobo (*Pan paniscus*), is limited to areas of tropical rain forest in the region bounded by the Zaire and Lualaba rivers in Zaire.

There are three subspecies of chimpanzee: the Western subspecies (*P. troglodytes verus*), the Central (*P. troglodytes troglodytes*), and the Eastern (*P. troglodytes schweinfurthi*). These three subspecies differ mainly in their complexion color. Experts do not agree about the proper classification of the pygmy chimpanzee. Some regard it as a subspecies, but most classify it as a separate species within the genus *Pan*. All chimpanzee populations are in jeopardy today, and chimps are no longer found in some countries that were once part of their range.

Common Chimpanzee

(Pan troglodytes)

ESA: Endangered

IUCN: Endangered

Weight: Males average 88 lb. (40 kg); females, 66 lb. (30 kg)

Length: Males, 30–36 in. (77–92 cm); females, 28–33 in. (70–85 cm)

Diet: Omnivorous

Gestation period: 203–244 days

Longevity: Unknown in the wild; up to 54 years in captivity

Habitat: Tropical forest, savannah woodlands

Range: Africa

THE LIFE CYCLE of the chimpanzee mirrors the human life cycle in many ways. For instance, males and females become sexually mature around the age of 13. The chimpanzee's brain is similar to ours and possesses high intellectual capacity. Chimps express a wide range of emotions that are similar to those of humans; they demonstrate unique problem-solving abilities. Several chimps have been taught successfully to use human sign language. Although their sensory abilities are similar to those of humans, their sense of smell is probably more highly developed than ours. The genetic similarity of humans and chimps has made chimps desirable as subjects for behavioral and biomedical research. Unfortunately, this is one reason for their decline in the wild.

In appearance, chimps have mainly black coats, with some white hairs on the muzzle. Their skin is light, and only the face is pigmented. Both sexes tend toward baldness. Their ears are noticeably large and protrude from the head. As with all great apes, chimps have no tail.

Tool makers and hunters

Although their thumbs are rather short, the chimpanzee has highly developed manual dexterity; they often make and use tools. Their behavior is also very adaptable. For example, in West Africa chimpanzees have been found using stones to crack nuts, while this behavior has never been observed in East Africa. In Tanzania's Gombe National Park, the famous naturalist Jane Goodall has seen chimpanzees poking grass stems into mounds to extract crunchy termites. They have also been seen rubbing leaves on their bodies to clean off dirt and blood. They may chew up leaves and wad them into a sort of sponge, which they insert into tree holes to soak up water. Stones and sticks are used as weapons, mainly in battles with baboons. It appears that small groups of chimpanzees will master a specific activity and their offspring will then imitate them.

Chimps are omnivorous. Their usual diet is fruit, but they also eat leaves, buds, seeds, pith, bark, insects, birds' eggs, fish, and meat. They spend up to seven hours a day feeding, and are particularly fond of ripening fruit. Chimps are, nonetheless, partial to meat. In the Gombe reserve, they form hunting parties of up to 30 adults and

The pygmy chimp is only slightly smaller than the common chimpanzee, but its head is more rounded and it is smaller, giving it a more juvenile appearance. This chimp is very agile and performs acrobatics in the trees.

Common chimpanzees are very similar to human beings in a number of ways: they display a wide range of emotions, have excellent problem-solving abilities, and similar physical traits.

juveniles that will hunt and kill baboons, young bush bucks, bush pigs, and their favorite target, red colobus monkeys. Cannibalism also occurs. It was once believed this only occurred when males snatched the infants of another community. However, Goodall has reported on three occasions that a female and her daughter seized and ate the infants of two other females within their own community.

Social behavior

Long-term field studies have shown that chimps are gregarious and highly social animals, but experts say their social groupings are "fluid" or flexible. Chimps live in communities ranging from 20 to over 100 animals. Within these communities, smaller parties consisting of two to ten animals constantly form and re-form as the animals travel in search of favorite foods. When food is scarce, individuals are often seen alone.

The strongest bonds are between mothers and their offspring. Infants are highly dependent upon their mothers for at least the first five years of life; they often maintain this relationship for many years after they are old enough to be self-reliant.

Males appear to be the most permanent members of a community, defending the group's territory against outside males. Upon reaching sexual maturity, however, females may transfer to a new community.

When a female is in estrus she often travels in the company of males and will mate frequently.

The similarities between chimps and humans becomes more obvious when watching the chimps' social behavior. Chimps have a rich system of communication based upon vocalizations, facial expressions, body postures, and gestures. When excited, chimps often perform dramatic displays, complete with screaming, shaking branches, scurrying up and down trees, slapping the ground, and drumming. They pant and hoot to make contact between distant groups or individuals, and they make loud high-pitched barks to issue a warning. Even their facial expressions can signal their emotional state. Adults appear to be grinning when they are frightened, and infants obviously pout when they cannot have their way. Chimps groom each other to reduce tension and satisfy the need for physical contact.

The threat

The common chimpanzee is becoming increasingly threatened in the wild. There is little survey data over much of the chimpanzee's range, making population estimates difficult. However, there are probably no more than 12,000 found in the western region and few of these are in protected areas. Chimpanzees are most common in central Africa, where perhaps 80,000 occur, chiefly in Gabon and Congo. In the eastern region, approximately 8,000 are known to occur outside Zaire and this subspecies of chimpanzees is considered severely threatened.

Chimpanzees once occupied an area about the size of the United States, but now they are under siege, living in shrinking patches of wilderness surrounded by farms and buildings. Although it is illegal to kill, capture, or sell chimps in most African countries, many orphaned baby chimps arrive on tourist beaches in Spain, where they are used by beach photographers as a prop.

Such baby chimps have become orphaned because their mothers were killed when the infants were captured. For every chimp alive in places such as Spain, ten will have died in the wild. The trade in chimpanzees is banned under the Convention on International Trade in Endangered Species of Wild Fauna and Flora (CITES). Sanctuaries in Gambia and Zambia care for chimps that are orphaned or confiscated

Chimps face three major threats: loss of their habitat, being hunted for their meat, and falling prey to poachers who sell them for use in biomedical research. If the chimpanzee is to escape endangerment in the 2000s, there must be better enforcement of anti-poaching laws and more protected areas.

Pygmy Chimpanzee

(Pan paniscus)

ESA: Endangered

IUCN: Endangered

Weight: Males average 86 lb. (39 kg); females, 68 lb. (31 kg)
Length: Males, 29–33 in. (73–83 cm); females, 28–30 in. (70–76 cm)
Diet: Omnivorous
Gestation period: 230–240 days
Longevity: Unknown
Habitat: Tropical rain forest
Range: Democratic Republic of Congo

THE PYGMY CHIMPANZEE is hardly smaller than its chimpanzee relatives, but its more rounded head and slighter build make it look more juvenile. The pygmy's build produces the illusion that it has longer arms. Pygmies are agile and acrobatic in trees, and can leap at heights that would terrify most humans.

The skin and coats of pygmy chimps are like those of the common chimpanzee—mostly black, with white hair on the muzzle, and light skin. Pygmy chimps will eat snakes, rodents, caterpillars, and sometimes crabs and fish.

Their social behavior differs from that of the common chimp. Females are usually sexually receptive, and females and males maintain a strong bond. Males often associate with their true brothers but will also spend time with other males. Pygmy chimps are less aggressive than are common chimps. Some experts believe that of all the primates, pygmy chimp society most closely resembles our own.

The problem

The pygmy chimp is threatened in the wild because of its low reproductive rate. Females are not sexually mature until age 13 and give birth every six years. With limited population and range, this low birth rate does not help their status in the wild.

The pygmy chimp is rare in captivity, and no successful breeding has taken place. Only 10,000 to 20,000 pygmy chimpanzees remain in the wild, compared to some 54,000 in the early 1970s. However, there is evidence of new populations in the southen part of this chimp's range. In Zaire, it is protected by law but enforcement is poor. Pygmy chimpanzees are hunted there for food to supply local labor forces. In some cases, this chimpanzee is hunted for medicinal purposes. Like the common chimp, international commercial trade is banned. Pygmy chimps are hunted for dietary and religious purposes, but the biggest factor in their demise is habitat destruction. Slash-and-burn agriculture and logging have consumed huge portions of their range. These chimps are protected by law, but the enforcement is poor. Pygmy chimpanzees are not known to exist in any African national park. The most urgently needed conservation measure is to establish a reserve in their natural habitat.

Sarah Dart

CHIMPANZEE
Africa

PYGMY CHIMPANZEE
Africa

CHUBS

Class: Actinoperygii

Order: Cypriniformes

Family: Cyprinidae

Chubs belong to a diverse family of fishes called Cyprinidae, which includes carps, minnows, shiners, daces, and others. Worldwide, there are over 1,500 species of Cyprinidae—50 kinds of chubs exist in North America alone. While chubs occupy many areas in the United States and North America, many of the endangered chubs are located in the western and central United States, where water projects have severely degraded habitat and diverted water for urban and agricultural use.

Chubs occupy a variety of habitats from small and clear slow-moving streams to large, rushing channels feeding mountain streams. Despite this difference they share a common need for a clean stream bottom of sand or gravel. Soil erosion and siltation caused by deforestation, agriculture, or other human pursuits, and water diversion and damming, have combined to jeopardize the existence of many chubs. Chubs vary widely in size from two inches to over 15 inches (5 to 38 centimeters). All fins lack true defensive spines, and they have no teeth. However, the inside of the mouth is partially lined with teeth-like structures called pharyngeal teeth, which help hold, crush, and swallow food.

All cyprinids, including chubs, have an internal organ called the Weberian apparatus. This is comprised of bones that connect the fish's gas bladder to its inner ear, and is responsible for their keen sense of hearing. The gas bladder helps regulate buoyancy.

Alvord Chub

(Gila alvordensis)

IUCN: Vulnerable

Length: Up to 5 in. (13 cm)
Reproduction: Egg layer
Habitat: Springs, streams, and ponds
Range: Oregon and Nevada

LIMITED TO A SMALL area called the Alvord Basin in southeastern Oregon and northwestern Nevada, the Alvord chub is a vulnerable chub. Luckily, much of its range lies inside the protection of the Sheldon National Wildlife Refuge in Nevada. If managed properly, this fish is not in immediate danger of extinction.

All of the collection sites for this versatile member of the Cyprinidae family fall within Sheldon Refuge's Virgin Creek drainage and the Trout Creek drainage in Oregon; these are the only year-round bodies of water in the area. Despite its shrunken range and low numbers, the Alvord chub is not fussy. It lives in springs, creeks, ponds, lakes, and reservoirs, and tolerates a wide range of water temperatures. It likes water depths from three inches (7.6 centimeters) to three feet (1 meter) over bottoms that vary from silt to gravel, and can live with or without vegetation. But the Alvord chub does have limits and will not inhabit water over 88 degrees Fahrenheit (31 Celsius).

The Alvord chub has gray-white coloration overall, with a darker back. This loner has a single dorsal fin on the back and a faint horizontal band on the sides, from the head to the end of the belly. The tail is somewhat forked and the lighter cheeks stand out against the darker gill covers. Not a long-lived fish, this chub probably endures for four or five years. During its life the Alvord chub eats primarily insects, but also consumes other small bottom-dwelling animals and microscopic zooplankton.

Both water and suitable habitat in this chub's range are scarce. Efforts to save this species must include maintaining the water levels in the streams and ponds in which it lives. It does not compete well with other fish, but it does tolerate rainbow trout, which is unusual because it is so much smaller than the trout and could easily become a meal for the larger fish.

Bonytail Chub

(Gila elegans)

ESA: Endangered

IUCN: Endangered

Length: 21½ in. (55 cm)
Reproduction: Egg layer
Habitat: Swift river currents and reservoirs
Range: Utah, Arizona, and Mexico

THIS LARGE RIVER fish is steadily losing ground to the forces of human alteration of habitat and increasing demands for water. Sightings are very rare. The bonytail chub used to inhabit rivers in Wyoming, Colorado, and New Mexico, but today the species is limited to Lake Mohave and Lake Havasu, and in the Colorado River from Lake Powell upstream to the Green River in Utah. It craves deep, fast-flowing water, a condition that is increasingly scarce in the western United States, but the remaining bonytails live in reservoirs and fish hatchery ponds.

Distinctive features

This unique-looking chub is large and reaches almost 2 feet (6 meters) in length. It is well suited for river life and has a pointed snout, broad body, and extremely narrow tail. The appearance of the tail is what gives it its name. Like its close cousin, the humpback chub, this chub has a distinctive hump on its neck, but it is less pronounced than the humpback's. The bonytail chub is a strong swimmer and it is aided by a highly forked and pointed tail fin, along with triangular-shaped body fins for low drag in fast water. This chub has a fairly uniform dark brown color on the back and sides and has a lighter to white belly. The body, tail, and gill covers are armored with scales for protection in the river environment.

The history of the Colorado River's use by people mirrors the history of this chub and other threatened Colorado River fishes. Before numerous dams were built on the main stem of the river and its tributaries, the river flow and temperature varied according to the seasons. Winter and spring brought high flows

and low temperatures, while in summer and fall the river environment reflected the higher temperatures and lower rainfall of the seasons. It carried tons of sediment regardless of the time of year, and was always a murky reddish color. The bonytail chub and 15 other native fish evolved under these conditions.

The 1930s ushered in an era that forever changed the face of the river. Huge hydroelectric, irrigation, and flood control dams such as Hoover Dam, Glen Canyon Dam, and Parker Dam dramatically changed the way water flowed into the river. This severely affected the habitat of all river fishes, inundating hundreds of miles of prime breeding and feeding areas. River water behind the dams became clear and cold all year; flood cycles were disrupted and environmental cues to trigger spawning vanished in many stretches of the river. Loss of water to evaporation and diversion for irrigation compounded changes to the river. Also, deforestation and overgrazing by cattle led to runoff, the lowering of water tables, and the deterioration of water quality.

As a final insult, officials decided to eliminate "trash fish" from many of the newly formed reservoirs and restock them with non-native trout and other game fish. Hundreds of gallons of powerful poisons were dumped into the river, killing all of the fish in the treatment areas.

The bonytail chub breeds in reservoirs and, probably, in quieter river pool areas, but the breeding success rate and total numbers of the chub are continuing to decrease. It will not spawn in water below 65 degrees Fahrenheit (18 Celsius), a fact that is most probably contributing to its decline. The chronically cold outfall from dams renders much of its previous spawning grounds unusable.

Efforts to restore bonytail chub numbers are at present underway. Fish culturists are raising this fish at Dexter National Fish Hatchery in New Mexico and plan to reintroduce them into the upper Colorado River in Arizona.

The bonytail chub lives in swift flowing water. Adaptations that help it survive in this habitat include a highly forked and pointed tail fin, along with triangular-shaped body fins for low drag in fast water.

Borax Lake Chub

(Gila boraxobius)

ESA: Endangered

IUCN: Vulnerable

Length: 2½ in. (6 cm)
Reproduction: Egg layer
Habitat: Pools and outflows
Range: Borax Lake, Oregon

The Borax Lake chub is restricted to a single lake in the Alvord Basin of Oregon. It is the only fish inhabitant of that lake.

THIS LONER RELIES on the geothermal nature of Borax Lake; hot springs keep the lake and surrounding pools at balmy temperatures of between 63 and 90 degrees Fahrenheit (17 to 32 Celsius) throughout the year. This is one of the few fish in North America that can tolerate these warm water temperatures. Because the Borax Lake chub is adapted to this particular environment, transferring some of the fish to other lakes as a means of increasing its range would be very difficult, if not impossible. Unfortunately, the only suitable home for this chub has been threatened by human exploitation of the natural resources. As a result, several geothermal pool sites next to the lake have dried up, and fish have been lost. However, progress to save this fish is being made. A legal ruling now prohibits development that would disturb the geothermal environment within a 1-mile (1.6-kilometer) radius around the lake. The Nature Conservancy has acquired a 10-year lease to a 0.25-square mile (65-hectare) parcel of private land that includes portions of Borax Lake. In addition, the entire

1-square mile (260-hectare) area is designated as critical habitat by the United States federal government, which affords further protection for this species.

This small, attractive chub has olive-green and silvery-purple coloration over most of its body, while the belly is silvery white. It has a bold stripe down the length of its back and narrower stripes down each side. The fins are clear with some pigmentation of the dorsal fin on the back and on the forked tail fin. The Borax Lake chub has a large head and a plump belly, but then the body and tail are streamlined behind the belly. This fish has many scales embedded into the skin.

This chub eats a wide variety of foods including insects and their larvae, algae, and microscopic animals. The tastes of the Borax Lake chub change according to the seasons and the abundance of the food. With little competition, this chub has learned to eat many foods.

Early spring usually brings on the breeding season, but curiously, mature eggs have been found in females from September to January, which shows that they can spawn almost any time of the year. This trait is very uncommon in North American fishes; preserving this species will give scientists the opportunity to understand it better.

Charalito (Chihuahua) Chub)

(Gila nigrescens)

ESA: Threatened

IUCN: Critically endangered

Length: 8 in. (20 cm)
Reproduction: Egg layer
Habitat: Pools of small streams
Range: New Mexico and Chihuahua, Mexico

MOST COMMONLY CALLED the Chihuahua chub in the United States, this rare fish is found only in the small Mimbres River of southwestern New Mexico and the Guzman basin in Chihuahua, Mexico. Loss of habitat seems to be the primary reason for the decline of this fish. Poorly thought-out flood control activities, such as construction of levees and alteration of river banks, destroy areas that this and many other fish need for survival. Much of the flow in the Mimbres River is diverted by nearby landowners for use in agriculture and ranching. These changes can be very destructive, stripping vegetation and exposing soil to erosion. This leads to more flooding and encourages more stream modification to prevent it. This vicious cycle has nearly wiped out this vulnerable chub in New Mexico and Chihuahua.

New sighting

Until 1975, scientists thought the Chihuahua chub was extinct in the United States. However, during a summer project with the Endangered Species program, a high school teacher named Bill Rogers found a population of Chihuahua chubs in the Mimbres River. Amazingly, the last recorded find of Chihuahua chubs was sighted in 1853.

This fish is a medium-sized chub with a slender body and pointed head ideal for gliding through river currents. The back and sides are an attractive silvery green and the belly is tan and white. Mild green stripes run from just behind the gills to the end of the belly. The fins vary in shape from triangular to oval and the tail fin is forked and blunt. The male Chihuahua chub has longer pectoral fins (just behind the gills) than the female, but both sexes become a more distinctive red-orange color during courtship and spawning. Because of their choice of habitat, Chihuahua chubs are very susceptible to changes in stream banks and water flow.

They rely on deep pools and undercut banks on the outer edges of river bends to offer them some protection.

When banks are modified for flood control, undercuts are the first features to go. Water diversions turn what were deep pools into shallow puddles.

This chub is also up against competition from the introduction of foreign invaders such as rainbow trout, largemouth bass, and longfin dace. Trout and bass are both competitors and potential predators.

The Chihuahua chub was thought extinct in the United States until 1975 when a population was found in the Mimbres River. The last recorded sighting had been 122 years earlier.

Charalito Saltillo (Humpback Chub)

(Gila cypha)

ESA: Endangered

IUCN: Vulnerable

Length: 12½ in. (32 cm)
Reproduction: Egg layer
Habitat: Deep water canyon areas and pools
Range: Colorado, Utah, and Arizona

THE HUMPBACK CHUB inhabits the Colorado River system across three states. Despite this seemingly vast range, this abused fish is in extreme peril of extinction. Its problems stem from the changes that humans brought to its habitat.

Once the flow and temperature of the Colorado River varied according to the seasons. Winter and spring brought high flows and low temperatures, while in summer and fall the river had higher temperatures and its levels fell because of less rainfall. It carried tons of sediment regardless of the time of year and was always a murky reddish color. The humpback chub and 15 other native fish inhabitants of the Colorado River evolved under these conditions.

With the 1930s came the building of massive dams for irrigation, flood control, and the generation of hydroelectric power. Hoover Dam is probably the most famous. These dams inundated hundreds of miles of prime breeding and feeding areas. River water behind the dams became clear and cold all year, flood cycles were disrupted, and without those environmental cues, spawning suffered.

Many non-native trout and other game fish were added to the river to eliminate so-called "trashfish" from many of the newly formed reservoirs. Hundreds of gallons of powerful poisons were dumped into the river, killing any and all fish in the treatment areas.

Once distributed throughout the Colorado River basin, the humpback chub is now restricted to isolated populations. Blocked by Hoover Dam, this species is no longer found below the dam along the border of Arizona and California. A population persists in the Grand Canyon between the Hoover and Glen Canyon dams. The Green River in Utah, a major tributary of the Colorado, holds several populations. Humpback chubs used to inhabit the Green River as far north as Wyoming until the Flaming Gorge Reservoir was constructed and all fish were poisoned. The

The humpback chub has a vast range, but this has not saved it from being an extremely endangered species.

Yampa River in Colorado, a tributary of the Green River, also holds small populations.

The main stem of the Colorado River at the Utah-Colorado border generally marks the eastern limit of their range. However, occasionally fish move farther upstream as far east as Palisades, Colorado.

The humpback chub is appropriately named and is supremely designed for life in a large river system like the Colorado. Fisheries scientists believe that the prominent hump just behind the head acts like a keel and improves the fish's stability in swift currents. The distinctive forked tail fin, slender tail, pointy snout, and triangular body fins all aid in streamlining the humpback chub to minimize the effort needed to swim.

This chub has a plain pattern of coloration changing gradually from olive green on the back to white on the belly, and the fins are white or clear. The eyes are

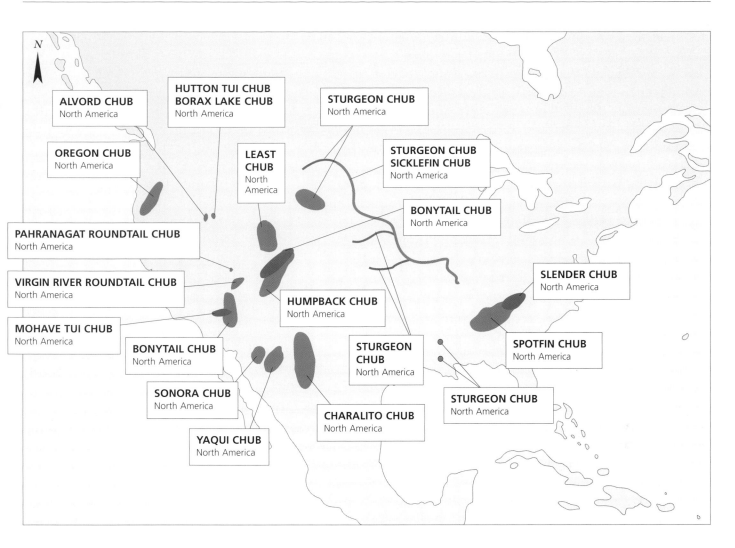

small but taste and smell are probably well developed, traits that are not unusual for fishes of the cloudy Colorado River. The humpback chub population in the Grand Canyon spawns in May and June in the Little Colorado River of Arizona. Because of colder water temperatures, Green River fish breed a bit later in June and July. Both sexes develop breeding colors; males turn red-orange on the sides and the cheeks turn bright yellow. Females sport a light orange color on the sides and at the base of the anal fin.

Recovery teams are trying to maintain five populations of humpback chub throughout the Colorado River system. Given the continued pressures of water use, alteration of habitat by dams, and competition from non-native fishes, prospects for a recovery are in doubt.

Least Chub

(Iotichthys phlegethontis)

IUCN: Vulnerable

Length: 2 in. (5 cm)
Reproduction: Egg layer
Habitat: Dense vegetation over lake or river mud
Range: Bonneville basin, Utah

THE LEAST CHUB is under attack from many different sources, and they are all contributing to the decline in numbers of this fish. It is a tasty food item for birds, mammals, and amphibians and, when present in large numbers, is preyed on by other fish. This fish's habitat is threatened by decreasing water tables and live-stock pollution. Its home is drying up and being poisoned.

The most difficult problem is that least chubs are breeding with other species such as the Utah chub and speckled dace—a genetic threat that dilutes the genes of the existing populations and could lead to extinction.

Desert dweller

This small chub makes its home in Utah. It used to be found throughout the Bonneville basin of northwestern Utah but now can be located only in springs of Snake Valley, particularly Leland Harris Spring, in the western part of the state. Introduced gamefish, other chubs, and bullfrogs are steadily eating the remaining populations. Gulls and ducks eat their share as well, but predation by native animals was always natural—it is the predation by non-native species which is new and adding the pressure.

This short-lived and slow-growing desert dweller is brightly colored; the male is olive-green on the back and silvery blue on the sides, separated by a gold horizontal stripe. In some males a second gold-red stripe below the first starts at the base of the pectoral fins just behind the gills and runs to the anal fin. Topping off the well-dressed look of the male least chub are amber-yellow fins from head to tail. The female is not nearly so spectacular and settles for pale olive on the back, silver on the sides and belly, and pale white fins.

Least chubs consume copious amounts of algae and some insects and other small invertebrate animals. They breed in the spring after their first year of life in mats of algae and other vegetation. Their eggs take only two days to hatch after they sink and stick to whatever they touch. After hatching, young fry live on their yolk for several days and then begin to feed.

Least chubs today live in Leland Harris Spring but also will inhabit gentle rivers, creeks, ponds, and swamps. They tolerate alkaline water quite well and look for areas with a clay, mud, or peat bottom. Unfortunately, floating peat in the Leland Harris Spring is particularly attractive

and inviting to cattle, and as they try to walk out onto the mats for a drink, they often fall into deep unseen pools and drown.

The U.S. Bureau of Land Management controls the land occupied by the least chub and has tried to minimize damage to their remaining populations. Only time will tell if their efforts are successful.

Oregon Chub
(Oregonichthys crameri)

ESA: Endangered

IUCN: Vulnerable

Length: 2 in. (5 cm)
Reproduction: Egg layer
Habitat: River pools
Range: Oregon

THIS SMALL CHUB is restricted to the Willamette River of Oregon and is only one of two members of this genus. The Umpqua chub, a fish that occupies the Oregon's Umpqua River, used to be called the Oregon chub as well but scientists recently gave it status as a separate species.

A moderate-current river fish, the Oregon chub, like its relative the slender chub (also threatened), depends on its sight to find and catch food items. Intense logging and the increased soil erosion that results from these practices may be contributing to the decline of this fish. As trees are stripped from large clear-cut areas, soil is more easily washed into rivers. The increased cloudiness (called turbidity) of

the water and accumulation of silt on the bottom makes the Oregon chub's search for insects and small river animals increasingly difficult.

The Oregon chub has an odd-looking, highly scaled body similar to that of the larger bony-tail chub. The rather plump belly section is offset by the slender, narrow tail. It has a highly forked tail characteristic of strong swimmers. This chub is usually found over rubble and large gravel and among vegetation used for cover. Some food items tend to congregate in these aquatic plants. The Oregon chub breeds in early spring in still water. Little else is known about its habits.

Once abundant in the Willamette River system, the status of this fish is now vulnerable. As logging intensifies and soil erosion continues, this species could be in even greater jeopardy in the future.

Pahranagat Roundtail Chub
(Gila robusta jordani)

ESA: Endangered

Length: 6 in. (16 cm)
Reproduction: Egg layer
Habitat: Spring pool
Range: Ash Springs, Nevada

NO FISH LIVING in the Great Basin of the western United States is as endangered as the Pahranagat roundtail chub. Only a few dozen adult fish remain in existence at one small, isolated site: Ash Springs in eastern Nevada. This rare chub is one of four subspecies of the roundtail chub; its very close relative, the Virgin River chub (*Gila robusta seminuda*), is also endangered.

Foreign invaders, disease, and predators have all been responsible for the decline of this fish.

The Oriental snail was introduced into Ash Springs and has had a devastating impact on this chub by bringing in parasites. Non-native speckled dace compete for food and habitat. Birds feed on the Pahranagat roundtail chub and, unfortunately, this fish is susceptible to capture by hook and line. Because there are so few left, however, capturing or harassing this fish is not allowed. The limited space and food in their isolated spring mean there is little opportunity for growth in numbers or expansion of range.

Ash Springs is only 16-feet long by 10-feet wide and 8-feet deep (5 by 3 by 2.5 meters). It flows into the White River but is quite a bit higher in elevation than the river itself. This chub seeks pools and slow-moving water, and shallow rapids and falls prevent movement to the river. This subspecies hides in undercuts in the pool and stream areas of the spring.

The Pahranagat roundtail chub consumes algae almost exclusively. When offered insects, the fish refused to eat. Some scientists believe, however, that small fishes also are a part of its diet. Living three to five years, this chub spawns in February and March in the stream sections of the spring.

Water temperatures in the spring are coolest during this time of year and may be most suitable for reproduction. Adult fish are blotchy over the back and sides and sport olive-green background coloration.

This stocky fish has a narrow and long snout, a narrow tail, and the back is slightly humped.

Virgin River Roundtail Chub

(Gila robusta seminuda)

ESA: Endangered

Length: 12 in. (30 cm)
Reproduction: Egg layer
Habitat: River undercuts and boulders
Range: Virgin River of Utah, Arizona, and Nevada

THIS CLOSE RELATIVE of the Pahranagat roundtail chub (and subspecies of the more common roundtail chub) used to be found throughout the lower reaches of the Colorado River's tributary, the Virgin River, in Utah, Arizona, and Nevada.

When the Hoover Dam was built in the 1930s forming Lake Mead, the mouth and much of the Virgin River was flooded by the new reservoir. Now this fish is confined to a much smaller stretch of the Virgin River and is blocked by Lake Mead from entering the main stem of the Colorado River.

Swift, murky water

Technically, this fish could swim across the reservoir to reach the middle section of the Colorado. But the Virgin River roundtail chub will only tolerate swift, murky river water; the clear and calm waters of Lake Mead are no place for this river fish. Once again, human intervention has led to a severe reduction in the range of a native fish and has put the Virgin River roundtail chub in peril of extinction and on the list of endangered fishes.

While it is known that the Virgin River roundtail chub is an isolated subspecies of the roundtail chub (*Gila robusta*), some biologists say that its physical characteristics resemble those of both the roundtail chub and the bonytail chub (*Gila elegans*). Like the bonytail, the Virgin River roundtail chub is relatively large and streamlined with triangular body fins that cause less drag in river currents.

The roundtail chub has a bulbous belly and a narrow tail with a deeply forked tail fin. The Virgin River roundtail chub is well scaled for protection from abrasion in fast flowing water. It has a glowing silvery appearance overall with little other coloration. The base of the fins are mildly yellow and the dorsal fin is somewhat darkened.

Varied diet

The Virgin River roundtail chub eats insects, some vegetation, and other smaller fish when available.

This chub spawns in the spring and seeks cover in rivers from undercut banks, boulders, and other large objects.

If this subspecies is to survive, care must be taken to prevent destruction of its remaining habitat on the Virgin River and prevent further loss of the enduring populations to pollution or other similar catastrophes.

Sicklefin Chub

(Macrhybopsis meeki)

IUCN: Lower risk

Length: 3½ in. (9 cm)
Reproduction: Egg layer
Habitat: Murky stream over sand
Range: Missouri and Mississippi Rivers

THIS RIVER FISH is ideally designed for life in large and murky, fast-flowing streams and is found only in the main channels of the Missouri and Mississippi Rivers. While not immediately threatened with extinction, the reproductive and feeding habitat of the sicklefin chub has been systematically destroyed. Two factors, siltation and the construction of dams, have led to this decline.

Dam problems

The sicklefin chub has a decided preference for clean gravel or sand in which to spawn and feed. Siltation resulting from deforestation and soil erosion has ruined many of this chub's preferred areas and forced the remaining populations into smaller and smaller stretches of river. Construction of dams have not only turned many segments of the Missouri and Mississippi Rivers into large reservoirs, but they have changed the nature of the rivers downstream. Dams cause material suspended in the water to settle, effecting the water quality below dam outlets, and drastically alters the normal seasonal changes in water flow.

Feeding habits

As with most river fishes, the sicklefin chub is slender and streamlined in shape. It has small eyes that are partially covered by skin to protect them from the abrasive, silty current and relies more on taste than sight to find and discriminate between various food items. The small whiskerlike barbels on the mouth are packed with sensors and used for that purpose. Additionally, the sicklefin chub has numerous taste buds on its skin to help in its searches. Food preferences of this fish are not known but it is a bottom feeder that locates its food by taste. Small bottom-dwelling insects and other invertebrates probably are its foods of choice.

The name "sicklefin" comes from the shape of its pectoral fins just behind the gills. They are unusually long and slender, and are used to maneuver in swift currents. All body fins are triangular in shape to reduce drag and the tail fin is deeply forked for efficient swimming. This chub overall is lightly colored with a yellow-brown and silvery back and silvery-white lower sides and belly. The sicklefin chub breeds in the spring but unlike many fishes, skin coloration of either sex does not change during the breeding season.

Seasonal dilemma

During the summer, water that is normally warm and muddy becomes clear and cold as water from below the surface of the reservoir is released. The sicklefin chub, because it has adapted to different conditions, is forced to avoid these areas. River management policies that are sensitive to the needs of river fishes like the sicklefin chub could halt further destruction of habitat and aid the recovery of this important species of fishes.

Slender Chub

(Erimystax cahni)

ESA: Threatened

IUCN: Vulnerable

Length: 3 in. (8 cm)
Reproduction: Egg layer
Habitat: Warm river currents over fine gravel
Range: Tennessee

A VICTIM OF THE coal industry, water development projects, and deforestation, the slender chub is struggling to cope with a world of pollution and altered habitat within its native river system. A major industry in eastern Tennessee, the home of the slender chub, is coal mining. Acid runoff into the Clinch and Powell Rivers from these mining operations, and increased levels of sedimentation, are forcing this chub into an ever-smaller range. Dams and other similar water projects also are undermining the slender chub's ability to inhabit unpolluted areas.

When a dam is constructed on a river and a reservoir is formed behind the dam, water at the bottom of the reservoir is colder than water at the surface. Often only the frigid water at the bottom is allowed to flow downstream. For the slender chub, a fish that prefers the warmer waters of an unob-

Sonora Chub (Charalito Sonorense)

(Gila ditaenia)

ESA: Threatened

IUCN: Vulnerable

Length: 5 in. (13 cm)
Reproduction: Egg layer
Habitat: River pools and headsprings
Range: Arizona and Sonora, Mexico

structed river, the construction of dams and the release of cold water is truly detrimental to their continued survival.

Deforestation for lumber and agriculture adds another problem. When trees are removed from hillsides, the soil on those hills becomes less stable and eventually erodes into nearby streams. These sediments reduce water clarity and therefore the ability of visual-feeding fish, including the slender chub, to find food. More importantly, sediments fill and destroy clean gravel areas used by the slender chub for breeding. This fish is currently known only from the Clinch and Powell Rivers in northeastern Tennessee. No population estimates are available.

This small fish lives up to its common name: slender. Its sleek, streamlined body has a pointed snout, large eyes, and a well-scaled body to prevent abrasion in the river environment. Body coloration is olive on the back and cream on the underside with silvery sides; thin dark stripes run from just behind the head to the base of the blunt, forked tail. The

The slender chub lives in Tennessee, where a great deal of coal mining takes place. This industry changes the water habitat of the chub. Because of this, the slender chub's range is continually decreasing in size.

clear body fins are triangular in shape and several spots mark the base of the tail fin.

The slender chub feeds on insects and small mollusks like snails, and will occasionally consume small freshwater clams. This chub is a May spawner that seeks very small gravel in which to lay its eggs.

The slender chub begins breeding during its second year of life. Most slender chubs live about four years.

Slowing the decline

The destruction of slender chub habitat could be slowed by the use of environmentally sensitive mining techniques and the maintenance of buffer zones between mining and lumber operations and nearby streams.

These changes would increase the cost of mining, but would have the benefit of saving the slender chub from extinction.

TRULY A DESERT fish, the Sonora chub occupies small streams of the Sonoran Desert in southern Arizona and northern Mexico. In Arizona, the only population can be found in Sycamore Canyon downstream from a small spring. Farther south in Mexico, the Sonora chub tends to be more numerous and grows to a larger size. As is the case with most endangered fishes, destruction of habitat and introduction of non-native fishes threaten the Sonora chub. Also, this chub has a relatively small range and for these reasons is considered threatened by extinction.

Ironically, the Sonora chub is part of a very diverse, rich biological community. Many plants and animals that are otherwise rare or not found in other parts of the United States and Mexico can be found fairly routinely in the Sycamore Canyon system.

The Sonora chub is well adapted to its environment and has developed traits to deal with the heat and lack of water. Dur-

The Sonora chub is supremely adapted to its habitat in the deserts of Arizona and Mexico. This fish has been known to survive in little more than a trickle of water during times of drought.

ing times of drought, it moves to areas of shade in deeper stream pools and under stream banks to wait out the hot and dry weather.

The Sonora chub is a tenacious fish, and in extreme cases has been found in little more than a trickle of water. Its ability to withstand severe temperature swings is truly amazing. Curiously, researchers have found that after a drought subsides and water is once again more plentiful within the stream, the Sonora chub is reluctant to leave these protected areas for other acceptable areas. Because of this reluctance, those looking for the Sonora chub have been led to the conclusion that the fish was extinct in that location.

The Sonora chub is an attractive fish that can vary in size from 5 to 10 inches (13 to 25 centimeters). It has triangular body fins and a fork-shaped tail fin. This chub has an olive-brown back that lightens to a greenish cream on the belly. Each side is marked with a thin, iridescent yellow stripe between two darker and wider stripes that run from just behind the head to the base of the tail; the base is marked by a subtle dark spot. During breeding season in early spring the base of the fins, except the dorsal fin and the tail fin, become red and the belly produces an orange cast in both sexes.

Favorite foods

The favorite foods of the Sonora chub are insects and algae, but they will take advantage of opportunities to consume other available food items.

Spotfin Chub

(Cyprinella monacha)

ESA: Threatened

IUCN: Lower risk

Length: 3½ in. (9 cm)
Reproduction: Egg layer
Habitat: River current over silt
Range: Alabama, Georgia, North Carolina, Tennessee, Virginia

LOCATED PRIMARILY in Tennessee, the spotfin chub is under assault from the same enemies as the slender chub. A victim of the coal industry, water development projects, pollution from local communities, and deforestation, the spotfin chub is struggling to cope with an altered habitat. A major industry in eastern Tennessee and western North Carolina is coal mining. Although this chub prefers medium to large-size rivers, acid runoff from mining operations and increased levels of sedimentation are forcing the spotfin chub into an ever-smaller range. Dams and other water projects are also undermining the spotfin chub's ability to find unpolluted areas. When a dam is constructed on a river and a reservoir is formed behind the dam, water at the bottom of the reservoir is colder than water at the surface. In many situations, only the frigid water at the bottom flows downstream. For the spotfin chub, a fish that prefers the warmer waters of a flowing, unobstructed river, the construction of dams and the release of cold water can be extremely detrimental to its survival.

Deforestation for lumber and agriculture adds a third dimension to the picture. When trees are removed from hillsides, the soil on those hills becomes less stable and eventually erodes into nearby streams.

These sediments reduce water clarity and the ability of all visual-feeding fish, including the spotfin chub, to find food. More importantly, sediments fill and destroy clean gravel used by the spotfin chub for breeding.

Rescue strategies

The destruction of the chub's habitat could be slowed by using environmentally sensitive mining techniques and the maintenance of buffer zones between mining and lumber operations and nearby streams. These changes would increase the cost of coal mining but may well save this chub from extinction.

The spotfin chub is named for the spot at the base of the dorsal fin on the back and on its tail. Slightly larger than its neighbor the slender chub, the spotfin chub is even more narrow and streamlined in appearance. The sleek body has a green back and silvery sides and belly. Mature males are more spectacular and sport a brilliant turquoise-blue on the back and sides. Triangular body fins and a forked tail fin reduce drag and aid swimming in the river currents. The purpose of the enlarged anal fin is to help keep the spotfin chub in a slight head-down position as it swims in search of bottom-dwelling insect larvae.

The spotfin chub probably spawns from late May to early July after its first full year of life. Its lifespan is about four years.

Sturgeon Chub

(Macrhybopsis gelida)

IUCN: Vulnerable

Length: Less than 1 in. (2 cm)
Reproduction: Egg layer
Habitat: Murky river shallows over gravel
Range: Missouri River basin and lower Mississippi River

THIS RIVER FISH is ideally adapted for life in large and murky fast-flowing streams, and is found primarily in the main channels of the Missouri River and its principal tributaries. It is also found in the main channel of the lower Mississippi River in Mississippi and Louisiana, and some can be found in streams in northeastern Wyoming.

While not immediately threatened with extinction, the feeding habitat of the sturgeon chub has been systematically destroyed and the fish is now in even greater danger than its neighbor the sicklefin chub.

Ruin of habitat

Two factors, siltation and the construction of dams, have led to this decline. The sturgeon chub has a decided preference for clean gravel or sand in which to spawn and feed. Siltation resulting from deforestation and soil erosion has ruined many of this chub's preferred areas and forced the remaining populations into smaller and smaller stretches of river. Construction of dams has not only turned many segments of the Missouri and Mississippi Rivers into large reservoirs, but has changed the nature of the rivers downstream. Dams cause suspended material to settle, significantly change water quality below dam outlets, and drastically alter normal seasonal changes in water flow.

Keeled scales

As with most river fishes, the sturgeon chub is slender and streamlined in shape. Its body scales on the back and sides each carry a small projection called a keel. The purpose of the keels is not specifically known but they may help the sturgeon chub orient itself in the river current. The body is covered generously with taste buds to locate food, the eyes are small and of relatively little use in the murky water, and the

The spotfin chub is named for the spot at the base of its dorsal fin on the back and on its tail.

snout is long and flat to reduce drag in currents. The light brown back is covered with dark spots, the sides are silvery, and the belly is silvery-white. The lower lobe of the deeply-forked tail fin is darker than the upper lobe and the body fins are triangular in shape. Neither sex develops brightened or changed breeding coloration but the male does produce nodule-like tubercles on its pectoral fins just behind the gills. Little is known about the daily feeding habits or breeding requirements of this increasingly rare fish.

Recovery measures

Better river management policies that are sensitive to the needs of river fishes such as the sturgeon chub are the only way forward to halt further destruction of habitat and aid the recovery of this important species of river fish.

Hutton Tui Chub

(Gila bicolor ssp.)

| ESA: Threatened |

Length: 13 in. (33 cm)
Reproduction: Egg layer
Habitat: Slow-moving water near vegetation
Range: Oregon

THE VARIOUS SUBSPECIES of tui chub (*Gila bicolor*) cover a broad area of the western United States, including large areas of Oregon, California, Nevada, and parts of Idaho. Until recently this prolific and adaptable fish had thrived well and occupied territory in a wide variety of habitats and climates.

Several distinct subspecies, however, are restricted to limited areas of desert basins where the removal of water for irrigation threatens their continued survival. The Hutton tui chub is one

of those desert subspecies that is threatened in this way.

The Hutton tui chub is a fairly chunky fish with large scales covering most of the body. Body coloration varies from dark olive or brown on the back to white or silvery on the belly, breast, and throat. Few if any spots or blotches mark the body. The fins are rounded and the tail is blunt but deeply forked.

In older fish a hump may form behind the head but this is much less pronounced than the much more prominent hump of their cousins, the humpback chub and the bonytail chub.

Not finicky

The Hutton tui chub is not a discriminate eater and will eat whatever is available and appropriately sized. It prefers insects that live on the river bottom or among aquatic plants.

This chub spawns from late April to late June over gravel and sand in shallow water. The eggs hatch after slightly more than a week. Newly hatched fish will start to feed on floating plankton and organic material.

Difficult choice

As a whole, the tui chub is not considered either a threatened or endangered species. However, several of the subspecies, including the Hutton tui chub, are in danger of extinction.

As is the case with many fishes, an unfortunate choice must be made between adequate water supply for a vulnerable species and the needs of people.

Mohave Tui Chub

(Gila bicolor mohavensis)

ESA: Endangered

Length: 13 in. (33 cm)
Reproduction: Egg layer
Habitat: Slow-moving river areas near vegetation
Range: Mojave River, California

THE MOHAVE TUI chub is another desert subspecies of the tui chub (*Gila bicolor*). The appearance and feeding habits of the Mohave tui chub are similar to those of the Hutton tui chub. The tui chub is not an endangered species, although several of the subspecies are threatened with extinction, and one of these is the Mohave tui subspecies.

A troubled habitat

The Mohave variety is threatened by loss of habitat and invasion by more aggressive invaders like the common carp into its range. Despite the high reproductive rate of this fish and other factors that originally helped to establish the Mohave tui chub within its range, it simply cannot compete with such formidable opponents.

The sole remaining natural range for this chub is the Mojave River in southern California. As with other rivers, the Mojave River is under assault by people's requirement for water, and as a receptacle for the industrial, agricultural, and residential wastes that they produce.

Greater threat

However, the greatest threat to the continued existence of the Mohave tui chub is the arroyo chub, a non-native species introduced to the Mojave River.

The arroyo chub and Mohave tui chub readily cross-breed to create a hybrid, lessening the numbers of purebred species. Fortunately, concerned experts recognized the problem and transplanted some purebred Mohave tui to other isolated locations within southern California and to an area near Warm Springs Resort. Because of the efforts of these individuals and some added protection due to state and federal law, the Mohave tui chub has at least a fighting chance for recovery.

Owens Tui Chub

(Gila bicolor snyderi)

ESA: Endangered

Length: 13 in. (33 cm)
Reproduction: Egg layer
Habitat: Slow moving river areas near vegetation
Range: Owens River, California

UNTIL RECENTLY THE Owens tui chub was a prolific and adaptable fish. Removing water for irrigation threatens its survival.

The sole remaining natural range for this chub is the Owens River in eastern California. As with other rivers, the Owens River is used by people for drinking, irrigation, and as an

The tui chub is a species with many subspecies. It inhabits a broad area of the western United States, including large areas of Oregon, California, Nevada, and Idaho.

unfortunate receiver of the wastes they produce. A diversion of water from the Owens River to the Los Angeles area has drastically changed the habitat of the river; many formerly acceptable areas are gone, are occupied by more aggressive non-native species, or are now unacceptable.

Cross-breeding threat

Like the Mohave tui chub, the Owens tui chub is also threatened by cross-breeding. Another introduced tui chub subspecies, *Gila bicolor obesa*, interbred with a population in Crowley Lake near the Owens River. As a result, that population was lost. Despite its high reproductive rate, this tui chub cannot survive with these forces at work.

The Owens tui chub is a fairly chunky fish with large scales covering most of the body. Body coloration varies from dark olive or brown on the back to white or silvery on the belly, breast, and throat. The fins are rounded and the tail is blunt but deeply forked. As with the Hutton tui chub, older fish may have a hump behind the head that is less pronounced than that of the humpback chub and bonytail chub.

Omnivorous feeder

The Owens tui chub is an opportunistic feeder and will eat whatever is available.

This fish prefers insects that live either on the bottom of the river, or among aquatic plants. Spawning takes place from late April to late June, and the Owens tui chub distributes its eggs over gravel and sand in shallow water. The sticky eggs cling to leaves or the bottom, and then hatch out about a week later.

Yaqui Chub
(Gila purpurea)

ESA: Endangered

IUCN: Vulnerable

Length: 4 in. (10 cm)
Reproduction: Egg layer
Habitat: Stream pools and vegetation
Range: Arizona and Sonora, Mexico

NAMED AFTER THE Rio Yaqui basin which it inhabits, the range of the Yaqui chub (like the Sonora chub) barely penetrates into the United States. This fish is restricted to the southeastern corner of Arizona in a stream called Leslie Creek and the San Bernardino National Wildlife Refuge. The Yaqui chub once occupied other nearby areas but those populations have been lost.

The principal threats to the Yaqui chub are destruction of habitat by people and livestock, and the introduction of predatory, non-native fishes. Because it is beyond the reach of most efforts in the United States to save this species, the Yaqui chub must rely on the efforts of the Mexican government and also on international environmental organizations to maintain its remaining habitat, and to reverse the insults of the past.

Compared to its neighbor and relative the Sonora chub, the Yaqui chub is quite plain in appearance. The female has an overall yellow-brown appearance but is somewhat lighter on the underside. The flashier male is a silvery steel blue throughout much of the year. The faint horizontal stripe on each side is difficult to see near the head but sharpens and darkens slightly toward the tail. The stripe ends in a prominent triangular spot at the base of the tail. This stream dweller has clear triangular-shaped body fins and a blunt, forked tail. The body is stout and more chunky than the Sonora chub. The Yaqui chub also is a close relative of the humpback and bonytail chubs as proven by its mild hump just behind the head. This chub breeds during spring and early summer as water temperatures increase and the young can grow to half of their adult size by the following year.

The Yaqui chub is primarily a vegetarian and eats algae until the occasional insect, spider, or smaller fish comes along. The desert environment for the Yaqui chub is harsh and opportunities to eat foods other than algae cannot be passed by.

Saved by science

Without the initiative of fisheries experts in 1969, the Leslie Creek population would not exist. As the range of the Yaqui chub in Arizona diminished, biologists moved some fish from Astin Wash to Leslie Creek. Coincidentally, after the fish were moved, the spring that supplied Astin Wash failed and all fish in the wash died.

This recovery effort had the effect of saving the last remaining U.S. population of this chub. Today, all other populations are located in the desert environment of Sonora, Mexico, but even locating specimens in Mexico is difficult at best.

William E. Manci

PERIODICAL CICADAS

Class: Insecta

Order: Homoptera

Family: Cicadidae

Residents of the eastern United States are familiar with periodical cicadas even if they've never seen one, because cicadas can produce an amazingly noisy sound. On warm summer days the males serenade their females hour after hour, for days at a time, in an effort to find a mate. Although cicada serenades are often referred to as songs, these shrill, high-pitched sounds swell in crescendo, shrieking louder and louder until they appear to be almost roaring in unison. To the female cicada this may sound romantic, but to humans it is often annoying.

Insect experts also believe these songs encourage the gathering of males and repel predators. All species of cicadas sing, but their serenades are particularly noteworthy during the early summer months of any year, when a mass emergence of periodical cicadas occurs.

The sudden debut of millions of cicadas into certain geographic regions is an amazing phenomenon to witness. Some cicada populations, or broods, have 13- and 17-year cycles between emergences. This emergence occurs when an entire generation of insects crawls out of the soil and climbs to nearby trees to begin their mating songs, and thereby signals the change from an immature stage to an adult stage.

Cicadas possess specialized organs for the production and reception of sounds. Their noise-making apparatus is among the most highly perfected of all the insects. The typical cicada sounds are produced by a pair of timbals, which are drum-like organs located in a cavity of the male's abdomen. Females lack these "drums" and so are silent. This shell-shaped organ is ribbed, and the cicada tugs at it with powerful muscles to cause vibrations that produce its song. Rhythmic movements of the cicada's abdomen vary the quality and intensity of the timbal sounds.

Both males and females have specialized organs for hearing known as tympana. Like the timbals, the tympana also occur in pairs. Tympana are located in the abdomen and consist of an air-filled cavity covered by a tightly stretched and brightly colored membrane that resonates. Both timbals and tympana play such a vital role in the life of the cicada that to accommodate them, many other abdominal organs are greatly reduced in size.

Species recognition

Each species of cicada can be distinguished by the shape of its timbals, which makes every species' song unique. Each species sings with a different rhythm, so the cicadas can recognize their relatives from afar.

Like all insects, periodical cicadas have three main body regions: the head, thorax, and abdomen. Cicadas are members of the insect order Homoptera, which includes such relatives as plant and leaf hoppers, white flies, aphids, and scale insects. Cicadas can be distinguished from other Homoptera by their shape and size. The most prominent facial features are their egg-shaped, bright red, protruding compound eyes. Two or three smaller simple eyes, known as ocelli, lie between the larger compound eyes and are usually brightly colored. A pair of small, whiplike antennae are also obvious. The primary facial plate, known as the *clypeus*, is bowed outward, as if inflated. At its lower end are the mouth parts that are specially adapted to penetrate the woody tissue of tree branches to suck out the sap. Adult cicadas have large, membraned wings that are held in a

Cicadas are members of the insect order Homoptera, which includes such creatures as aphids and white flies.

roof-like posture over the abdomen. The body of the cicada is often black or dark brown with orange markings.

Cicadas insert their eggs in groups of slits called "splinter pockets," which they cut into the twigs of various trees and shrubs using a saw-like, egg-laying appendage, called an ovipositor. The eggs are laid in groups, or "egg nests," of as many as 50 eggs. Because females live as long as three weeks, a single female may make 20 or more egg nests and lay more than 600 eggs during her brief lifetime. Twigs are often so damaged by the egg slits that they wilt and fall to the ground. This natural pruning can result in better foliage growth in future years, although younger trees can die from this assault.

The long sleep

After the immature nymphal cicada emerges from the egg, it drops to the ground and burrows into the soil to feed on tree roots. Most cicadas require two or more years to complete their development. The mature nymphs remain in the soil until conditions are favorable, when they crawl above ground and molt, turning into adults. Despite the lengthy development, the emergence of adults is synchronized, with hundreds of thousands, known as a brood, emerging all at the same time. Adults of the genus *Magicicada*, the periodical cicadas, are active in May and June.

Approximately 1,500 species of cicadas are known around the world, from tropical and subtropical regions. In North America, there are about 175 species primarily in the United States. The periodical cicadas of the eastern

United States are interesting because of their long life cycle, number of broods, and their folklore. In many rural areas people still view their appearance with superstitious concern. Many tribes collected cicadas as food.

Six species of the genus *Magicicada* live in the eastern United States, distinguished by their size, color, song, and placement of the ovipositor. Their life cycles span 13 to 17 years.

Several broods of cicadas have become extinct as their woodland habitats are transformed into urban and agricultural uses. As

The mass emergence of the periodic cicada has been viewed as a bad omen. Even today the appearance of these insects prompts superstitious concern.

habitat destruction increases, more and more broods consist of fewer and fewer populations, hence the broods become more vulnerable to extinction. Because of their lengthy life span, habitat protection will be an important part of any conservation effort. More studies are needed to identify the endangered broods and their locations in North America.

Richard A. Arnold

Lake Victoria Cichlids

(Haplochromine spp.)

IUCN: Endangered

Class: Actinopterygii
Order: Perciformes
Family: Cichlidae
Length: Varies
Reproduction: Egg layers
Habitat: Open water, shoreline, and bottom environments
Range: Lake Victoria, Eastern Africa

IN 1988, the World Conservation Union (IUCN) listed 596 freshwater fishes that were threatened or in danger of extinction. Almost half of those fishes reside in Lake Victoria in eastern Africa. Without question, Lake Victoria contains the single largest group of imperiled fishes in the world. The single overriding factor that has been identified as the cause of this ecological catastrophe is the introduction of the predatory Nile perch (*Lates niloticus*) into Lake Victoria.

As one of the largest lakes in the world, Lake Victoria boasts many different habitats and a corresponding diversity of fish species. Out of approximately 400 species that have been identified, 250 to 300 of these species are known as haplochromine cichlids. However, some 200 haplochromine species have disappeared. The haplochromine cichlids have evolved into an amazing number of physical, behavioral, and reproductive varieties throughout the lake's

different ecological habitats. As humans began to exploit Lake Victoria for its bounty of high-quality foods, with improved fishing methods, cichlids and other fishes began to feel the impact. The seemingly endless catch of fish in the lake started to dry up. To further compound the problem, the Nile perch (from northeast Africa) was intentionally introduced into Lake Victoria in the late 1950s. It preyed on the native fish populations and they soon began to decimate. The reason for the introduction was better sport fishing: fishermen wanted to catch much larger fish in beautiful Lake Victoria.

The Nile perch, which can reach 300 pounds (136 kilograms), would feed on the smaller, less-desirable cichlids, thereby increasing their own size.

Despite their seemingly endless physical and behavioral differences, cichlids possess many similar physical characteristics. This is *Haplochromis compressiceps*, whose common name is the Malawai eyebiter.

The more hospitable cichlids were no match for the aggressive Nile perch. Additionally, four species of tilapia were introduced to "improve" the fishery.

The position of the cichlids in Lake Victoria today is very unstable. A much larger effort is needed to collect reliable data so that scientists can examine even a small number of the threatened cichlid species. Lack of reliable information is hampering efforts to develop a recovery plan. Unfortunately, researchers have enough data to know that more than 40 percent of the native haplochromine cichlids have

273

already become extinct. The irony is that fishermen in some areas of Lake Victoria have fished the Nile perch below its sustainable levels as well.

Some biologists believe there is no possibility for recovery from this ecological disaster, and that the situation will only get worse. The Nile perch fishery is now a strong economic force that provides a steady income to many local residents.

Even if measures were taken to try to eliminate the Nile perch from Lake Victoria, its extermination would be impossible. A reasonable approach would be to stabilize the situation in some way (as yet undetermined) to save as many of the remaining species as possible. The lessons learned in Lake Victoria must also be applied to other large African lakes such as Tanganyika

LAKE VICTORIA CICHLIDS
Africa

and Malawi, to prevent a similar catastrophe from occurring. The recovery plan includes the following: an educational effort to underscore the importance of haplochromine cichlids; an increased effort to conserve and raise existing captive stocks in North America and Europe for research and educational purposes; and an assessment made to determine the status of the wild populations.

This recovery plan is thought to be ambitious and will be difficult to implement.

First, haplochromine cichlids are hard to identify. The color patterns of sexually mature males are the only reliable identification method, but only a handful of experts can differentiate between the species. Second, the genetic purity of captive fish will be hard

The Texas cichlid (*Hericththys cyanoguttatum*) looks very different from its African relatives and aptly demonstrates the diversity of this species. The fish has a striking appearance, with attractive markings.

to maintain. While these fishes rarely interbreed in the wild, interbreeding in a captive environment is common. Apparently, small and confining tanks and aquariums can lead to the development of hybrids.

To date, more than 30 species are held in captivity. A species survival plan has been initiated that includes lakeside propagation and reintroductions. Kenya, Tanzania and Uganda have also signed an agreement to establish a commission to coordinate conservation and management of Lake Victoria.

William E. Manci

CISCOES

Class: Actinopterygii
Order: Salmoniformes
Family: Salmonidae

Ciscoes, members of a larger group commonly called whitefish, live in the icy waters of North America and prefer large lakes that have been known over the years for their pristine conditions. Centuries ago, Lake Superior, Lake Michigan, Lake Huron, and other large lakes were relatively untouched by humans. Fish populations, including the ciscoes, flourished in clean water and were not threatened by foreign, non-native fishes. Population explosion on the continent and the expansion of industry brought pollution, over-fishing, introduction of foreign predators, and an ever-increasing influence by people on the biological balance of these lakes.

Ciscoes used to be considered a delicacy in the United States before the 1950s as a smoked product, and fishermen went out of their way to find new and better equipment to catch these prized fish. By the late 1960s and early 1970s, ciscoes had been fished to a point where there simply were not enough fish left to justify a catch.

Pollution in the forms of sewage and industrial waste, and predation by the invading sea lamprey added additional threats. Today, in North America three species of cisco and three other whitefish are on the verge of extinction.

Ciscoes and other whitefish are related to salmon, trout, and grayling (Salmonidae), and have an interesting background. A long history of controversy arose over their classification and naming. During their heyday as food fish, ciscoes were marketed as "chubs" or "herring."

The true chubs that we know today are very different from the "chubs" of yesterday and are classified as cyprinids, not salmonids. However, fish experts admit to some confusion and disagreement when it comes to naming these deep-water dwellers. Eighteen North American species of whitefish (including ciscoes) are included in the subfamily Coregoninae. Some argue that this group should be given family status. Others claim it is a subfamily under the family Salmonidae.

The confusion is compounded by a disturbing evolution in the life of the ciscoes. Even before their numbers dwindled dramatically in the 1960s, experts struggled with the appropriate naming of individual cisco species. A catastrophic result of the endangerment of some of these fishes has been their interbreeding with similar and more populous cisco species, thereby creating a muddle of genes. If this indiscriminate interbreeding continues, the already fine lines between the 14 freshwater species in the genus *Coregonus* will disappear.

Shortjaw Cisco

(Coregonus zenithicus)

IUCN: Vulnerable

Length: 12 in. (30 cm)
Reproduction: Egg layer
Habitat: Water of deep lakes
Range: Canada, Great Lakes

THIS SPECIES GETS its scientific name *zenithicus* from the city of Duluth, Minnesota, also known as "The Zenith City." The complete range of this fish is not fully known, but it once roamed Lakes Michigan and Huron in great numbers. Today, it is believed to be extinct in those waters. Some fish can be found in Lake Superior and in some of the larger lakes of Canada as far north and west as Great Slave Lake in the Northwest Territories.

Over-fishing and loss of spawning habitat in all parts of its range have caused the greatest damage to the well-being of this endangered species.

The shortjaw cisco varies in size depending on the location of a particular population.

The Great Lakes version has an overall coloration that is silvery. The back is light green, the sides are a brilliant silvery purple color, and the belly is white.

The dorsal fin on the back matches the back in color or is somewhat darker, as is the highly forked tail fin. Other fins are white or only lightly colored. The shortjaw cisco has the characteristic turned-up jaws and snout. The shortjaw ciscoes that remain today spawn in the fall. Populations in the northern part of their range spawn early in the season, while the Lake Superior fish probably spawn as late as December. They seek water as deep as 600 feet (183 meters) to live and feed, but move to shallower water over a clay bottom to lay their eggs. Males develop nodule-like tubercles over parts of the body and fins during breeding season.

When given the opportunity, the shortjaw cisco can be long lived, reaching ten years of age or more. Their principal foods are small fish and planktonic shrimp.

This cisco used to be a major part of the diet of lake trout and burbot in the Great Lakes. Commercial fishing for ciscoes, lake trout, and burbot and attacks on all three by sea lamprey have decimated their numbers, and the dwarf populations in inland lakes are still prey for lake trout. Parasitic worms may also play a role in the declining health of many shortjaw cisco populations.

This is one of the problem fish for fishery biologists. There are marked similarities between the shortjaw cisco and other species of ciscoes. In addition, there is suspected interbreeding with more plentiful ciscoes. Because of these two circumstances, doubts linger about the true range of this shortjaw cisco. Dwarf populations found in some inland lakes also cloud the situation. Unless more work can be done to clarify some of these disputes, a realistic picture of the shortjaw cisco's numbers will not be available.

Ciscoes live in the cold waters of North America. For many years these whitefish were considered a delicacy as a smoked product. Uncontrolled commercial use of the fish has played a major role in their declining populations. This is the bloater cisco (*Coregonus hoyi*).

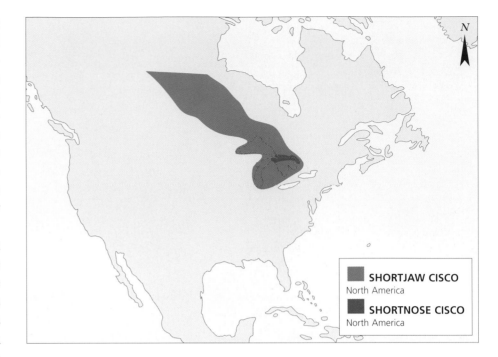

| SHORTJAW CISCO |
| North America |
| SHORTNOSE CISCO |
| North America |

Shortnose Cisco

(Coregonus reighardi)

IUCN: Critically endangered

Length: 11 in. (28 cm)
Reproduction: Egg layer
Habitat: Open water of deep lakes
Range: Lake Huron

THE SHORTNOSE CISCO was one of the most important commercial species in the Great Lakes Basin until at least the late 1940s; populations thrived in Lake Superior, Michigan, Huron, Ontario, and Nipigon. In Lake Ontario, this cisco was a prized catch and was considered an excellent fish for smoking and eating, despite its smaller size.

Today, the shortnose cisco has been all but eliminated; a small population in Georgian Bay of Lake Huron is all that keeps the species alive.

This fish is similar in coloration to the shortjaw cisco, with an overall silvery appearance, iridescent sides, and white belly, but the difference is it has a distinctive light green, straw-colored back. Like the shortjaw, the shortnose has a dark dorsal fin on the back and dark forked tail fin; other fins are white. The "cisco-like" turned-up snout and deep belly are very pronounced.

Little is known about the breeding and living habits of the remaining Lake Huron population. Historically, the shortnose cisco spawned in the spring at depths over 100 feet (30 meters) over sand, silt, and clay. As a whole, male ciscoes live from six to eight years, but females tend to live longer than males. The shortnose cisco has a preference for planktonic shrimp and small fish. It will accept other planktonic animals, insect larvae, and fingernail clams as food items.

This cisco was named for the American fishery scientist Jacob Reighard.

William E. Manci

Malagasy Civet
(Fossa fossa)

IUCN: Vulnerable

Class: Mammalia
Order: Carnivora
Weight: 2¼–4½ lb. (1–2 kg)
Length: 16–17 in. (40–43 cm)
Diet: Carnivorous
Gestation period: 82–89 days
Longevity: 11 years in captivity
Habitat: Near streams in forests
Range: Madagascar

THE FAMILY KNOWN as Viverridae is made up of 36 genera and 71 species. These animals can be found in southwestern Eurasia, the East Indies, Africa, and Madagascar, and there are certain species that have been introduced to regions where they do not occur naturally.

Civets are related to the more familiar mongoose family, as well as to other unusual species of mammals, such as, genets, linsangs, and fossas.

These carnivores are small to medium sized and are found in a variety of patterns, including stripes, spots, and uniform colors. In general, they are forest inhabitants, but also occur in dense brush and thick grass.

The viverrid diet seems to consist of small vertebrates and

Civets are part of the family Viverridae, which is made up of 71 species. This is *Arctogalidia trivirgata stigmatica*, or the small-toothed palm civet. This particular species can be found in Assam, Indochina, and from the Malay Peninsula to Sumatra, Banka, Java, and Borneo. Species can also be found on numerous small nearby islands of the East Indies.

various invertebrates; occasionally they will take vegetables, fruit, bulbs, and nuts.

Endangered island

The Malagasy civet is just one of many species that have declined in numbers on the island of Madagascar since the arrival of human beings. Once found in forested regions throughout the island, the Malagasy civet now appears to be restricted to the eastern and northwestern evergreen forests.

The Malagasy civet is a long slender animal that belongs to the same family of small hunting carnivores that includes the mongoose and the genet. The Malagasy civet has pale, reddish-brown fur and four rows of dark brown spots that run the length of the body and flanks. These spots merge, becoming stripes as they run on to the tail. The underside is paler with less noticeable spots. This civet has very slender limbs and appears adapted to running down prey.

Varied diet

This species is nocturnal and shelters during the day in crevices and hollow trees. It is

The Malagasy civet is a nocturnal hunter and will eat a wide variety of foods, including birds, insects, crustaceans, eels, and rodents.

MALAGASY CIVET
Madagascar

believed that a civet will hunt its prey wherever it finds it, on the ground or in trees.

The civet prefers rodents, frogs, and small eels, but also eats crustaceans, worms, insects, and

small birds. It seizes and kills prey with wide-open jaws, and holds its prey during eating with its forelegs.

Reproduction

Mating pairs will mark and share a territory, and communicate with each other and their young by using a limited set of vocalizations. Courtship is brief, lasting only 15 to 20 minutes. After a gestation of about three months, the female gives birth to the single, 2¼- to 2½-ounce (65- to 70-gram) offspring, sometime between October and January. The male is excluded from the den during birth, and for a month after the birth. The offspring can walk at about three days of age and begins eating meat at about one month of age. Despite these early developments, weaning does not occur until approximately 2 to 2½ months of age. It is thought that the young leaves its parents when it is about one year old.

At risk

Studies on the decline of this interesting viverrid have been few. Loss of habitat and unrestrained hunting are two of the major factors that contribute to the rapid reduction in both the numbers and range of the Malagasy civet. Since both of these factors have played a role in threatening many other species on Madagascar, plans to save such species and the Malagasy civet are desperately needed. Only with prompt action will we be able to save this species, as well as saving one of the most interesting and isolated communities on the planet.

Terry Tompkins

CLAMS

Freshwater "clams," "mussels," and "oysters" are vernacular (regional dialectal) names applied to bivalved mollusks that occur in the rivers and lakes of every continent except Antarctica. Most of them, including the following species, are not really clams, mussels, or oysters.

They are in fact a kind of ancient bivalve that is quite apart from those familiar marine groups. In the Northern Hemisphere these animals belong primarily to the Family Unionidae. Pearlymussels reach their greatest diversity in eastern and central North America, where over 300 species are known to have occurred in recent times.

However, of those, a dozen or more are now extinct, and over 50 of them are endangered or are facing extinction in the near future. They have reached this stage due to the actions of man.

Birdwing Pearlymussel

(Lemiox rimosus)

ESA: Endangered

IUCN: Critically endangered

As its common name indicates, this mussel somewhat resembles a bird's wing. The shell is elliptical and thick, with irregular radiating ribs—the "feathers" of the wing. Shells of juveniles are dark green, but they become dark brown or black with increasing age. The interior of the shell is iridescent white. The birdwing pearlymussel is small, only reaching 50 millimeters in length. Historically this species lived in much of the Tennessee River system in North America, but today it is limited to small populations in the tributaries.

Once a prolific inhabitant of the Tennessee River system, the birdwing pearlymussel now inhabits the river tributaries, but in smaller populations.

The cracking pearlymussel can be found in small numbers in the Clinch River. When it dies, the shell dries out and cracks, hence its common name.

N

BIRDWING PEARLYMUSSEL
North America

BIRDWING PEARLYMUSSEL

CRACKING PEARLYMUSSEL
North America

Cracking Pearlymussel

(Hemistena lata)

ESA: Endangered

IUCN: Critically endangered

The shell of the cracking pearlymussel is very elongate and thin, often cracking as the shell dries after the death of the animal. The shell lacks sculpture. The outside is yellowish or tan-colored with radiating broken rays of dark green. The interior of the shell is iridescent white, salmon, purple, or orange colored. Shells may reach 90 millimeters in length. Once widely distributed in the Ohio River system (including the Tennessee and Cumberland Rivers) of North America, it has been extirpated from most of its range. Today it is found in the Clinch River.

Dromedary Pearlymussel

(Dromus dromas)

ESA: Endangered

IUCN: Critically endangered

The shell of the dromedary pearlymussel is rounded in outline, usually rather flattened, and thick. In some river reaches the shells have a single row of large irregular knobs on each shell; in other places the shells may be nearly smooth. The outside shell is yellowish or tan-colored with fine radiating dashed lines of dark green. The interior of the shell is iridescent white to salmon or orange colored. Shells may reach 4 inches (10 centimeters) in length, but more usually are 2⅓–2¾ inches (6–7 centimeters). Originally found throughout the Tennessee and Cumberland River systems of North America, today this pearlymussel is limited to small stretches of those rivers.

The dromedary pearlymussel inhabits very limited portions of the Tennessee and Cumberland River systems. Like other pearlymussels, pollution and run-off from agricultural land are the agents of its decline.

Green Blossom Pearlymussel

(Epioblasma torulosa gubernaculum)

Tubercled Blossom Pearlymussel

(Epioblasma torulosa torulosa)

ESA: Endangered

IUCN: Critically endangered

These subspecies exhibit pronounced sexual dimorphism in the shells—males and females look very different from each other. The female shell is elliptical with an expanded posterior portion. The male shell is more pointed posteriorly. The male and female shells both have a single row of irregular knobs on each shell. They both have tan to

DROMEDARY PEARLYMUSSEL
North America

greenish shells with numerous fine radiating rays of dark green. The interior of the shell is an iridescent white. Both sexes of this pearlymussel attain a maximum size of 2⅓–2¾ inches (6–7 centimeters) in length.

Possibly extinct

The green blossom pearlymussel is considered the Tennessee River headwater form of the big river tubercled blossom pearlymussel. The tubercled blossom pearlymussel is considered by many people to be extinct, and some experts believe that the green blossom pearlymussel has also suffered this fate

Littlewing Pearlymussel

(Pegias fabula)

ESA: Endangered

IUCN: Critically endangered

Individuals of this small, peculiar species have quadrate shells, sometimes becoming a pronounced point at the posterior end. The shell is thick, without sculpture, and has several broad green, black, or brown rays on an off-white shell. Most specimens are highly eroded. The interior of the shell is iridescent white or flushed with salmon. The littlewing pearlymussel reaches only 30 millimeters in length, but usually is much smaller.

Known from the Tennessee and Cumberland Rivers in North America, the littlewing pearlymussel is now limited to just a few localized populations.

White Catspaw Pearlymussel

(Epioblasma obliquata perobliqua)

ESA: Endangered

IUCN: Critically endangered

Like other members of the genus *Epioblasma*, this species exhibits pronounced sexual dimorphism in the shells. The female shell is quadrate with a peculiar serrated expansion posteriorly. The male shell is pointed posteriorly. Female shells have radiating threads corresponding to the serrations, while male shells lack pronounced sculpture. Both have greenish shells with numerous fine radiating rays of dark green. The interior of the shell is iridescent white. Specimens rarely exceed 50 millimeters in length. The white catspaw occurred in tributaries, such as the Maumee River, of the western basin of Lake Erie in the North American Great Lakes.

Today this species may be restricted to 7½ miles (12 kilometers) of a single creek.

On the verge of extinction

The seven freshwater mussels described here are but a few of the more than 50 that are considered Federally Endangered by the United States Fish and Wildlife Service. According to that agency, freshwater mussels are more imperiled than any other group of organisms in North America. In addition to the endangered species, a dozen or more additional mussel species have become extinct in the past 200 years. All of these appear to have been driven to that end by the activities of mankind. There is no single cause for their demise. Rather they seem to have succumbed to an accumulation of impacts until they could tolerate no more. Pollution, impoundment, and overharvesting all contributed to the loss of these animals. Freshwater mussels live buried in the bottom of rivers, streams, and lakes where they filter microscopic food from the water. This food consists of single-celled organisms, fungal spores, and fine detritus. Many species live up to 200 years, although most individuals live for 20–30 years. This is an unusually long lifespan for an invertebrate animal. As adults, mussels seldom move unless stranded by low water, yet they historically lived in nearly every body of fresh water. They have a wide distribution because freshwater mussels are dispersed by having a parasitic larval stage, called a glochidium (pl. glochidia), that attach to the fins

The tubercled blossom pearlymussel is a critically endangered species, in fact, many experts believe it to be extinct or on the verge of extinction. This pearlymussel inhabits portions of the Tennessee River, where it was once fairly widespread.

and gills of fishes. There the larvae remain for days or months until they eventually drop from the fish and begin life as a juvenile mussel. Mussels cannot complete their life cycle without passing through this parasitic stage. By hitching a ride on a highly mobile host such as a fish, the mussel is dispersed far beyond the limits of its own movement. Although this is a highly successful adaptation, it has become one of the causes of their increasing scarcity.

It is becoming apparent that many types of mussels are host specific. That is, they cannot successfully use any species of fish as a host, but are limited to a few types of fishes instead. For example, some mussels may only parasitize sculpins and darters while being unable to utilize min-

281

nows and bass. If these necessary hosts are absent, the mussel cannot successfully reproduce because the parasitic stage cannot be bypassed. It is suspected that some mussel species are becoming rare for just this reason. As the ecology of a river becomes impacted by human actions, fish species may be lost.

The littlewing pearlymussel has very few localized populations. Like other pearlymussels, it has been harvested for the pearl button industry and as material for the cultured pearl industry.

Any mussels in that river that relied on those fish as hosts will eventually be lost as well.

Agents of extinction

Because mussels filter very fine matter from the water to eat, they are susceptible to overloads of sediments and other materials that are introduced by mankind. These pollutants foul and smother the mussels' gills or, in the extreme, bury them. Runoff from agricultural lands, construction sites, deforestation, and mining all contribute to this problem. Often this runoff is accompanied by chemical pollutants as well: road salt, fertilizers, petroleum products, pesticides, altered pH, and heavy metals. Although mussels have existed for at least 250 million years, and have survived many natural runoff catastrophes, it is the continuous and widespread assault by human-

caused runoff that has affected them so badly.

One of the most devastating actions of mankind on mussels is the impoundment of free-flowing rivers. Water is dammed for many purposes: hydroelectric power, mills, navigation, and recreation. All these have a profound impact on the physical properties of the river and its biota. A river typically has high habitat heterogeneity—riffles, runs, pools, meanders, tree canopy cover, and shoals. It is a general rule that the more types of habitat that are available, the more types of plant and animal life can be supported. Conversely, loss of habitat heterogeneity leads to loss in biotic diversity. When a river is impounded, many of the original habitats are lost or dramatically altered. Riffles, runs, and shoals are lost. Canopy cover becomes insignificant. The result is a loss of diversity in impoundments, including mussels and their necessary host fishes. In addition, moving water has the capacity to transport sediments, but as water velocity decreases these sediments begin to fall to the bottom. In impoundments, water once free-flowing becomes sluggish. Sediments once carried away and flushed from the river now rain down to the bottom, and in the process, slowly bury the mussels.

If not smothered by the accumulating sediments, mussels in impoundments face other problems. The water at the bottom of an impoundment may become cold and oxygen-depleted. The reproductive cycle of freshwater mussels is dependent on water temperatures rising during the spring. But in impoundments these environmental cues may be

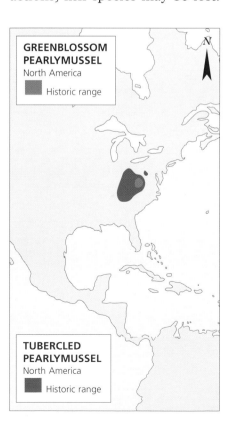

GREENBLOSSOM PEARLYMUSSEL
North America

Historic range

TUBERCLED PEARLYMUSSEL
North America

Historic range

LITTLEWING PEARLYMUSSEL
North America

lacking, resulting in the mussels never reproducing.

Dams represent obstacles to the movement of host fishes. It has been shown that low-head dams as small as one meter high have limited the distributions of fishes and their corresponding mussel parasites. Even if fish ladders are present, not all types of fishes can use them. For mussels, the result is a lack of the proper host at the proper time. Without these hosts, the mussels can never reproduce. In North America, some rare mussels are surviving in impoundments, but without reproducing, apparently because of a loss of their hosts. When these mussels eventually die of other causes, these species will become extinct.

These problems are the result of mankind's degradation of the mussels' habitat and are not directed at the mussels themselves. However, several human activities have a direct bearing on mussels. Since the 1800's mussels have been commercially harvested, historically for making pearl buttons, and recently as material for the cultured pearl industry. Although the exact amount of mussels that have been taken for these purposes will never be known, it is presumed to be many thousands of tons. Because mussels are so slow-growing and produce so few juveniles, under this degree of exploitation mussels probably do not constitute a renewable resource. Because of this, commercial harvest has been outlawed in many parts of the United States.

A new, gravely serious threat to mussels has recently emerged in North America: exotic zebra mussels. These prolific invaders apparently were transported to North America from Europe in the ballast water of a trans-Atlantic cargo ship. The first individuals appeared in the Great Lakes in the 1980s. Since then they have been transported throughout much of eastern and central North America, from Canada to the Gulf of Mexico. Zebra mussels do not require a host for reproduction. They spin tough fibrous threads, called the *byssus*, to anchor themselves to objects. Unfortunately they overwhelm native mussels, robbing them of food and oxygen and "sewing" their shells shut. Native mussels have been driven to near extirpation by zebra mussels in many areas. Although zebra mussels do not fare well in flowing rivers, many of North America's rivers have been dammed, creating impoundments ideal for the proliferation of the exotic species.

To add to these problems, we now know that juvenile mussels have different habitat requirements from adults. Once the juveniles drop from their host to the bottom, they dig into the sediment and remain buried for several years. Unlike the adult, they do not feed with their gills, but gather food with ciliary tracts on their feet from the interstitial spaces between sediment particles. Toxicological tests suggest that adults and juveniles have different tolerances to pollutants as well. What may be tolerable to an adult may be lethal to a juvenile. Because of these very different requirements, it is likely that some mussel populations that outwardly appear healthy may in fact consist solely of adults.

Protection and recovery

The species described above are listed as Endangered by the United States Fish and Wildlife Service. This action offers some protection for these animals, with the eventual goal of "delisting" them. A delisted mussel species is one that has increased in population size and distribution to the point where it no longer is in jeopardy. This endangered status protects the mussel from outright destruction from commercial harvest, poaching, or personal collecting. More importantly, it also regulates what may be done to the mussel's habitat. Rivers having endangered mussels may no longer be dredged, impounded, polluted, or otherwise altered without consultation with the Service. When habitat alteration is unavoidable (to replace or repair a bridge, for instance), the Service suggests mitigation practices that will minimize habitat loss: bank stabilization, erosion control, or even the relocation of mussels to another place. The

Service also funds mussel surveys and basic research. In addition to the federal government protecting mussels, many individual States also have lists of endangered species. These species may not be federally endangered (rare nationwide) but are imperiled within the boundaries of the state. State endangered species have much the same protection as federal ones within that state.

Research in the last 20 years has demonstrated that freshwater mussels are much more complex organisms, with complicated life cycles and habitat requirements, than was ever imagined. However, we also now have a much better idea of how to manage and conserve them. Rescuing these endangered animals requires focus in three critical areas: adult requirements, juvenile requirements, and host requirements. We know that adults and juveniles have different needs. It is not sufficient to manage the habitat of one stage if the other's basic requirements are not met as well. The addition of a host creates a unique conservation problem. Because the host is a necessary part of the

The white catspaw pearlymussel has a greenish shell with an iridescent interior. It is a small shell, rarely more than 50 millimeters long. It inhabits tributaries of rivers in the Great Lakes.

mussel life cycle, it is necessary to manage two species in order to save one. Fishes have very differing needs from mussels, including different foods, different tolerances, and different distributions. This makes the recovery of mussel species much more complicated.

However, recent advances in our knowledge of these animals have led to some promising conservation methods. Hosts can be determined in the laboratory by trial and error. With this information we can parasitize hosts in captivity, recover the juvenile mussels, rear them to an appropriate size, and release them to bolster existing populations and reestablish lost ones. This has already been successfully accomplished for one endangered mussel. Even if we do not know the proper hosts, it may be possible to raise the parasitic larvae in artificial media, thus avoiding the need for a host. This method has yielded some promising results.

Finally, individuals of existing populations of endangered mussels may be reintroduced to areas of their historic range to reestablish the species. This prevents the possibility that the last remaining population could be destroyed by an unforeseen environmental disaster; establishing multiple populations assures that one or more will survive. This technique has been successfully used on the birdwing pearlymussel.

G. Thomas Watters

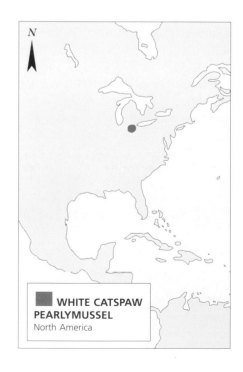

N

WHITE CATSPAW PEARLYMUSSEL
North America

GLOSSARY

actinopterygii: the scientific name for bony fish

albino: any organism lacking color in the skin or fur; albino species have pink eyes, while albino fish often have no functioning eyes

anther: at the tip of the filament of the stamen, it is made up of pollen sacs that contain grains of pollen

apically: relating to, or situated at the apex

arboreal: living in or adapted for living in trees; arboreal animals seldom, if ever, descend to the ground (see terrestrial)

aves: the Latin scientific name for birds

barbels: a slender growth on the mouths or nostrils of certain fishes, used as a sensory organ for touch

bipedal: any organism that walks on two feet

bract: a leaf at the base of a flower stalk in plants

buff: in bird species, a yellow-white color used to describe the plumage

byssus: strong, fibrous threads for anchoring bivalved mussels

calyx: the green outer whorl of a flower made up of sepals

captive breeding: any method of bringing several animals of the same species into a zoo or other closed environment for the purpose of mating; if successful, these methods can increase the population of that species

carnivore: any flesh-eating animal

carnivorous: flesh eating

clear cutting: a method of harvesting lumber that eliminates all the trees in a specific area rather than just selected trees

clutch, clutch size: the number of eggs laid during one nesting cycle

corolla: the separate petals, or the fused petals of a flower

cotyledon: the first leaf developed by the embryo of a seed plant

decurved: curving downward; a bird's beak is decurved if it points toward the ground

deforestation: the process of removing trees from a particular area

diurnal: active during the day; some animals are diurnal, while others are active at night (see nocturnal)

dominance: the ability to overpower the behavior of other individuals; an animal is dominant if it affects others of its own species in a way that benefits itself; also, the trait of abundance that determines the character of a plant community: grasses dominate a prairie, and trees dominate a forest

dorsal: pertaining to or situated on the back of an organism; a dorsal fin is on the back of a fish

ecology: the study of the interrelationship between a living organism and its environment

ecosystem: a community of animals, plants, and bacteria and its interrelated physical and chemical environment

endangered species: any species on the verge of becoming extinct; disappearing from the wild forever

endemic: native to a particular geographic region

estrous: the time period when female mammals can become pregnant

exotic species: a plant or animal species that is not native to its habitat

feral: a wild animal that is descended from tame or domesticated species

fishery, fisheries: any system, body of water, or portion of a body of water that supports finfish or shellfish; can also be used as an adjective describing a person or thing (for example, a fisheries biologist)

forest: a plant community in which trees grow closely enough together that their crowns interlock to form a continuous overhead canopy

fry: young fish

gene pool: the total hereditary traits available within a group; when isolated from other members of their species, individual organisms may produce healthy offspring if there is enough variety in the genes available through mating

gestation: the period of active embryonic growth inside a mammal's body between the time the embryo attaches to the uterus and the time of birth; some mammals carry dormant embryos for several weeks or months before the embryo attaches to the uterus and begins to develop actively, and this dormancy period is not part of the gestation period; gestation period is the time length of a pregnancy

granivore: any seed-feeding animal

granivorous: seed feeding

guano: manure, especially of sea birds and bats

habitat: the environment where a species is normally found; habitat degradation is the decline in quality of a species' home until it can no longer survive there

halophyte: salt lover

hemiparasitic: obtains water and nutrients from the roots of other plants

herbivore: any plant-eating animal

herbivorous: plant eating

hibernate: to spend the winter season in a dormant or inactive state; some species hibernate so that they can save energy during months when food is scarce

hierarchy: the relationships among individuals of the same species or among species that determine in what order animals may have access to food, water, mates, nesting or denning sites, and other vital resources

home range: the area normally traveled by an individual species during its lifespan

hybrid: the offspring of two different species who mate; see interbreed

hybridization: the gradual decline of a species through continued breeding with another species; see interbreed

immature(s): a young bird that has not yet reached breeding maturity; it usually has plumage that is different from that of an adult bird of the same species

in captivity: a species that exists in zoos, captive breeding programs, or in private collections, perhaps because the species can no longer be found in the wild

incubation: the period when an egg is kept warm until the embryo develops and hatches

indigenous species: any species native to its habitat

inflorescence: a group of flowers that grow from one point

insecta: the Latin scientific

name for insects

insular species: a species isolated on an island or islands

interbreed: when two separate species mate and produce offspring; see hybrid

invertebrate(s): any organism without a backbone (spinal column)

juvenal: a bird with an intermediate set of feathers after its young downy plumage molts and before growing hard, adult feathers

juvenile(s): a young bird or other animal not yet mature

lore(s): the irregularly shaped facial area of a bird between the eye and the base of the beak

mammalia: the Latin scientific name for mammals

migrate, migratory: to move from one range to another, particularly with the change of seasons; many species are migratory

milt: the reproductive glands of male fishes; also, the breeding behavior of male fishes

mollusca: the Latin scientific name for mussels, clams, and snails

mucronate: having a sharp terminal point

nocturnal: active at night; some animals are nocturnal, while others are active by day (see diurnal)

nomadic species: a species with no permanent range or territory; nomadic species wander for food and water

old growth forest: forest that has not experienced extensive deforestation

omnivore: any species that eats both plants and animals

ornithologist(s): a scientist who studies birds

pelage: the hairy covering of a mammal

perennial: persisting for several years

plumage: the feathers that cover a bird

prairie: a plant community without trees and dominated by grasses; a grassland; often incorrectly used synonymously with plain or plains, which is a landform feature and not a plant community

predation: the act of one species hunting another

predator: a species that preys upon other species

primary forest: a forest of native trees that results from natural processes, often called virgin forest

primate(s): a biological ranking of species in the same order, including gorillas, chimpanzees, monkeys, as well as human beings (*Homo sapiens*)

range: the geographic area where a species roams

recovery plan(s): any document that outlines a public or private program for assisting an endangered or threatened species

relict: an isolated habitat or population that was once widespread

reptilia: the Latin scientific name for reptiles

riffle(s): a shallow rapid stretch of water caused by a rocky outcropping or obstruction in a stream

riparian: relating to plants and animals close to and influenced by rivers

roe: fish eggs

rufous: in bird species, plumage that is orange-brown and pink

secondary forest: a forest that has grown back after cutting, forest fire, or other deforestation; secondary forests may or may not contain exotic tree species, but they almost always differ in character from primary forests

sedentary species: one that does not migrate

serpentine: mineral rock consisting of hydrous magnesium silicate. It is usually a dull green color, and looks mottled

siltation: the process of sediment clouding and obstructing a body of water

species: a distinct kind of plant or animal; the biological ranking below genus; a subspecies is an isolated population that varies from its own species

stamen: the male reproductive organs of a flower, consisting of the pistil and anther

stigma: upper part of a carpel in a flower, that receives pollen grains during pollination

taxonomy: the science of biologically ranking plants and animals, arranging the relationships between species

terrestrial: living in or adapted for living principally on the ground; some birds are terrestrial and seldom, if ever, ascend into trees (see arboreal)

territory: the area occupied more or less exclusively by an organism or group, usually defended by aggressive displays and physical combat

tribe: a more specific classification within the biological rankings of family or subfamily

tubercle: a prominent bump on a fish's spine

veldt: a grassland region with some scattered bushes and virtually no trees; other terms are *steppe*, *pampas*, and *prairie*

ventral: on or near the belly; the ventral fin is located on the underside of a fish and corresponds with the hind limbs of other vertebrates

vertebrates: any organism that has a backbone (spinal column)

water column: the zone of a pond, lake, or ocean below the surface and above the bottom that holds free-swimming or free-floating fish and other animals and plants

weir: a dam or other obstruction in a stream that diverts water

woodland: a plant community in which trees grow abundantly but far enough apart that their crowns do not intermingle, so no overhead canopy is formed

xerophyte: a plant adapted for life with a limited water supply

INDEX

The scientific name of a plant or animal is entered in *italics*; its common name is in roman type. Page numbers in *italics* refer to picture captions.

Abbott's Booby 171
Abruzzo Chamois 244, 246
Acinonyx spp. 248–251
Agelaius xanthomus 157
Alabama Cavefish 241–242
Alvord Chub 256
Amblyopsis spp. 242–243
Apennine Chamois 244, 246
Apodemia mormo langei 190, 191
Asiatic Cheetah 250, 251
Audubon's Crested Caracara 228–230, *229, 230*

Bagre de Muzquiz (Mexican Blindcat) 158–159, *159*
Bahaman Swallowtail Butterfly 191
Bay Checkerspot Butterfly 192
Bird's-Beak 150–152
Birdwing Pearlmussel 279, *279*
Bison 153–155
Bison spp. 153–155
Bitterling, Tokyo 156, *156*
Blackbird, Yellow-shouldered 157
Black Caiman 223–225, *224*
Blaine Pincushion 205–206
Blindcat 158–160
Blue-eye, Honey 161
Blue Prairie Violet Butterfly 191–192

Boa 162–165
Bobcat 166
Bobwhite, Masked 167–169, *167, 169*
Boloria acrocnema 192
Bonobo (Pygmy Chimpanzee) *252, 255*
Bontebok 170, *170*
Bonytail Chub 256–257, *257*
Booby, Abbott's 171
Borax Lake Chub 258, *258*
Boxwood, Vahl's 172–173, *172*
Broadnosed Caiman 225–226, *226*
Bubalus bubalis 183–184, *183*
Buckwheats 173–182
Buffalo, Water, Wild Asiatic 183–184, *183*
Bushbaby, Zanzibar 184–186, *184*
Bushchat, White-browed 187, *187*
Bustard, Houbara 188, *188*
Butterfly 189–194
Buxus vahlii 172–173, *172*

Cachorrito 195–204
Cactus 205–220
Cahow 221–222, *221*
Caiman 223–226
Caiman latirostris 225–226, *226*
Callophrys mossii bayensis 191
Camel, Wild Bactrian 227–228, *227*
Camelus bactrianus 227–228, *227*
Caracara, Audubon's Crested

228–230, *229, 230*
Cat 234–240
Catfish 231–233
Catlet, Incomati Rock 233
Cave Catfish 231
Cavefish 241–243
Chamois 244–246
Charal 246–247
Charalito (Chihuahua Chub) 258–259, *259*
Charalito Saltillo (Humpback Chub) 260–261, *260*
Charalito Sonorense (Sonoro Chub) 265–266, *266*
Chartreuse Chamois 244, 246
Cheetah 248–251, *249, 250*
Chihuahua Chub 258–259, *259*
Chiloglanis bifurcus 233
Chimpanzee 252–255
Chirostoma regani 247
Chlamydotis undulata 188, *188*
Chub 256–270
Cicadas, Periodical 271–272, *271, 272*
Cichlids of Lake Victoria 273–274
Cisco 275–276
Civet, Malagasy 277–278, *278*
Clam 279–284
Clarias cavernicola 231
Clay-loving Wild-Buckwheat 173–175
Colinus virginianus ridgwayi 167–169, *167, 169*
Common Chimpanzee 252–255, *254*
Cordylanthus spp. 150–152

Coregonus spp. 275–276
Cracking Pearlymussel 279, *279*
Cualac tessellatus 203–204
Cushenbury Buckwheat 175–176, *176*
Cyprinella monacha 266–267, *268*
Cyprinodon spp. 195–199, 200–203, 204

Damaliscus dorcas dorcas 170, *170*
Dromedary Pearlymussel 280, *280*
Dromus dromas 280, *280*

El Segundo Blue Butterfly 191
Epicrates spp. 162–165
Epioblasma spp. 280, 281, *284*
Erimystax cahni 264–265, *265*
Eriogonum spp. 173–182
Euphilotes spp. 191
Euphydryas editha bayensis 192
European Bison 153–154, *154*
Eyebiter, Malawi 273

Felis spp. 166, 238–240
Flat-headed Cat 235, *236*
Fossa fossa 277–278, *278*

Galago zanzibaricus 184–186, *184*
Giant Catfish 232–233
Gila spp. 256–261, 262–263, 265–266, 268–270
Graphium lysithous harrisianus 192–193

Greater Large Blue Butterfly 191

Green Blossom Pearlymussel 280

Gypsum Wild-Buckwheat 177–178

Hatchet Cactus (Peyotillo) 207–208, *207*

Haplochromine spp. 273–274

Haplochromis compressiceps 273

Harris' Mimic Swallowtail Butterfly 192–193

Hemistena lata 279, *279*

Hericththys cyanoguttatum 274

Homerus Swallowtail Butterfly 193

Honey Blue-eye 161

Houbara Bustard 188, *188*

Humpback Chub 260–261, *260*

Hutton Tui Chub 268–270, *269*

Icaricia icarioides missionensis 191, *193*

Incomati Rock Catlet 233

Iotichthys phlegethontis 261–262

Iriomote Cat 235–237

Knowlton Cactus 208–210, *208*

Lange's Metalmark Butterfly *190*, 191

Large Alcon Blue Butterfly 191

Large Blue Butterfly 191

Large Dusky Blue Butterfly 191

Large Scarce Blue Butterfly 191

Least Chub 261–262

Lemiox rimosus 279, *279*

Leopardus tigrinus 237–238, *238*

Little Spotted Cat 237–238, *238*

Littlewing Pearlymussel 280, *282*

Lloyd's Mariposa Cactus 210–211

Lotis Blue Butterfly 191

Lycaeides idas lotis 191

Macrhybopsis spp. 264, 267–268

Maculinea spp. 191

Magicicada spp. 272

Malagasy Civet 277–278, *278*

Malawi Eyebiter 273

Marbled Cat 238–239

Masked Bobwhite 167–169, *167*, *169*

Megupsilon aporus 199–200

Melanosuchus niger 223–225, *224*

Mesa Verde Cactus 211–213, *212*

Mexican Blindcat 158–159, *159*

Mission Blue Butterfly 191, *193*

Mohave Tui Chub 269

Mona Boa 162, *163*

Mussels, Freshwater *see* Clam

Myrtle's Silverspot Butterfly 192

Northern Cavefish 242, *242*

Oncilla *see* Little Spotted Cat

Oregon Chub 262

Oregonichthys crameri 262

Oregon Silverspot Butterfly 192

Ornithoptera spp. 193, 194

Owens Tui Chub 269–270

Ozark Cavefish 242–243, *243*

Pahranagat Roundtail Chub 262–263

Pakistan Sand Cat 239, *240*

Pangasianodon gigas 232–233

Pan spp. 252–255

Papasula abbotti 171

Papilio spp. 190–191, 192

Parides ascanius 192

Pearlymussels 279–281, 284

Pediocactus 208–210, 213–214, 214–216, 218–219

Peebles Navajo Cactus 213–214, *214*

Pegias fabula 280, *282*

Pelecyphora aselliformis 207–208, *207*

Peyotillo (Hatchet Cactus) 207–208, *207*

Phreatichthys andruzzi 243

Poblana spp. 246–247

Polyborus plancus audubonii 228–230, *229*, *230*

Prietella phreatophila 158–159, *159*

Prionailurus spp. 235–237

Pseudomugil mellis 161

Pterodroma cahow 221–222, *221*

Puerto Rican Boa 163–164, *164*

Pygmy Chimpanzee *252*, 255

Queen Alexandra's Birdwing Butterfly 193, 194, *194*

Rebel's Large Blue Butterfly 191

Regal Fritillary Butterfly 191–192

Rupricapra pyrenaica ornata 244, 246

Rusty Spotted Cat 240

Salt Marsh Bird's-Beak 150–151, *150*

San Bruno Elfin Butterfly 191

San Rafael Cactus 214–216, *215*

Satan eurystomus 160

Saxicola macrorhynca 187, *187*

Schaus Swallowtail Butterfly 190–191

Schlesser Pincushion 216–217, *217*

Sclerocactus spp. 205–206, 210–213, 216–218, 219–220

Scrub Buckwheat 178–179

Shortjaw Cisco 275–276

Shortnose Cisco 276

Short-tailed Swallowtail Butterfly 192

Sicklefin Chub 264

Silversides *see* Charal

Slender Chub 264–265, *265*

Smith's Blue Butterfly 191

Soft Bird's-Beak 151–152, *152*

Sonora Chub 265–266, *266*

Southern Mountain Wild-Buckwheat 180–181

Speoplatyrhinus poulsoni 241–242

Speyeria spp. 191–192

Spotfin Chub 266–267, *268*

Steamboat Buckwheat 181–182, *182*

Sturgeon Chub 267–268

Tanakia tanago 156, *156*

Texas Cichlid 274

Tokyo Bitterling 156, *156*

Toothless Blindcat 159–160, *160*

Trogloglanis pattersoni 159–160, *160*

Tubercled Blossom Pearlymussel 280, *281*

Umcompahgre Fritillary Butterfly 192

Vahl's Boxwood 172–173, *172*

Viola pedatifida 191–192

Virgin Islands Tree Boa 164–165

Virgin River Roundtail Chub 263

Water Buffalo *see* Buffalo, Water

White-browed Bushchat 187, *187*

White Catspaw Pearlymussel 281, *284*

Widemouth Blindcat 160

Wild Asiatic Water Buffalo 183–184, *183*

Wild Bactrian Camel 227–228, *227*

Winkler Cactus 218–219, *218*

Wisent (European Bison) 153–154, *154*

Wood Bison 154–155

Wright Fishhook Cactus 219–220, *220*

Yaqui Chub 270

Yellow-shouldered Blackbird 157

Zanzibar Bushbaby 184–186, *185*

REFERENCE